CHRISTIANITY
AND IGBO CULTURE

CHRISTIANITY AND IGBO CULTURE

A STUDY OF THE INTERACTION OF CHRISTIANITY AND IGBO CULTURE

BY

EDMUND ILOGU

Reader in Religion, University of Nigeria, Nsukka

WITH A FOREWORD BY DR. M. A. C. WARREN

NOK PUBLISHERS, LTD. - 1974

New York - London - Enugu

First published in the United States of America
by NOK Publishers, Ltd.
150 Fifth Avenue
New York, New York, 10011

PRINTED IN HOLLAND

First published 1974

Library of Congress Catalog Card Number
International Standard Book Number 0-88357-030-0 (cased)
International Standard Book Number 0-88357-031-9 (paper)

Dedicated to

Rosemary Uzoamaka Abiodun Ilogu,
who has enriched my *faith* through endurance;

Simon Mgbeodinma Amamgbo,
who in *love* of the "brother" put me through school;

The memory of the late Reverend Abel Ekpunobi, (died 1973)
who made me *hope* for an indigenous Church in Iboland.

A religion that took no account of people's way of life, a religion that did not recognise spots of beauty and truth in their way of life, was useless. It would not satisfy. It would not be a living experience, a source of life and vitality. It would only maim a man's soul.

James Ngugi, *The River Between.*

CONTENTS

FOREWORD

Canon Ilogu has been a friend for many years, and more than once a welcome guest in our home. Twice, I have had the unforgettable experience of being in the country of the Ibos, and I have paid brief visits to many of the places mentioned in this book. For good measure, I can add that, in 1869, my grandfather, a naval officer, visited Onitsha, where he landed to salute the Obi. So I have an hereditary link with the Ibo people! Yet, for all this, I am not qualified to evaluate this serious study of Ibo culture and the world-view of the Ibo people, or to assess in detail the legitimacy of every detail in the author's argument.

But I have two qualifications which, perhaps, entitle me to accept the privilege of writing this Foreword. Apart altogether from the gift of friendship with many Ibos, and not least with Canon Ilogu, I have had the advantage of very close links with the Ibo people during the traumatic experience of the civil war. And I am acutely conscious of the present situation of the Christian Church in that country.

It is therefore with complete confidence that I endorse the urgency of the author's attempt to consider the proper role of the Christian Church in this hour of Ibo history, an hour of destiny for all Nigeria's peoples.

Great and legitimate use has been made by theologians in recent years of the quite distinctive meanings of two Greek words, used to designate "time". *Chronos* is clock time, time as measured by the sequence of events, of day and night, of year following year. *Kairos* is time understood in depth, a moment or a period seen as offering meaning, judgment, opportunity—and *urgency for decision.* The importance of this book is that it takes the *kairos* of today seriously.

Canon Ilogu is concerned to show how the traditional life of the Ibos has, over the last hundred years, been disorganised by Western commerce (preceded by the voracity of the the Western slave trade), by the impact of Christianity, and by the increasing secularising of life in the technological revolution now taking place at an ever increasing pace.

What is the role of the Christian Church in this situation? This book offers an answer based on an impressive range of study, historical, sociological and theological, all mediated through an Ibo's own experience of the traditions of his people, his experience of the Christian Faith, and his involvement in the world of the second half of the 20th Century.

He writes wistfully, partly in sorrow, partly in anger at the failure of the 19th Century Christian missionary impact to understand the religion and the *mores* of the Ibo. For the uninitiated reader it is perhaps important for it to be noted that, for the first 25 years of this missionary impact, all the missionaries were themselves Africans, and not a few with an Ibo heritage. It is not at once obvious that men having names like Crowther, Taylor, Perry, and Johnson were Africans, not Englishmen. It was they who laid the foundations of the Christian Church in the Ibo country. The English missionaries who followed come in, however, for some quite legitimate criticism for their failure in imagination, their insensitivity to the depths in African experience, and their censoriousness: though, in regard to this last point, it is fair to say that they, and their like, were just as censorious about their contemporaries in England!

But our author strikes a fair balance. He is less concerned with the past than with the present *kairos*. How can the Church offer a cement to the Ibo people now living under such intolerable pressures? The answer of this book is that, while maintaining its full Christian allegiance, the Church can offer just such a cement by taking much more seriously some of the "natural" religion inherent in the Ibo consciousness, and baptising its symbols. He has some very practical suggestions which emerge convincingly out of his detailed argument.

Will the Church see the urgency of the present *kairos*? If it does, then, in addition to the particular proposals advanced, there is here an approach which, faithfully explored, will offer a real opportunity to demonstrate that the Ibo people can find in the Christian Faith and in the Christian Church a fulfilment of all that is most profound in their religious heritage. In the Gospel the Ibo people will discover that for them also "the desire of all nations has come".

MAX WARREN

PREFACE

A good deal has been said, and sometimes written, about the foreign nature of the Church in Africa. More time and energy have been expended in blaming it all on early missionaries than in providing constructive literature on how this foreignness can be changed so as to make Christianity as African as its universal nature indicates. This book, therefore, is an attempt to provide some concrete theological and sociological suggestions how Christianity can be related to some aspects of African culture. Because of the vastness of the African continent, generalizations about the continent are avoided. Specific study of a particular people—the Ibo of South-eastern parts of Nigeria—was made in some depth and patterns of Ibo life, values, and therefore culture, are brought into the Christian milieu to indicate how such African cultural patterns can be baptised into the Christian Church. This we believe will, in course of time, help to end the unnecessary foreign garb put on the Church in Africa.

No doubt, many of the Ibo patterns indicated in this study can be identified in various parts of Africa with some minor, and possibly some major variations, as the case may be. What is important is the realisation that we can no longer neglect patterns of our way of life, which by and large, have grown out of our non-Christian religious past. The future of Christianity in any part of Africa, will largely depend on how well we can graft the realities of this our religious cultural past on the vitality of the Christian present. We hope that this Ibo example will serve as a useful introduction to what surely will be the one demanding task of all theologians concerned with the Christian presence amid the African people, namely, the expression of Christianity in an African way of life.

This book grew out of the doctoral dissertation presented to the Faculty of Theology in the State University of Leiden. My thanks, therefore, are due to Professor Dr. E. Jansen Schoonhoven who supervised my thesis as well as to Professor Dr. J. H. M. Beattie who advised me on the anthropological aspects of my work. Other Professors in the Faculty have been very helpful in advising me on the ethical and the historical aspects of the dissertation. It will be invidious to single out some for special mention leaving out others. I must, however, express my gratitude to Professor Dr. M. de Jonge, then the dean of the Faculty, who together with my "Promotor" obtained the necessary permission from the Netherlands Ministry of Education for me to complete my studies at the University. Without the financial grant from the Theological Education Fund, and the leave of absence granted by my own University (the University of Nigeria, Nsukka), I could not have utilized the opportunity at Leiden. The Government of the United States of America awarded me the Fulbright-Hays Fellowship as Visiting Scholar at the University of Chicago during the Fall of 1973. It gave me the opportunity to discuss with some American scholars in the field of the Sociology of Religion in particular and Religion and Culture in general. Some of the insights gained then are reflected in this book, for which I am grateful.

Finally my thanks are due to my many Dutch friends as well as to the staff of the library at the C.M.S. Headquarters in London, the staff of the library of the African Study Centre, Leiden and the staff of the Inter-University Institute for Missiological and Ecumenical Research at 43 Boerhaavelaan in Leiden for their courteous and untiring efforts to assist with books, archival materials and secretarial services, without which, no study could ever bear fruit in the form of a book.

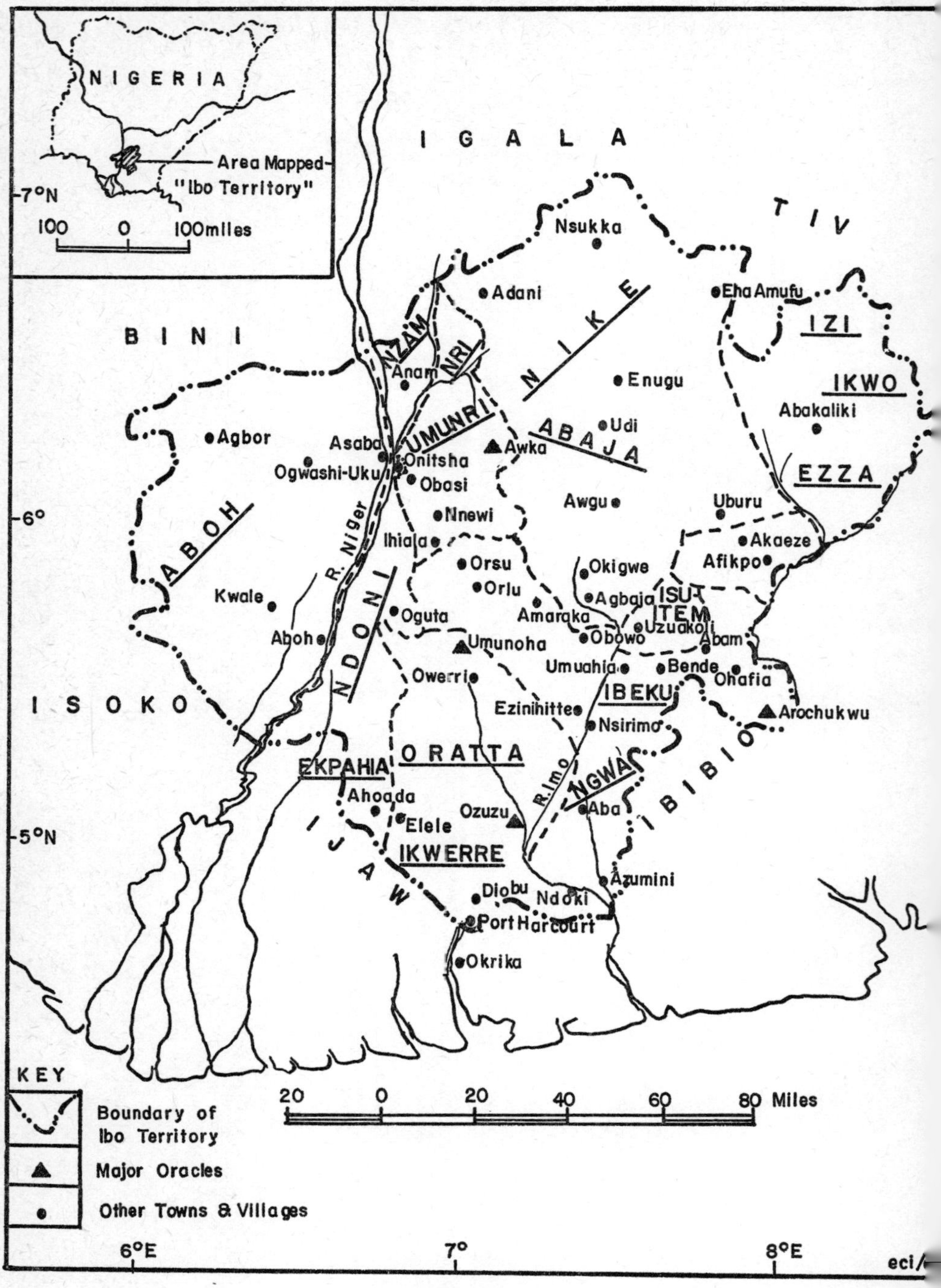

Map of Ibo Territory

CHAPTER ONE

INTRODUCTION

The Ibo, Who they are and where they live

Where the Ibo came from and when, will remain for a long time a matter of conjecture because of the absence of helpful records or archaeological finds by which we can determine date of settlement or place of origin. Dr. Talbot speaks of the migrations set in motion in Egypt in 1870 B.C. by such events as the Nubian wars of Amenemhat I or the conquest of Egypt somewhat later by the Hyksos. These movements are believed to have led some Egyptians to settle in the Yoruba country of Ọyọ and in certain Ibo subtribal areas. [1] Elliot Smith has mentioned some similarity in customs and practices between the Ibo and the ancient Egyptians such as mummification, circumcision, incision, tattooing, the use of the boomerang, serpent and sun worship. [2] More recently a Nigerian, after visiting the British Museum, wrote: "Any observant Ibo or student of Ibo life and culture after close examination of the Egyptian apartment of the Museum will at once begin to ponder in himself what was the original home of the Ibo. This calls for an intensive study. Paintings, wood carving and mode of burial point to a common origin." [3] There has been no such intensive study yet, and so this theory of Egyptian or North African origin of the Ibo, or even Hebrew origin like that claimed by Yoruba scholars for their own tribe, [4] will still remain a conjecture. What is certain is that the Ibo, even if some of them came from Egypt originally, do contain people from other migration movements. (The Onitsha Ibo is said to come from Benin, and the Nri group from Idah.) A few scholars are now prepared to accept that what is at present Awka division, which includes Nri clan, and the Orlu division which includes another widely travelled group of people of Nkwerre and Amigbo (the original home of King Jaja of Opobo fame), is the core of Ibo

---

1 P. Amaury Talbot, The Peoples of Southern Nigeria, Vol. 1, London: Oxford University Press, 1926, p. 19.

2 Referred to by Talbot, *op. cit.*, p. 22.

3 V. Nworah Umunna in *Western Equatorial Africa Church Magazine* of June, 1938.

4 Cf. S. O. Biobaku, The Egbas and Their Neighbours, London: Oxford University Press, 1957, p. 1.

settlement. From here there was a dispersion to the south and to the east. The recent archaeological find at Igbo Ukwu, which Professor Shaw tentatively attributes to the court of the Priest Kings of the Nri people, gives more weight to this hypothesis.[5] These various migration groups arrived at different times only to occupy contiguous geographical units which today include all of Abakaliki, Onitsha, Enugu, Owerri and Umuahia Provinces within the East Central State, some Ikwerre areas of the Rivers State, and parts of Benin, Warri and Delta Provinces in Mid-western Nigeria. Approximately the Ibo live within latitude 5°-7° North of the Equator and longitude 6°-8° East of the Greenwich line. In the absence of reliable and up-to-date population census of Nigeria, the rough estimate of the present Ibo population will be about nine million.

The word Ibo is now used to indicate a language group as well as a culture group. This was not the case some ninety years ago when people from this language group preferred to designate themselves by their clan names. A man from Onitsha for example would refuse to call himself an Ibo but rather an Onitshaman. This changed attitude is significant because it indicates the acceptance of the common factor in culture as well as in the language of the Ibo, despite the fact that there are many subcultural areas as well as many dialects of the one Ibo language. For the purpose of this study we will follow the Forde and Jones division of Ibo land into five subcultural areas,[6] "subcultural" because sharing in the common Ibo cultural pattern, they show some distinguishable cultural differences: (i) Northern or Onitsha Ibo which includes towns like Awka, Udi, Enugu, Enugu-Ukwu, Nsukka, Aro Ndizuogu, Onitsha, Agukwu Nri, Igbo Ukwu and Ihiala. This is the area from which two thirds of the samples of cultural, ethical and religious factors were collected during my field work. It is also the area in which there has been the greatest evidence of the interaction of religions and cultures which have led to the ethical problems we want to examine. (ii) Southern or Owerri Ibo: Within this subcultural area are important clans like Isu Ama, Oratta-

[5] See G. I. Jones, The Trading States of the Oil Rivers, London: Oxford University Press, 1963, p. 30. See also Thurstan Shaw, Igbo-Ukwu-An Account of Archeological discoveries in Eastern Nigeria, in 2 vols, London: Faber and Faber for Institute of African Studies, London and the University of Ibadan, 1970.

[6] See D. Forde, and G. I. Jones, The Ibo and Ibibio Speaking Peoples of South-Eastern Nigeria, London: Oxford University Press for International African Institute, 1950, p. 10.

Ikwerri, Ohuhu Ngwa, and Isu Item. Important towns in this group are Aba, Umuahia Ibeku, Owerri, Ahoada, Okigwi, Orlu (One third of the data was collected from this area, especially from Aba.) (iii) Western Ibo: As the name suggests this is that part of Ibo land which is in the Mid-Western State of Nigeria and includes towns like Asaba, Agbor, Kwale, Illah and Aboh. (iv) Eastern or Cross River Ibo: This area is surrounded by the Efiks and the Ibibio whose language most Ibo from there speak. Important places include Abam, Ohafia, Afikpo, Arochukwu and Abriba. (v) North Eastern Ibo: This is a small subcultural area in which the interaction of religions and cultures seems to be less intense than in other areas. Places of interest here include Ezza, Uburu, Okposi and Abakaliki.

The existence of these various subcultural areas is largely due to the various sources of the different migration groups that now make up the Ibo speaking people. The existence of so many subcultural areas is also due to the absence of any central unifying political organization. I will show in the course of the discussion the common cultural factors that bind these subcultural areas together. Nevertheless we must begin to appreciate, from the onset, some form of diversity which exists both in religious as well as ethical practices, as well as in some details of culture patterns. It is therefore necessary for me to use more frequently the Northern Ibo subcultural area in illustrating details of religious life and culture, but when discussing elements that are common to all Ibo people, I will illustrate from any part of Iboland.

A feature of Iboland which is also found in most parts of Africa is the acceptance of the idea that any agnatic group can move away from one district to go and settle in another and mix with earlier settlers. Physical mobility has therefore become an accepted pattern of culture among the people. Today, with a very high population density in some Ibo areas (about 711 persons per square mile) resulting in the difficulty of finding enough food through agriculture to support the population, many Ibo people migrate to different parts of the country. With this physical mobility goes the spreading of the Ibo way of life in other parts of Nigeria as well as adapting the Ibo way of life through influences from other parts of the country. And although there is always unwillingness and resistance on the part of various ethnic groups in Nigeria to accept openly influences from other groups, yet no study of interactions in the ethical values of Iboland can neglect completely the effect of this dispersion of Ibo people throughout Nigeria. This trend was badly halted by the recent civil war. Yet in the study of culture contact and ethical problems of Iboland, one easily notices the two way traffic in the effect of such contact upon those who stay behind at home and those who migrate to other places. Our study is concerned with the Ibo in Iboland and yet Iboland would definitely be different without the influence from these contacts of Ibo people with the Northern or with the Western parts of this federation as it obtained before the crisis of 1966.[7]

Source Materials and Methods used in Gathering Data

This study, as the title suggests, is both sociological[8] as well as theological, especially theological interpretation of missionary activities. Both the traditional society of Iboland, and the Christian Church that has grown up, contain beliefs and values as well as social structures and institutions, the one conditioning the other or influencing or being influenced by the other. There is a very thin layer separating belief patterns from social life in any so called "primitive" society. The "theologians" of pre-literate societies used to be the social analysts of their community. The prohibitions of gods and goddesses prescribed the structure of social interactions and behavioral patterns. Therefore the relationships between different members of Ibo traditional society were, by and large, determined and upheld by what the ancestors, as spirits of the departed and messengers of the Supreme Deity had ordered. There are bound to be weaknesses in this combination of sociological insight with theological problems as neither the methods nor the demands of either of these two disciplines can possibly be fully developed, especially from the particular position of some fundamentalist theologians. The empirical observations and theoretical analysis consistent with the sociological tradition is not very easily transferable to the theological attempts of describing "revealed" beliefs, values and the contents of human-divine relationships. But insofar as the interaction of any group of religions of any given community (as in this case Christianity and the traditional religion

---

[7] For a very useful discussion on the influence of physical mobility on Ibo receptivity to change, see Simon Ottenberg's essay "Ibo Receptivity to Change" contributed in *Continuity and Change in African Culture* edited by W. R. Boscom and M. J. Herskovits, The University of Chicago Press, 1959, p. 140.

[8] I use the word "sociological" here as an umbrella or convenient term to cover what could be ethnographical and social anthropological study. See "Other Cultures" by John Beattie for differences between sociology, social anthropology and ethnography.

among the Ibo) involves that community also in cultural or social change, the best method of handling our study is suggested by the combination of a theological and a sociological approach. Furthermore this study is meant to be of some practical help to the Church, at least that part of it in Iboland. The Church is both a social institution as well as a "dogma-bearing" and a "dogma-teaching" body. Therefore too exclusive a theological study, especially of a Church within an area of rapid social change, robs that Church of an insight into the social realities and influences upon it from the community in which it exists.

The data used in this study were collected from sources that are partly documentary and partly oral. Parish magazines, newspapers, published synod reports and missionary historical records and materials in archives have been consulted. A good deal of information was obtained from interviews I conducted with elders of the Church and the leaders of traditional religious systems and organizations in different parts of Iboland, especially in Northern Ibo area. References are made in footnotes and in the text to many authors from whose work I have benefited. It has been possible therefore to check oral information with some written records. Sometimes some opinions expressed in reports from missionaries and synod records have been checked against oral information received from old men whose understanding of traditional religion and culture is still authentic, although mellowed by the experiences of the passing years and enlarged by contact with influences from Christianity and Western culture. Nevertheless the limitation imposed upon data gathered through oral information is recognized and allowance made for such limitation which can arise from three possible sources: (1) the traditional etiquette of the Ibo to give the kinds of answers considered pleasant and welcome to a stranger enquirer, Nigerian or foreign; (2) claims of superiority by one village group over another by which some facts are exaggerated by representatives from various village groups; (3) general lack of coherence in religious concepts leading to surprise reactions when research enquirers seek for deeper and more involved information from interviewees. Such further questionings are either dodged or the answers obtained become vague and difficult to analyze.

Questionnaires were sent out to a random sample of students, village elders and town elite. About half of the questionnaires were returned. Replies received through these questionnaires have been analyzed and useful data collected which are summarized under four headings and appear in various parts of the discussion in this study: (1) religious beliefs and practices which relate to the organization of traditional society; (2) some areas of ethical conflict between Christianity and Ibo traditional religious culture; (3) disorganization of ethical and social behaviour and social expectation resulting from confused cultural institutions such as religion and education; and (4) the incidence of unorthodox Churches which results from the search for cultural meaning and identity as well as the search for unity of experience through more traditionally based and therefore indigenised "Christianity."

Aim and the Theoretical Approach of the Study

This study of the interaction of religions, cultures and ethical practices is also a study of a phase of social change. Murdock's theory of social change is found useful in this investigation. In his view, cultural change occurs "whenever social behaviour persistently deviates from established cultural habits in any direction, it results in modifications first in social expectations and then in customs, beliefs and rules." [9] In other words social change is due to the existence of social malfunctioning of the institutions of the society concerned because the experiences, ethical values, ideologies and activities of such society can no more be accommodated within its institutions. There are four processes noticeable in social change which are relevant to the emergence of new ethical guidelines: Innovation, Social Acceptance, Selective Elimination, Integration.

(1) Innovation can be of various kinds, like invention, where innovation involves the transfer of elements of habitual behaviour from one context to another. The most common as well as the most important kind of innovation is cultural borrowing. This is the process of diffusion of some elements of an alien culture through contact which could be either face to face or from "distance." Trade, missionary enterprise and political conquest are more common agents of this kind of cultural borrowing. Incentive is essential in cultural borrowing, as such borrowing will only occur, if the alien culture proves demonstrably rewarding and more satisfying to the needs of the society. Prestige of the alien culture and absence of social prejudice against it facilitate the rate of diffusion. In most situations what is

---

[9] George Peter Murdock, How Culture Changes, quoted by John Eric Nordskog in Social Change, New York: McGraw-Hill Book Company, Inc., 1960, p. 87.

borrowed is only the general idea of the alien culture trait, the specific form of its expression in the new situation is supplied by the genius of the people. In other words, no item of culture borrowed from one culture area develops exactly the same as in its original habitat.[10]

(2) Social Acceptance: This stage inevitably follows the innovation. If the social experience of the people can develop structures of action and of thought congenial to the newly borrowed aspects of culture, then internal or vertical diffusion takes place spearheaded by members of the society rather than by the foreign innovator or source of the cultural borrowing.

(3) Selective Elimination: Newly socially accepted innovations compete with survivals, the less adaptive elements in the new are thrown away, and what looks like the survival of the fittest in organic nature takes place. This is the stage of interaction between the new and the old in the ethical practices and cultural life in the Ibo today.

(4) Integration: This is the stage when the new had found institutions able to express itself, when social relationships and social expectations are more clearly defined once more to generate clear ethical practices. There can never be complete equilibrium in culture, inasmuch as the nature of social action and thought, (the stuff of which culture is made) involves change. The rate of integration and internal adaptation is no doubt higher in a "settled" culture than in a culture undergoing rapid social change as a result of culture contact. Cultural lag which is the term used to describe the period of time between innovation, for instance, in the form of cultural borrowing, and integration is a conflict period, hence rapid social change involves painful changes in role playing, institutional functions and social relationships. Integration is reached when such conflicts and pains remain unnoticeable.[11]

The theoretical approach of this study therefore is that Iboland has come into contact with the Christian religion and Western culture. This contact creates significant alteration in the life condition and behaviour patterns of the people. The situation under which collective behaviour expresses itself is changing; habitual and traditional actions

---

10 Hence the difficulty of having throughout the world a common Christian culture which early missionaries thought they could establish in Iboland, backed up by definite Christian ethical principles. More on this in subsequent chapters.

11 Murdock, *op. cit.* For a good discussion on the social anthropologist's approach to the study of Social Change see John Beattie, Other Cultures: Aims, Methods and Achievements in Social Anthropology, London: Cohen and West, 1964, pp. 241-264.

are becoming more difficult because their basis in customs, social ethos and expectations is being destroyed. New responses are seeking new bases on which to build themselves. This is the stage in social change known as selective elimination. This study is an attempt to analyze this "selective elimination" process and through such analysis to reach some conclusion which is the thesis of the study, namely that the surest basis on which new responses can be built is through the values, the ethos and the customs derived from religion. It is further argued that Christianity could be the religion to do this for Iboland, provided that it is Christianity which has established deep roots in the cultural soil of Iboland. Hence the belief that there is the possibility of the emergence of a viable Christian ethic in an African background.

In adopting this theory of social change and giving emphasis to normative considerations based on religion, we are not unmindful of the many debates going on as to what is the more appropriate theory of social change. Owing to the dynamic nature of society including the self regulating quality of social units, the older deterministic theories with emphasis on groups and economic *cum* technological causes of change, do no longer satisfy. Others like the role/status theory or the structural-functional theory have been advanced.[12] Emphasis is more and more being placed now on the study of change through exploring in detail the ramifications of particular actions, so as to indicate how new types of social situations, relationships and values are emerging. This will help to indicate the direction of change.[13] Instead of studying "one theory oriented" pattern of social change the tendency now is to study situations. The segmentary society of Iboland seems best studied through such situational analyses in which elements of religious functionalism, conflicts between the traditional culture and the invading Western Christian culture, together with areas of consensus among them, are carefully examined.[14] It is

---

[12] See Richard M. Henderson, The King in Every Man: Evolutionary Trends in Onitsha Ibo Society and Culture, New Haven and London: Yale University Press, 1972, pp. 1-26 where the author makes an inclusive survey of the theories of social change anthropologists and sociologists have advanced together with his suggestion that an evolutionary system which includes many facets is a more satisfactory theory of social change.

[13] See Norman Long, Social Change and the Individual: A Study of the Social and Religious Responses to Innovation in a Zambian Rural Community, Manchester: The University Press, 1972, p. 10.

[14] See also J. Milton Yinger, Sociology Looks at Religion, New York: The Macmillan Company, 1963, p. 40, where the author indicates five possible angles from which students of religion view the influence of religion on social change.

from an understanding of the crisis of change in an African society that a workable ethics for such a society will emerge.

Scope of the Enquiry

The scope of this study as suggested by the title concerns the interaction between Christian ethics and Ibo traditional morality. It is therefore necessary that some definition be made. It is a study of the interaction of religions and cultures, a study of the resultant effect of Christianity in its contact with an African type of traditional religion. The cultures that are interacting are the technical, secular and Christian tainted Western culture and the African type of culture extant in Iboland, which had for many years expressed itself in religious terms of ethical and customary practices. We do not intend to study in this enquiry culture as such in its complex and far reaching meaning.[15] We are only interested in culture insofar as it is closely related to religious ethics which is the main topic of our study. For although religion is one of the basic institutions of culture (and there are other basic institutions like the family, education, politics and economics) yet it is religion which gives to culture ultimate orientation and direction. This it does, not only in the values and beliefs which it upholds, but also by the way religion creates the patterns of relationships between individuals and groups, through the values by which such individuals and groups make choices and thereby develop culture. It is because of this kind of involvement of religion in the culture, traditional and modern, of Iboland that we concern ourselves only up to that point with Ibo culture. Otherwise our central concern is with the interaction which Christianity today has with Ibo traditional religious life and values. In this interaction we will leave alone such

---

Yinger prefers to work from the perspective in which "religion is part of a complex interacting system. On some particular issue and from the perspective of a given point in time, religious developments may best be understood as responses to fundamental changes in their social environment. The new religious forces then 'feed back into' the system from which they came, influencing the course of its development. On another issue, viewed again from a given point in time, religious change may be the *dynamic factor* (my italics). The influences thus set in motion become, in turn, conditioning and constraining forces that affect the religion which released them." We accept this perspective and study the ethics of social change situation of Iboland through ethnohistory, Christian history and the impact of technology and secularization.

[15] Cf. E. B. Tylor's definition of culture as ... "that complex whole which includes knowledge, belief, art, morals, law, custom, and any other capabilities and habits acquired by man as a member of society." Primitive Culture, London: John Murray, 1871, Vol. I, p. 1.

possible and certainly rewarding enquiries into the interaction that the various sects or denominations of Christians make upon each other. For example, the more individualistic Protestant approach to theology has its social encounter with the more institutional approach of the Roman Church within the one Christian group in Iboland, resulting in various ethical emphases. This is different from the interaction which Christianity has with traditional religion and social customs. But because to pursue the former would make the scope of our enquiry too wide, that area of interaction between the various groups of the many Christian bodies in Iboland, will be left out. Attention will be paid to the emergence of many prophetic and sometimes unorthodox Churches which have sprung up possibly as a means of solving, too easily, the problems created by the interaction of Christian ethics and traditional morality. We will endeavour to examine how far these new Christian offshoots, that are sometimes unorthodox Churches, come into being as the answer to the people's demand for cultural unity, personal identity and social security through a religion expressive of their understanding of the true meaning of life and its ethical demands. In discussing these points, we have selected three Ibo areas (Ihiala, Nsukka, Aba) for closer study as well as three Ibo institutions (*Ọzọ* title, polygamy and the extended family). It is hoped that such closer study will lead towards the clarifications of concepts of Church growth in Iboland, through a greater understanding of the ethical significance of social change brought about by Christianity in that part of Africa. The study will end by examining our concept of Church growth in the light of the views of men like Kraemer, Visser 't Hooft and Van Leeuwen and conclude whether or not, from the thesis we have proposed, there can be Christian ethics in an African (that is non-Christian) background.

CHAPTER TWO

IBO TRADITIONAL SOCIETY

Kinship, Institutions and Cultural Patterns

Umunna (*Patrilineage*)

The localised patrilineage (*Umunna* [1]) is the central or basic social unit of Ibo society. It is made up of the descendants, in the male line, of a founder ancestor by whose name the lineage is sometimes called. At the bottom of the lineage are families of men, their wives and children living in homesteads surrounded by a mud wall. Sometimes the homesteads contain within the walled compounds not only men, their wives and children, but also patrilineal cousins. Sometimes brothers with their own respective wives and children live within one walled compound. [2]

The size of a lineage (*Umunna*) varies. There are segmentations into major sublineages and minor sublineages. Very often members of *Umunna* occupy a single hamlet of scattered homesteads.

Ebe, Ebo, Ogbe, Ama. These Ibo words are used to designate a group of villages or "the land and homesteads along a given path" (*ama*). [3] There are two kinds of villages: a village made up of various homesteads or compounds whose owners are members of the lineages that claim ultimate common descent. The other kind is a cluster of hamlets made up of homesteads or compounds whose occupants are members of various lineages, all of which do not claim ultimate common descent, and therefore can intermarry. The village in this latter instance is mainly a geographical unit providing some considerable solidarity based on neighbourhood rather than on immediate "blood relationship".

---

[1] Various terms are used in different parts of Iboland for the lineage unit which we describe here as *Umunna*, for example *Onu Ama* is used in Orlu area; some use *Agburu, ndi be* (the people of...). Whatever the term, the characteristics are common: allegiance to an ancestor "father", one shrine, one totem animal and no intermarriage among the members.

[2] This is what older writers on Ibo society call "the extended family" and Uchendu calls "the compound". See V. C. Uchendu, The Igbo of Southeast Nigeria, New York: Holt, Rinehart and Winston, 1965, p. 40.

[3] Daryll Forde and G. I. Jones, The Ibo and Ibibio-speaking Peoples of South-Eastern Nigeria, London: Oxford University Press, 1950, p. 17.

Various villages or subclans group together to form what the Ibos call *Obodo* or *Mba*, that is the "village group" or town. [4] The village group (*Obodo, Mba*) is in most cases the highest political unit, and centre of the modern forms of development and co-operative activities in what Uchendu calls "helping the town to get up". [5]

Let us illustrate Ibo various kinship net work with Ihiala a "village group" in Ihiala Division in Northern Ibo area. There are two subclans, Ezi and Ihite. Ezi has five *Ebe* (quarters or group of villages) and Ihite also has five *Ebe*. Hence in music and parables, as well as in myths, Ihiala is spoken of as the people of ten *Ebe*, (*Ebe leri* Ihiala). One of the *Ebe* in Ezi is Amamumu (the descendants of Amumu, one of the original inhabitants of the "village group"). This has ten *Umunna* units. One of the *Umunna* units is Nwajiobi — a lineage having within it three major sublineages known as Umu-Umerue, Umu-Ogamanya, Umu-Asodike. Umu-Asodike again divides into two minor sublineages known as Umu-Mgbeafulike and Umu-Nwaku. Thus all members of Umu-Nwajiobi regard themselves as *Umunna* (the highest unit of Umunna, that is a lineage); again all members of Umu-Asodike (one of the children of Nwajiobi) regard themselves as *Umunna* (a smaller unit of *Umunna*, that is a major sublineage); and all the children of Nwaku (a son of Asodike) also regard themselves as *Umunna* (the smallest unit of *Umunna*, that is a minor sublineage).

Therefore all Umunwajiobi regard themselves as "brothers". Then all Umu-Asodike regard themselves as closer "brothers" and all Umu-Nwaku regard themselves as closer "brothers" still. Hence the word *Umunna* applies to three levels of lineage relationships in this case; viz. all Umu-Nwajiobi is one *Umunna*. All descendants of Asodike (one of Nwajiobi's children) are one *Umunna* within the Umu-Nwajiobi *Umunna*. And then finally all descendants of Nwaku (one of Asodike's children) constitute *Umunna*. So that when a member of Nwaku speaks of his *Umunna* he could mean one or all of these three.

---

[4] The term "village group" is preferred to "town" because Iboland is predominantly agricultural, and various homesteads are separated by farms and gardens, making it difficult for the term "town" to be applied to such a unit. But because such peoples share a market place, possibly one ruler and an assumption of common ancestry (remote) possibly a common *Ọzọ* title rank, they regard themselves as a unit—a "town" *otu mba, otu obodo*. For growth of modern towns see chapter V.

[5] Uchendu, *op. cit.*, p. 34 ff. For "village group", Church life and modern interactions, see chapter V.

To illustrate subclans and lineages of Ihiala

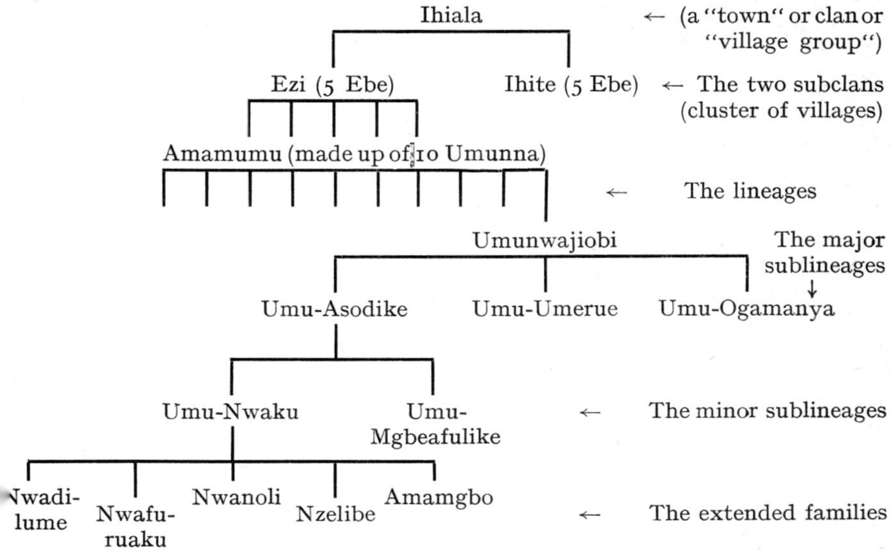

There is an *Okpara* or head of all Nwajiobi as well as the *Okpara* or heads for Umu-Asodike, Umu-Umerue and Umu-Ogamanya. Umu-Nwaku also has its own *Okpara* or head. All Umunwajiobi has one or two gods and shrines in common, but also each of the three sub-lineages in Umunwajiobi has its own particular ones. In addition Umunwajiobi together with the two other lineages that make up the *Mbara* (village) of Akpaka has common gods, common shrines and a common square. So a young man born in Umu-Nwaku minor sub-lineage, for instance, shares in the extended family of his own father (say Nzelibe on the diagram), he also has his own Nwaku minor sublineage rights, his own Asodike major sublineage relationships, and his own Nwajiobi lineage membership. He also shares in the community life of the village known as Mbara-Akpaka, and he is in all things a member of Amamumu from Ezi subclan, and finally a son from Ihiala "village group" or "town".

He has some claims, and shares to certain extent, in the membership of his mother's family as *Nwadiala* (child of our daughter). This intricate network of relationships involved in the concept of the lineage structures of Ibo traditional life, is the basis for understanding the Iboman's social consciousness, the structures of his political, religious and economic concerns and the means of bringing up children in the customs, ethos and manners, that is to say, the culture of the people. Let us discuss these further.

Owing to the network of relations within the various levels of the lineage a man is always certain of "belonging". He has responsibilities and claims according to his status, age or ability. For example the work of building of a new house for any member of the sublineages is shared by his kinsmen. Equally so the farm work of the *Okpara* or the senior member of each unit is the responsibility of all the women and young men at least once in a while. No young man goes to another lineage to take a wife without some members of his own *Umunna* meeting representative members of the girl's own lineage. The marriage when consummated is in fact the joining together, for many things and the mutual interest, of these two marriage-related "lineages". There is a type of corporate personality shared by all the members of a given lineage. When a gifted speaker from one such lineage speaks with others from other "families" he may employ the singular first person while referring to all his people back at home. What idle boasts he may sometimes make, are regarded binding by all his people upon them all. There is even the practice which is dying out now, where debt owed by a member of such *Umunna* can be forcibly settled by the initiative of the creditor in seizing a goat, or any other such property, as may belong to any member of the debtor's Umunna or lineage. Births, deaths and memorials, or any of such occasions, are the concern of all the members of the minor sublineage at least and in some instances all the members of the lineage too.

Political Concerns

Each household has its head and each lineage, i.e., *Umunna* has its own. Most, if not all of such heads, are elderly senior titled men in those parts of the Iboland where the *Ọzọ* title exists. (We shall explain more fully what the *Ọzọ* titles are later, on pp. 30-33). When there is a dispute to be adjudicated publicly in the interest of a village made up of various *Umunna,* all the elders and heads of all the *Umunna* concerned would assemble at the senior *Okpara's Iba, Obi* or *Obu* (the nobleman's public meeting and ceremonial house) with their *Ọfọ* [6] sticks (emblem of being representatives of dead ancestors and of religious authority) and listen to the two sides of the quarrel and punish-

[6] See page 18 ff. below where we discuss more fully the meaning and significance and the various uses of the *Ofo* stick in Ibo religion and society. See also the glossary of Ibo words used in this study, Appendix I.

ment decided according to custom. The sort of things that are publicly judged include *aru* (pollution or abominations) which are against the earth goddess (*Ala*) believed to bring disintegration to the *Umunna*, village or town such as murder of a fellow townsman, incest, stealing of yam especially by an *Ọzọ* title person. [7] The punishment for such offences includes propitation of the earth goddess (*Ala*) by an *Ala* priest assisted by a priest from Nri town. The Nri people are said to be special priests of the gods in most parts of Iboland, their king being the only priest king known in Ibo stories of origin. The *Ọfọ* stick is believed to be effective only when ceremonially produced and "washed" by a Nri person. Where the culprit pleads innocence of the offence, the council of elders may direct that he swears by *Ala* or be taken to one of the four important oracles of Ibo society in order that the oracle may pronounce him innocent or guilty. If guilty, such person fails to return to the village but rather is "eaten up" by the oracle. In other cases the punishment for the offender might be that he be sold into slavery, as his continued existence in that village might bring great calamity, as punishment from the gods, upon the whole commune.

Various other groups apart from the "council" of heads of lineages carry out one form of political activity or the other. Senior married women enforce their own laws about markets, their cleaning and the cleaning of the springs from where water is collected. If matters are very difficult for the women "council", they refer to the most senior *Okpara* and his council. There are various age sets (people born within a five year period constitute one age set). Such a group is drawn from all lineages living within a locality like the village or *Mbara* or *Ebe*. Different age sets do different community duties depending on their seniority, for example, the five to ten years group

---

[7] In Chapters II and III I have avoided much references in footnotes to existing materials on Ibo religion and society. Materials that are available and which throw much light on points discussed here include: C. K. Meek, Law and Authority in a Nigerian Tribe, London: Oxford University Press, 1950; M. Green, Ibo Villiage Affairs (Chiefly with reference to the village of Umueke Agbaja), London: Sidgwich & Jackson, 1947; J. Harris, "Human Relationship to The Land in Southern Nigeria", A paper read before the American Anthropological Association and the American Association for the Advancement of Science at Philadelphia, December 28, 1940, published in *Rural Sociology*, n.d.; G. T. Basden, Niger Ibos, London: Seeley, Service and Co., Ltd., n.d.; G. T. Basden, Among the Ibos, London: Seeley, Service and Co., Ltd., n.d., republished by Frank Cass, London, 1966; I. Nzimiro, Studies in Ibo Political Systems: Chieftancy and Politics in Four Niger States, London: Frank Cass, 1971 and Berkeley and Los Angeles: University of California Press, 1972. For a more comprehensive list, see Bibliography at the end.

sweeps the village square, the fifteen to twenty years group makes the roads, and newly married wives clean the springs.

The *Otu Muo* (the masquerade society) members also perform some political duties: they guard the village against thieves, collect fines from people pronounced guilty of offences, and help in seeing that *aru* (pollutions) are not hidden. The warrior grade includes all able bodied men from twenty-one years up to about forty years. Although the elders have some judicial and political powers, Ibo society does not know anything like an oligarchy. As C. K. Meek aptly puts it, "The elders were a body of mediators and referees rather than of prosecutors and judges, and the community was a republic in the true sense of that term, i.e., a corporation in which government was the concern of all". [8]

Apart from the *Okpara* and titled men or heads of lineages, most places in Iboland have an *Eze* (King). Such Eze as are powerful enough to rule over extensive areas, exercise both priestly and social leadership through the *Okpara,* heads of families, lineages and clans rather than through their own staff. There were no *Eze* whose authority extended to very wide areas and so the Ibo did not in the past organize empires or kingdoms. Rather marriage, and common interests like defence against any warrior intruders, united many communes into voluntary confederations. [9]

To complete the picture of the traditional Ibo political institution mention must be made of the laws of the land which, by and large, are in the form of prohibitions, said to have been sanctioned by *Ala* (the earth goddess). These are the codes that regulate community life and yet they bear more religious significance, hence the leadership and the significance of the Ala priests and the diviners who say what customs or codes have been broken and what social, political and religious steps are to be taken to secure "justice" for god and man. Examples are (1) not to take the life of a member of the commune; (2) not to steal, especially yams, the staple food of the people; (3) not to commit incest; (4) not to defraud strangers (this practice is not common to most Ibo areas); (5) not to hide *aru* (pollution or abominations) that pervert the course of nature, e.g., hiding children born with teeth, or twins, or goats that deliver in the night time. These

---

[8] C. K. Meek, Law and Authority in a Nigerian Tribe, London: Oxford University Press, 1950, p. 130.

[9] See, Ikenna Nzimiro, *op. cit.,* for kingship in four Ibo areas.

and other examples will be fully discussed as part of Ibo ethics in chapter VI.

Religious Concerns

We will discuss Ibo religious beliefs and practices in the next chapter. What we wish to include here are those general patterns of religious concern that reveal the nature of the traditional society and its ethical demands. Each household has its shrines and local as well as special family gods. In Ihiala town, for instance, any titled man has the shrine of the ancestors called *Ndebunze*. This is always placed at a prominent part of the *Iba*, that is the public house where people are received. Carved panels are built into elevated floor space, with pots planted behind the panels immediately outside the house near which an *ogirisi* tree is also planted to indicate the principal shrine, that is the *Ndebunze* shrine. At the end of the main entrance way to the walled compound is the *Ihu Aho* shrine with the stick (cultus symbol) of *Chukwu* planted. All along this passage way are the shrines of local gods like, *Ihu Ulasi,* and *Ihu Agwunsi* and *Ihu Ala.* These constitute the personal domestic gods and shrines of any titled man, which he has gradually acquired as he takes one title after the other. In addition there are the shrines and gods of the various lineages at a central spot chosen by divinerpriests. Then there are the village shrines of *Ulasi Ogboro, Egbo Chukwu* and *Ihu Ndoro Ohia.* In Owerri area the shrines of *Mbari* houses built to *Ala* are prominent. In Awka area *Agbara* shrines are prominent.

Domestic shrines are given daily worship especially *Ndebunze* (ancestors). Others receive occasional worship, some quarterly and some monthly. Particular sacrifice of atonement is given to the lineage gods when and as ordered by the diviner for any member of the man's household, especially wives and married daughters. The lineage shrines as well as village gods are worshipped at specified months of the year, for instance, *Ifejioku,* the god of farms, is worshipped at public ceremonial by the middle of the third month, which is the same as March, before the start of a new agricultural season.

The chief characteristics of Ibo religious life are three, namely, variety, communality and utility. Variety exists in the number of gods, places where they are worshipped and the method and manner of worship. Young people can spend the greater part of the year accompanying their fathers to one kind of celebration or the other, without noticing too much monotony. Communality is the essence of the gods.

They are the common possessions and guardians of all. No one sins to the gods alone. Punishment for the sin of one man is visited on all. The blessings of the gods are also shared by all. No god and no act of worship is for mere love of the gods. Rather it is an act either of supplicating for benefits, or pleading for atonement. Utility, therefore, is the most important reason the Iboman can give for the existence of the gods. Hence all of his life activities are geared towards these gods, be it in the economic activities of planting food crops, or in the upbringing of his children, or in the more individual incidents of being born, being married and being buried. This idea of utility, therefore, is the third important feature of Ibo traditional religion.

The *Ọfọ* stick is very important in Ibo religion and life and should be discussed a bit more here. It is a stick of varying sizes from about two inches long, and half an inch in diameter, to something near five inches long and one and a half inches in diameter, becoming thinner towards the tail end. It is made out of a branch of the *Detarium Senegalense* tree. One of the special features of this tree is that the branches fall off from the parent trunk when they are fully grown. No cutting of the *Ọfọ* branch is done. It is believed that *Chuwku* (the great God) purposely created this tree to be sacred, and by the manner its branches fall off unbroken, he (*Chukwu*) symbolizes the way families grow up and establish new extended families and lineages. Therefore the *Ọfọ* made out of these branches is the abode of the spirit of dead ancestors, hence the authority and the sacredness of the *Ọfọ*, as well as the special place given to it as the emblem of unity, truth and indestructibility for the individual or the group possessing the *Ọfọ*.

There are various kinds of *Ọfọ* and various uses made of it. A young man acquires his first *Ọfọ* when he is initiated into his first *Ọzọ* title where titles are taken. In Nri and associated clans like Enugu Ukwu, when a young man makes the *Amanwulu* he is given the *Ọfọ* stick. The same thing happens when at Ihiala a young man is initiated into the *Oruru Ifejioku* or *Agwu Nsi* or *Akpa Aja*. The *Ọfọ* is consecrated by Nri priests (the Nri people are the original priest kings of Iboland) before it is given to the young man. As he advances into the more senior *Ọzọ* title he acquires more *Ọfọ* sticks. But the most important *Ọfọ* is the lineage one said to have been first acquired by the founder of the *Umunna*. If we are to take our Ihiala diagram (see page 13) the *Umunna Ọfọ* first owned by Nwajiobi would pass on to the oldest son, that is, the *Okpara* and head of Umunwajiobi lineage. At the death of such a head the next *Okpara* inherits it. To transfer any such *Ọfọ* a ceremonial washing is performed by a specially chosen priest, in which a cock is killed and its blood poured on the *Ọfọ*. The individual *Ọfọ* of an *Ọzọ* title man can only be inherited by his eldest son after all the burial rites have been performed. It is regarded as a calamity when a dead father has no sons to inherit his *Ọfọ*. Let me now mention some of the uses made of the *Ọfọ* stick:

(1) It is the means of prayer to the gods. The young man who first begins to supplicate the gods at his *Amanwulu* cultus symbol, strikes his *Ọfọ* to the ground as he makes his requests to *Chukwu* in front of the shrine of which ever particular god is worshipped at that time. (2) The *Ọfọ* is used for swearing in all grave cases. It is also used for cursing people. (3) When any *Ọzọ* title person speaks and kisses his *Ọfọ* stick, it is a sign of a most solemn protestation as to the gravity or the truthfulness of what he says. (4) The *Ọfọ* of the lineage is the outward symbol of the presence of the dead ancestors of the lineage or the clan and therefore must be displayed when all the living are assembled for important "family" discussion. (5) It is used by the *Ala* priests to remove the evil effects of abominations after the proper sacrifices have been offered. (6) Because the head of each level of the lineage is charged with holding the *Ọfọ* of that group, he becomes not only its political and social leader, but also that "family's" priest and uses the *Ọfọ* in blessing the people at all public worship. (7) Prohibitions are made with *Ọfọ*. When a husband does not want to accede to his wife's request he would strike the *Ọfọ* on the ground saying at the same time "If I will ever accede to this request of yours let this *Ọfọ* kill me". (8) All unpleasant decisions of the elders are enforced by the *Ọfọ*. If certain young men question the decisions of the elders in any matter, the elders may reconsider and cancel such decisions. But if the elders feel sure that their decision is not only just and good, but also the upholding of customs, the elders can say: "anyone who wishes to disobey this our decision, may this *Ọfọ* kill him", striking their *Ọfọ* on the ground. The protest dies down soon after such cursing with the *Ọfọ*. (9) The Diviner (*Nwa Dibia*) uses *Ọfọ* as one of the apparatuses of divination, as it is generally believed that the ancestors, whose spirits the *Ọfọ* represents, are always helpful in determining a successful result of the particular subject for which a client seeks divination.

Economic Concerns

Ibo traditional society knows only of subsistence economy and trade by barter. Self supporting family units do farm work on land sometimes commonly owned (by the male adult members of the lineage concerned) and sometimes on privately owned land. They alternate this farm work with the making of crafts of household necessities which are sometimes marketed. Land, food, crops, communal work, pure craftsmanship and attention to the gods of economic life are the main factors of such economy. Land can be grouped mainly into four kinds: that owned collectively by the minor sublineage, the farming of which is directed by the *Okpara*; personal lands which a man has received in pledge for cattle or services; sacred land (*ajo ofia*) which no one goes into except the priests of the gods to whom such lands are dedicated; virgin land which any enterprising man can enter, appropriate by cultivating it, or establish a new settlement on it. For serious economic purposes only farm lands provide avenues for producing food and other means of livelihood. Crops commonly planted are yam (and later cocoyams), cassava, beans, corn, maize, okra and all forms of vegetables. Palm trees, breadfruit trees (Ukwa, *Treculia Africana*) and pawpaws, pear trees (Ube, a tropical plant, *dacryodes edulis*) and plantains seem to grow on their own without any special replanting or much attention. The purpose for agricultural work is to provide food for the family, and for the many social feasts which custom demands from all the inhabitants of any locality at various times of the year. Livestock like cows, pigs, goats and chickens are reared. These animals together with food crops, especially yams and palm trees, constitute a man's wealth. Because agricultural work of this nature requires a large number of people, a wealthy man of the kind described here, is also expected to have many wives and many children. Communal farm work is practised by which young men and their wives work at least one day, in an eight day native week, for the *Okpara* of the lineage or even the head of the small extended family unit or even of the household.

The only "savings" practised among Ibos in traditional society seem to be what is saved in the *Ọzọ* title. All the *Ọzọ* titled men share in the various things and properties which the person to be initiated must pay at various stages before he is finally installed. In this way those who had spent so much of their property in taking their own title receive in many years some "income" with which to help themselves, especially in old age.[10] Moreover the extended family and lineage structures provide for relatives to look after their old men and women, and so there is not the economic incentive towards saving for the rainy days of old age.

Certain crafts were family concerns which only members of such a family learnt, practiced and taught their young ones. Wood carving, pottery, cloth weaving, blacksmithery and basket weaving were prominent among such crafts. Sometimes in certain places these crafts were not regarded as a means of securing economic well being, but rather a form of service to the community. Some blacksmiths did not charge for what they did, regarding their work mainly as religious duties to the god of the farmlands. At Ihiala there was a famous basket weaver who gladly received any presents that the village women gave to him in return for baskets he made for them. Almost all sculptures known in Iboland were devoted to religious uses and therefore not regarded as economic activity at all. Art in general did not in Ibo traditional society earn income for any artist. In fact economic activities as such were not clearly distinguished. Considerations about nobility through achieved status, plus privilege of birth, outweighed a purely economic pursuit for its own sake. Markets were widely scattered and each market became important due to those commodities which were best produced in the area where the market was situated. Uburu is the native salt and cow market, Onitsha yam and fish market, Eke Nkwesi near Oguta corn and maize market, and Uzuakoli was famous for slaves and the few imported goods of those days. There were no trade guilds as such but certain towns or village groups specialized in certain crafts and economic activities. For instance Awka was the centre from where many people travelled out to various Ibo communes as blacksmiths, medicine men (*dibia*) and wood carvers; Nri Agukwu was known for all forms of religio-economic activities like removing *aru* (abominations or pollution), tattooing or incision of the face with the *ichi* marks and the production and distribution of the *Ọfọ* stick, especially in the Northern Ibo areas; the Aros from Arochuku were foremost in trading in slaves and in escorting people to the Oracle of *Chukwu* in their land.

---

[10] The Isusu (thrift co-operative or improvement societies) which have become prominent in Ibo society in recent times might have arisen as an answer to the diminishing instances of *Ọzọ* title taking. See S. Ottenberg, "Improvement Associations Among the Afikpo Ibo", *Africa*, Vol. XXV, No. 1, January, 1955; M. M. Green, Ibo Village Affairs, London: Sidgwick and Jackson, Ltd., 1947, pp. 44-48.

Cultural Patterns and Customs

The cultural pattern that emerges through looking at the traditional social structures of Iboland as well as the institutions of family, religion and economic pursuits could be termed communalistic. Emphasis is placed on the commune rather than the individual, and moral obligations are regulated more by the demands of moral codes, tradition and custom than by the exercise of individual moral judgment and conscience. Yet the individuals' responsibility to the commune is clear and never shirked because social expectation as well as shared values are commonly observed and the social ethos of the village is jealously guarded and upheld both by religion as well as by the accepted practices and prohibitions of the community.

Omenani

The Ibo word used in describing custom is *omenani.* This word is sometimes interpreted as tradition. *Aru* (abomination or pollution) or *Nso Ala* (behaviour contrary to the laws of *Ala,* that is, the earth deity) are two words that are used when speaking of contraventions against approved social and religious norms. There are two main kinds of custom: customs that pertain to morality and those that are purely social and cultural. All the codes of morality are nearly always in the form of prohibitions sanctioned by the earth goddess (*Ala*), and communicated from her by the dead ancestors (*Ndichie* or *Ndebunze*) to the community. Examples of moral customs will be discussed later under morality. Social and cultural traditional practices are detailed for each activity that makes up the institutions of society. There are various *omenani* (customs) governing, for example, marriage, burial, offering of kola nuts, drumming or style of speaking. [11] This means that Ibo customs range from very serious subjects, like methods of social control, to the more minute demands of etiquette and polite behaviour. It is against tradition for a man who is not *Osu* (persons dedicated to a god as slaves of that god) to marry an *Osu* girl. It is against *omenani* (tradition or "custom") in some places to mourn aloud the death of any man on *Eke Ukwu* market day. It is against "custom" for a cock to crow in the middle of the night for this is *aru* or ritual pollution. It is against *omenani* or "custom" for a young man to say to an *Ọzọ* title man "*lie nsi*" (go and eat excreta). No

---

[11] Details of customs governing any institution will be given when discussing that institution, only general points are made here.

breach of *omenani* goes unpunished. Tradition prescribes the various things that must be done to take away the evil effects of such breaches, or else the spirits of the ancestors and *Ala* will plague the society. *Omenani* therefore becomes the means by which traditional Ibo society enforces conformity. Culturally speaking, *omenani* is the means by which the social ethos is measured, the values of the society are continued from one generation to another, and the processes of socialization through the education of the young ones are facilitated. Harmony and equilibrium are in this way maintained as every member of the society knows what to expect from his neighbours and what to give to them, simply by observing the well known customary way of behaviour and moral code, that is, *omenani*.

Because *omenani* is derived from the goddess of *Ala* and sanctioned by the ancestors, it is religious in nature, although it fulfils social, moral and cultural functions. It's hold on the community derives from the power of the goddess and the ancestors. Hence the unquestioned obedience which the community gives to it. In the absence of writing and formal school education, *omenani* becomes the means of summarizing the social philosophy and religious doctrine of the Ibo. Apart from those customs which are observed as laws or prohibitions and social codes, there are those which embody the myths of society expressed in the rituals of public worship and seasonal ceremonial observances. It is omenani or the customary practice to bury the navel cord that falls off from a new born child underneath the tap root of a fruit tree like *ube* (native pear tree, *dacryodes edulis*). Buried in this practice is the belief that we as human beings share life with *Ala* (earth), that we have our nature which is partly made of earth, and that our sustenance comes from the fruits of the earth and at death we rejoin in our bodies, the composition of earth whilst our soul joins our ancestors, who with the authority of *Ala*, rule and govern the earth on which the community builds its homes and society. On the day of celebrating *Obi Umuaka* (Hearts of Children) such a tree is chosen and a shrine constructed at which sacrifices are offered to remind teenage children of their relationship to *Ala* and to ancestors and to the community.

Another aspect of *omenani* is what is commonly called taboo or ritual avoidances. It is a ritual pollution in many Ibo areas to kill the *aka* snake or to eat the royal python. The python, for instance, is a totem animal supposed to embody the communal soul of the people and therefore sacred and shares with the *Ala* goddess in the protection of the community. Custom prescribes the appropriate sacrifice which the *Ala* priest will offer before the python is removed from any house into which it had crawled.

There are taboos or ritual avoidances which custom prescribes for persons holding specific office or position. *Ala* priests for instance, or *Ọzọ* title men, *dibia* or minstrels do observe taboos peculiar to their callings. Certain sacred bushes, groves and streams are not to be entered into by any other person than the priests or the initiated persons. Fishes in sacred streams are regarded as sacred and never to be caught or eaten. It is in the utter disregard of, and organized disobedience to, these taboos and customs of ritual avoidances that the conflict between Christianity and Ibo traditional life first started to manifest itself. Examples include: many Churches were built on sacred lands; many newly converted Christians did not only pollute the sacred streams by fishing in them but also ate those sacred fishes to show that they have turned their backs against such customs. We will discuss details of this kind of conflict later. Meanwhile let me mention the general ritual avoidances which could also be called *aru,* pollution or "abominations". These include homicide, kidnapping, birth of twins or deformed children, stealing of yams, conspiracy to commit a felony, evil sickness like chicken pox. When any of these "*aru*" takes place the *Ala* priest of the village or clan concerned prescribes the sacrifice of atonement and cleansing of the earth with a sheep after due punishment of the offenders. Twins or deformed children were killed, those guilty of homocide, kidnapping, stealing of yams or conspiracy were sold away into slavery so that their evils may not be repeated or their presence continue to annoy *Ala* and provoke her to punish the people.

The Individual and Group Life

From the discussion of the traditional Ibo lineage structure commonly called *Umunna,* it is already indicated that group life with its web of social life is very strong, and the ties of relationship far spread, and the pattern of life is communalistic. We will now describe the many institutions, organizations and activities by which this group life is integrated, continued and allowed to provide satisfying moral concepts of life for the individual, who willingly or unwillingly must share in the group life. The more religious activities, ceremonies and observances will be discussed in the next chapter.

A convenient starting point for the discussion of the way the individual shares in Ibo group life is the method of rearing children. Most traditional homes are polygamous, therefore the husband helps in constructing houses for each of his wives, sometimes in a semi circular position with his own house dominating at the centre. Each child lives with its mother in her house and is fed by her although the father during the harvest season may provide the raw food to be cooked. The father calls on any of his children to run errands for him or accompany him to family, lineage or village meetings, religious observances or any of the many social ceremonies of the village. Through these contacts those children who stay near their father learn the traditional ways and customs. Otherwise the duty of training the child in the manners, ethos and patterns of life in the community largely devolves on the mothers. The spirit of competition is engendered by the mothers who hate to see their own children become second rate in the estimation of their husband and the other members of the extended family. It is a common saying among the people that when a child misbehaves it is called by the mother's name. This saying may be true to a large extent yet the force that influences the life of a child socially and morally may not be that of his parents. It could well come from two other sources, namely members of the extended family and members of his age set or his play mates in general. Members of the extended family or the child's parents take it upon themselves to correct, teach and admonish the child. Sometimes a child's aunt or uncle or cousin can take away the child into his or her own household to rear, especially where the child's mother is regarded incompetent. Because the many members of the extended family sometimes live close together in a compound, a child is therefore always watched and guided by so many and could not afford to fool around. As the child grows up it joins the many young people of his *Umunna* and village in the many activities of his age set such as story telling, wrestling and moonlight plays. Boys and girls gradually learn to perform the various functions belonging to their particular groups, and through that process, learn early how to contribute to the well-being of their community. They also learn early what things are done and what things custom prescribes as not done. Various age sets prescribe their sanctions and enforce their own discipline. Hence the great influence they exercise in the upbringing and the training processes of young people in Ibo traditional society.

There is not too much difference in the methods employed in bringing up boys and girls. They both do household chores, farm work and village duties.[12] There are emphases upon the differences of duties in the adult life of boys and girls, for instance that a daughter marries into another family whilst a son continues the patrilineage, or that a daughter provides the bride wealth with which a son might find himself a wife. Sometimes the father-son relationship is more intimate than the father-daughter relationship, sometimes the opposite is the case. Mother-children relationship is generally more intimate than the father-children relation, and this is explained by the polygamous and house-building practices whereby the children live and grow up in the same house with their mother. The advantages[13] of these child-rearing practices of Ibo society for effective participation in group life are many. (1) The father image is not so dominant as to create complexes in adult life. The mother who seems to dominate over the earlier period of the child's life does not constitute a threat to the child, not even to a daughter. Rather the influence of peers leads to greater ease of adaptability and predisposes people to greater receptivity within or outside the culture. (2) Initiative and achievement are encouraged within group activities from an early age, for example, activities within one's age set such as story telling, wrestling or cleaning of the village square, dancing or drumming. (3) The attention paid by so many members of the extended family to the child, creates a sense of security and belonging which strengthens the concept of corporate conscience and family cohesion—very useful qualities for successful group life.

Age sets

Various Ibo communities use different methods in determining how people are classified into age sets. At Ihiala all children born within a five year period fall into one age set. In that town every village is divided into *Okpulo* and *Akaba* (people of the old settlement and people of the new settlement). This is a purely geographical division. All children in *Okpulo* play together, join masquerade societies together and engage in wrestling bouts together. This way, all those born within one age set know one another and stage contests with the

[12] Certain Ibo areas, for example Western Ibos of Asaba Division, do not take girls to farm work other than to collect crops and carry them home. Equally boys do not generally rub the mud floors and walls or cook. But in the Northern Ibo subcultural areas of our present Onitsha Division both boys and girls do farm work, and tidy up the house and collect water from the stream, etc.

[13] For the disadvantages created by Ibo child-rearing customs and the moral problems created for Christianity, see pages 136-137 (Chapter VI).

identical age sets of *Akaba* or adjacent villages. This is the major form age sets take for boys and girls, until later at about the age of 15 and over, boys organize themselves more formally for more adult participation in the community life. Girls try to get married according to their groups as both the girl and her family feel a sense of shame if girls of her age set have all gotten married leaving her behind. When they get married, girls' age set activities tend to end as they now join the families into which they have married. The men's age sets tend to continue into old age with more organizations in some parts of Iboland (e.g., Northern Ibo) than in others. In Awka, Onitsha, Nsukka and Cross River areas, or Afikpo, Abriba, Ohafia and Asaba men's age sets tend to be well organized with distinctive names, leadership and aims, and perform important social and political duties. From the age of ten onwards boys of various age sets perform such duties as cleaning the springs, village squares, market places and in some places the compound of the chief. They organize dance groups and drumming. As members of the masquerade societies they serve as village night guards, collectors of fines, prosecutors of all forms of offenders, and therefore protectors of public morality. Above the age of twenty-one they constitute the army of the village or clan and learn to shoot guns, stage mock battles especially at the funeral ceremonies of dead members, organize dances and chivalry displays. Both the younger sets and the over twenty-ones play special parts at public worship, with the latter group providing the sacrificial animal in certain village groups. In some places, for instance at Onitsha, men tend to take titles according to the seniority of their age sets, thereby constituting a hierarchy of councils that settle cases or advise the *Obi* (ruler) in the affairs of the community.

Married women in some places like Ihiala, Enugu Ukwu and parts of Nsukka organize their own age sets, not according to years of birth but according to the years when they get married into their husbands' families. Apart from the many religious, social and political functions age sets perform in Ibo traditional society, they also provide for young people training in group life, avenues for socialization and companionship which are very useful and integrative factors in the society. The age set as an institution, provides impetus towards achievements, ambition and hard work because no one likes to be left behind by the members of his own set. Parents strive hard to do the ceremonies that are relevant to the age sets of their children like initiation into the masquerade or *Muo* society, installation of the *chi* (guardian spirit) cult or *Iba nkpa* (fattening) ceremony for the girls. The children are urged by such parents to work hard in farms or in collecting palm nuts or in looking after livestock from which the parents derive the funds involved in these ceremonies. The strong achievement motivation among the Ibo is believed to be partly due to the influence of the age sets. At Ihiala for instance members of an age set arrange days on which to help a member in his or his parents' farm work. If the young man has no yams to plant nor land on which to plant them, he would try to pledge his labour to some one who could give him yams or land or both in return. This he does to avoid the shame of being let down before his age set, when it is his turn for members to come to work for him, and they are to be told there are no yams to plant or that there is no piece of land on which to plant. By this effort to save his face, the young man learns to struggle to possess yams and land and eventually achieve some success and become a man of some substance. In most places some age sets attempt to be self sufficient by raising funds through organizing dances and all forms of entertainment especially during the dry season when farm work is over and the moon shines brightly. Members are forced to discover talents for various activities, like being a leader of the chorus singing or trumpeter or dancer or being the leader of drummers and costume designers, even though such costumes are made of raffia or of wood masks! [See chapter VI pages 134-135 on the virtues which age sets help young people to develop.]

Marriage

Marriage, together with the many customs associated with it, is another avenue through which an individual shares in the group life of the Ibo community. Some of the less important features include betrothal from an early age of a girl to a boy, residence at intervals by the girl with the family of her future husband during which the girl's character and personality are observed. During this period also a familiarization process goes on between the families of the boy and the girl from the early days of the betrothal. Among its more serious features are the offer of a bride-wealth [14] by the family of the boy

---

[14] I have purposely used the word "bride-wealth" instead of bride price because in traditional Ibo society no "price" was ever fixed. Labour on the girl's parents' farm, offer of livestock like a goat or a cow, and fruits like coconuts made up the gifts offered. Westermann in The Africa Today and Tomorrow, uses the word "bride gift", London: O.U.P., p. 135; Forde and Jones in The Ibo and

to that of the girl, and various gifts from the girl's extended family to her on the day she goes finally to settle down in a new home with the husband. Such gifts include land, livestock and in some rare cases slaves to work for the new bride.

The rule of exogamy is rigidly applied to forbid marriage between any two members of the same lineage. If any kind of kinship relationship can be faintly established, marriage is forbidden, but if any had taken place unknowingly, due to the remoteness of the relationship, when such relationship is established no matter how vaguely, a sacrifice for the removal of *aru* or pollution or abomination is performed. The kinship relationship is severed by this special sacrifice consisting of kola nuts and sheep while the marriage is allowed to continue. When a lineage is very large, the rule of exogamy is applied within the minor and the major sublineages into which the lineage is subdivided. Where the bride-wealth is not paid a child born through the coming together of a man and a woman belongs to the woman's father's patrilineage. Even when a wife deserts her husband to live with another man in his home, unless the bride-wealth is completely refunded to the former husband, any child born by that woman belongs to the "legitimate" former husband. Divorce therefore is effected not only by the woman deserting her husband to live with another man, but in addition, by this second man refunding all the bride-wealth and expenses incurred by the first husband. In over eighty per cent of Iboland inheritance of the parents' estate and lineage is from the father's side. Only in places like Ohaffia [15] in the south-east of Iboland is lineage counted from a child's mother and inheritance is also from the mother's side, but residence is patrilocal. Thus a child is expected to be trained not by his father but by the mother's father or brothers.

Two families are linked together in a kind of "brotherly relationship" when a boy and a girl from these two families get married. Because of the systems of exogamy and polygamy large numbers of clans and lineages are in this way united for mutual assistance, defence, and trade.

Women when they get married share in the activities of their husband's lineage and yet they retain membership of their own father's

---

Ibibio Speaking Peoples of South Eastern Nigeria, use the word "marriage-payment". See also footnotes nos 15 and 16 in chapter V.

15 See Philip O. Nsugbe, Ohaffia: A Matrilineal Ibo People, Oxford: The Clarendon Press, 1974.

lineage. When someone's wife dies her corpse must be carried back by her father's lineage people, to be buried in her father's compound or in the compound of her father's eldest son where the father is long dead and the family has moved to a new settlement. The idea behind her being buried in her father's lineage's settlement is to make sure that her spirit joins her agnatic kin in the land of the dead. The husband pays quite a large quantity of things, including money in these days of money economy, for the services rendered by his dead wife's lineage in carrying and burying her corpse. Elderly wives who have many children are entitled to cows, cloths, goats and in more recent times, money. Because a married woman maintains links in two lineages, her husband's and her father's, some married women have played important roles in creating unifying influences in various parts of Iboland, especially in the absence of unifying political structures over an extensive area.

Ọzọ Title

The *Ozo* title has become a very important institution in Iboland and has led to quite a large body of literature.[16] There is also a great variety ranging from one part of Iboland to the other. At Awka, for instance, there are the junior and the senior titles, the former consisting of *Ime Amanwulu, Ime Chi* and *Ajigirija* and the latter consists of *Ime Ekwu, Ime-Ozo-Uno* and *Nnekwu-Ọzọ* when the initiated wears cotton strings on his ankles as the status symbol of his new social and religious standing. In neighbouring Nri there are a few more, the common ones being: *Agwu, Emume-Nwa, Fajioku, Okike-Amanwulu, Imachi, Nninwamadu, Ife-Akamkpisi, Ife-Agukwu* and the highest called *Ọzọ*. Compare these two with the practice at Amaruru group of villages in the Osu Ala-Miri clan of Orlu Division where there are only three kinds namely *Ime Uko, Ichi Ozo* and *Ahia Ọzọ*.

---

[16] Lengthy discussions are given about *Ozo* titles in C. K. Meek, Law and Authority in a Nigerian Tribe, London: O.U.P., 1950, Ch. VII. See also G. T. Basden, Niger Ibos, London: Seeley Service and Co., Ltd., n.d., p. 130, 133-135, 143, 193; M. M. Green, Ibo Village Affairs, London: Sidgwick and Jackson, 1947, p. 58, 214-215; D. Forde and G. I. Jones, The Ibo and Ibibio Speaking Peoples of South-Eastern Nigeria, London: O.U.P. for International African Institute, 1962, p. 19; and Jerry I. Orakwue, Onitsha Customs of Title Taking, Onitsha: The Renascent Africa Press, 1953. See also Richard N. Henderson, The King in Every Man: Evolutionary Trends in Onitsha Ibo Society and Culture, New Haven and London: Yale University Press, 1972, Chapter 7, pp. 247-266. — The *Ozo* title system: A Pathway to self purification (in Onitsha).

In Nsukka Division there are three principal ones, *Ele, Owa* and *Ọzọ* followed by the *Ichi* incision. In Owerri Division some clans do not have *Ọzọ* titles at all, others have a major one called *Onumonu.* In Onitsha town there are two main distinct groups of *Ọzọ* title namely *Ọzọ* and *Nzele.* The important thing which is to be emphasized about *Ọzọ* title here, is not its varied kind, or its various stages and modes of acquiring them, and the ceremonies or rituals connected with them. Rather the role of the *Ọzọ* title in establishing social or religious ranks, hierarchy and social privileges for the individual in his group life, is what we wish to underline. Later we will discuss the interaction Christian ethic is having with this *Ọzọ* institution. (see Chapter VIII).

The origin of the *Ọzọ* institution is difficult to trace. However it is safe to say that it grew out of the need for priests who would preside at extended family and lineage worship and supervise the cult of the ancestors and keep the family *Ọfọ* stick. Secondly it grew out of the economic needs of the peasant society and economy wherein young men could invest their agricultural wealth in the form of crops and livestock into the taking of the title from which they derive much dividend from the new entrants. In this way people secure for themselves means of livelihood in old age when they can work no more. Neither this sort of old age pension aspect, nor the priestly or political[17] importance conferred by the *Ọzọ* title, is accepted by the initiated to be the primary reason for the existence of the institution. The majority of the older initiates insists on the purely religious origin of the title as the most important reason for their taking it. They argue that the continuity of the lineage, clan or village depends on the existence of God-fearing men who share in the spirit of the land through their relationship with the earth goddess (*Ala*), and also know how to placate the spirit of dead ancestors and uphold the ordinances of the land. The *Ọzọ* title is said to be the religious means of achieving these ends. Therefore the individual who has taken on *Ọzọ* title must live a holy life, uphold publicly and privately the morality of the land and observe all the taboos, religious ceremonies and rituals of all the gods and goddesses of his community.

The privileges which the *Ọzọ* title man enjoys are many but the

---

[17] The younger and modern initiates recruited from the Christian elite argue that the most important aspect of the title is the political aspect of the institution. This is part of the moral problem created for the Church leaders which we shall discuss in full later. See Chapter VIII.

principal ones relate to political and social status. In most Ibo areas only the *Ozo* men hold political offices and represent their families and lineages in the village group councils or preside over settlement of cases, making of covenants and the establishment of new cults. Socially they belong to the noblemen's rank—a social status marked out by the honour accorded to those holding that position. They also take precedence in all public entertainments and feasts irrespective of their age. For instance at Onitsha the *Ọzọ* man, however young, is to be served first at public meals, he alone can carry and blow the elephant tusk, put eagle feathers on his cap, sit on a goat's skin on the dais, pour libations of wine to the spirits of dead ancestors, be the *Okpara* or head of his extended family or lineage. It will be an insult for anyone to address him in public other than in his title name. Only *Ọzọ* title men could greet one another with the double hand shake. The *Ọzọ* titled man used to be the "banker" for his community, because he was so trusted that people kept their precious properties with him. He is exempt from menial manual labour. At Nri any titled man convicted of stealing, automatically forfeits his title. Such is the great honour society bestows on the *Ọzọ* title holder that when he dies, especially in old age, his burial assumes pious and sacred form which indicates the people's belief that his spirit has joined the gods and the ancestors, and that he has become divine.

The cult of the ancestors is believed to have arisen partially as a means of continuing to reverence, even after their death, the noble life of some *Ọzọ* men.

What then is the *Ọzọ* title, and what are its main features? Briefly it is a religious *cum* social association into which men are initiated (sometimes with their wives) in various stages with religious ceremonies. It is not a cult. It has no seasonal or annual religious celebration or a chief priest to supervise its shrine as there is none. The members meet when there is some one to be initiated and the *Onyeisi Ọzọ* (the leader) functions at such times or at the burial ceremonies of one of its members. One of the features is *ibu aku Ọzọ*, that is the presentation of the appropriate *Ọzọ* wealth to its members in the form of goats, cocks, yams, fishes, salt, various kinds of palm wine and other drinks (cloth in some places). The presentation is done in various stages and at various occasions, sometimes spreading over one year. Another aspect is the various sacrifices given to various gods and at various shrines. Then there is the planting of the *Ọzọ* trees like *Oha, Ogirisi* or the installation of the ancestor shrine called *Ndebunze*, when the panel doors can be built in the *Iba* of the newly initiated. Another feature is the giving of an *Ọzọ* title name chosen by the initiate to convey the thought uppermost in his or the family's history at the time the title is being taken. Various families and villages or towns have a permanent prefix to their title names such as *Dim* (nobleman), *Eze* (king). [18]

In most Ibo areas the eldest wife of the title man takes her own title in that of her husband. Such woman commonly called *Lọlọ*, presents her own *Ọzọ* wealth which is shared among the already initiated women of the clan or the group. This bestows rank, privilege and economic advantages to the woman. If the *Lọlọ* of the *Ọzọ* man dies before him, he transfers the status, privileges and rights to the next senior wife. Seniority in this instance is not according to the age of the women concerned but rather according to the date when the wife settles down to her home in the husband's place.

At death all the *Ọzọ* titles which a man has acquired, may be in a period of time extending for over fifteen years, are removed from him in a very solemn religious ceremony which involves the sacrificial killing of some goats, cocks and cows. It is believed among most Ibos that although the *Ọzọ* man must be buried with the rites, ceremonies and pageantry pertaining to his rank, yet the practice of removing the *Ọzọ* in symbolic religious rites is to teach people that no one should carry title or rank to the gods; for before the gods all men are equal, and the only title or rank to be awarded in the land of the dead, is what the gods themselves give, according to the quality of life a man has lived in this world.

---

[18] It is interesting to observe here that certain village groups which had migrated from the same ancestor still retain a common prefix in their *Ọzọ* title name. For instance a group who now live at Ihiala after migrating from Nri still retain the prefix *Dim* as people do today in Nri town itself. This has given some further evidence to the claim of this lineage that they migrated from Agukwu Nri in Awka Division. For further discussions on the *Ọzọ* title see Chapter IV, pages 71-72; Chapter VIII, pages 224-228.

CHAPTER THREE

TRADITIONAL IBO RELIGIOUS BELIEFS, PRACTICES AND ORGANIZATION

DEITY, SPIRITS AND WORLD VIEW

The principal God of the Ibo is called *Chineke* or *Chukwu*. *Chi-ne-ke* literally means "the Creator God" whilst *Chukwu* (*Chi-ukwu*) means "the Great God". In the Onitsha areas where this variant *Chineke* is used, the emphasis is placed on the creative activity of the supreme being simply by the use of the one word. In other parts of Iboland where the variant *Chukwu* is used people sometimes add the word *Okike* and speak of *Chukwu-Okike* to imply the same idea of creation as is contained in the word *Chineke*. The central association therefore in the concept of the principal God is belief in a supreme source of beneficent creation. The great God (*Chi-ukwu*) is believed to be the author of heaven and earth who makes animal and plant life grow. As the source of human life, he gives to each man at the time of his birth that man's particular portion of the divine being called *Chi*. [1] It is this idea which also leads to the word *Chi-ukwu* which, as the name for the great God, explains that the individual *Chi* which each human being possesses derives from the great *Chi*—the over Soul who is the creator of all that has life and being.

Next to *Chineke* is a pantheon of gods: *Anyanwu* (the sun god), *Igwe* (the sky god), *Amadi-Oha* (the god of thunder and lightening) and *Ala* (the earth goddess).

Anyanwu, the sun god is worshipped prominently in Nsukka Division of the Northern Ibo subcultural area. Both private and public, cultus symbols of a plant with earthen bowl, placed at the base of the plant, are erected. Sometimes the sun god is worshipped and addressed in prayer as if he were the same as *Chineke*. At other times he is regarded as the messenger of the great creator God (*Chineke*) through whom fowl sacrifice tied on the top of a long bamboo pole should

---

[1] Cf. The Roman concept of Genius which Servius said was used to indicate the natural god of each individual place, or thing or man which accounted for the difference even between twin brothers. Quoted by T. R. Glover in The Conflicts of Religions in the Early Roman Empire, Boston: Beacon Press, Beacon Paperback, 1960, p. 15.

reach *Chineke.* A popular way of offering prayers to the sun god is by addressing him as the companion of the king of the heavens (*Anyanwu na eze-elu*). Apart from Nsukka Division other areas of Iboland offer prayers and sacrifices to the sun god when required to do so by a diviner for special purposes. For example, during a severe illness in which the sick person's breath is feared to be high and fast, the sun god is prayed to make the heart beat normal. The sun god, by and large, can be beneficent.

Igwe, the sky god is the husband of *Ala* who sends rain to moisten Ala so as to be productive. Not much worship is offered to this god as he is often better known through his "wife" the earth goddess, who happens to be the most important of these four gods of Ibo religion and life as we shall show later.

Amadi-Oha, the god of thunder and lightening is sometimes called *Kamalu* among the many Aro settlements and parts of the Eastern Ibo areas of Afikpo, Bende and Arochuku divisions. In his principal name *Amadi-Oha,* he is very prominently revered by the inhabitants of Owerri Province. He is the wrathful messenger of the supreme God, *Chineke,* who sends *Amadi-Oha* in the form of thunder to punish evildoers. Hence oaths are sworn by him and priests can curse suspected persons by him. He is not a beneficent god to whom various sacrifices are offered; rather occasional public appeasements are ordered by diviners so as to ward off impending doom from his wrath.

Ala, the earth goddess, is the most important deity in Ibo social life. She is the guardian of morality, the controller of the minor gods of fortune and economic life which we shall discuss presently. It is she who works in conjunction with the spirits of dead ancestors to order the prohibitions and the ritual avoidances. Many social offences become *aru* or pollution or abominations because they infringe the laws of the earth goddess. Because of her importance in ensuring health, agricultural fortune and hunting successes, she is well known all over Iboland. Most public worship of various communities is offered to the earth goddess as well as seasonal celebrations which relate to the various seasons of the year. Her shrine is found in most homes and public squares of any village.

Next in rank to this pantheon of four gods are innumerable minor deities which are sometimes personifications of the facts and features of nature and of daily life. Prominent among these minor gods (or godlings as some writers describe them) are *Ifejioku,* the god of farm work; *Agwu Nsi,* the god of divination and herbal medicine; *Ndebunze* or *Ndichie,* the deified spirit of dead ancestors; *Ikenga,* the god of adventure in hunting or business enterprise; tree gods like *Akpu, Orji* and *Ogbu* do exist. There are also river gods like *Ide-mili, Ulasi* or *Nwangene.* These godlings have their cultus symbols in public squares as well as in private homes but some like *Ifejioku,* receive much public sacrifice and command community worship with big celebrations at seed planting time and at harvest. River gods like *Ide-mili* and *Ulasi* are regarded as the "patron saints" in towns like Obosi and Okija. The prominent spirit in this group of spirit-gods is *Ndichie,* the deified spirit of dead ancestors. What makes *Ndebunze* or *Ndichie* a prominent feature of Ibo religious life is the belief that the dead ancestors are invisible members of the community. These spirits work conjointly with *Ala* (the earth deity) in protecting the community from harm in the form of famine or epidemics like small pox or abominations like the birth of children with a tooth on or the birth of twins. Various forms of worship offered to the ancestor spirit as gods, by which their cult remains prominent, will be discussed later. It is their religious significance in Ibo beliefs that is now being emphasized. The very important feature of Ibo social structure described as the lineage or *Umunna* is religiously upheld by the ancestor cult. People who trace their origin to common ancestors must keep together and help one another or else incur the displeasure of these ancestor spirits. After all, these ancestors, though dead, observe more acutely the activities of the living than the living themselves. As spirit-gods in the underworld, they share more fully in the omnipresence of *Chukwu* and his messenger, the goddess of morality, *Ala.*

This sketchy description of the deities and spirits of Ibo religion leaves them lifeless until one knows something of the world view which Ibo life and thought have built around these gods and spirits. Man is believed to be created by *Chi-ne-ke,* the creator God who also is the great spirit or the world's Over Soul. At the time of birth this great spirit *Chukwu* gives to each man a part of his divine nature called Chi which becomes the spiritual double of the man throughout his life. Whatever abilities, good or bad fortunes, successes, failures or weaknesses possessed by the man are often attributed to his *Chi.* Children of the same parents are therefore variously endowed by different kinds of *Chi.* Through this *Chi, Chineke* connects himself with all created human beings and the closer such men are to one ancestor the nearer they are to each other. Because individual *Chi* differs, every man is expected to prove of what kind his own *Chi* is, by various economic and social activities. This is the background of the strong achievement motivation said to be possessed by Ibo people. Early in a young man's life the parents help him to discover by divination which of the dead ancestors had possessed the kind of *Chi* with which their child is now endowed. Although the endowment of one's *Chi* may be small and inauspicious, it is believed that a man

Painting of Mbari House, the *Ala* (earth goddess) shrine at Owerri. A cultic mural emblem of "*Ala*", Earth Goddess of Iboland, photographed at Owerri. A coiled snake, especially when swallowing its tail, is an Ibo symbol of eternity.

through medicine, prayer and sacrifice, especially sacrifice to the ancestors, can finish his life more successfully than his *Chi* originally intended. But if after all such efforts have been expended, the man finally ends ignominiously, then his colleagues would acknowledge that he had tried but his *Chi* had not helped him much.

The creation of the universe is believed to be the work of *Chineke* and this creation is good. Evil, in the form of disease, death and atmospheric catastrophe, results from the work of evil spirits who abound in this world, including the spirits of displeased dead ancestors. The origin of these evil spirits is not clearly thought out in terms of the possibility of two sources of creation, one good and the other evil. What is clearly believed is that *Chineke* is a beneficent god who, although supreme, allows the existence of minor gods and spirits some of which could be evil. Because evil comes from these spirits, evil has not got the same ultimate origin or "everlastingness" of the goodness in *Chineke*'s creation. That is why man must find the sources of *Chineke*'s benevolence and engage them advantageously through medicine, which controls the spirit force within all life—animal, plant, rivers and rocks as well as human. It is this belief and practice which give rise to certain practices and concepts that are commonly described as magic. The Ibo strongly believe that the goodness of *Chineke* is superior to all the evil that might befall a man. Therefore all rites, ceremonies, sacrifices and other religious observances, either in ritual avoidances, ancestor worship or burial customs are strenuously pursued towards the one goal of falling in line with the goodness of *Chineke* which can free man from the machinations of the evil spirits. It is often surprising to many students of Ibo life and society why a culture that has so strong orientation towards individual achievement and competition does not have any noticeable incidence of suicide in accordance with the Durkheim model. [2] The explanation can be found in this Ibo belief that a man can come upon fortune and success any day, and that *Chineke* in his intentions for man is positively good. There is therefore no religiously rooted pessimism, no world denying religious creeds that create psychological complications from which man seeks escape through suicide. [3] The idea of evil spirit having a

[2] Emile Durkheim, Suicide: A Study in Sociology, translated by John Spaulding and George Simpson, New York: Free Press Paperback, 1968, part 3, Chapter 2, especially.

[3] Cf. G. Parrinder, "Here is no pessimism or other-worldly way of negation ... the aim of religion is positively this-worldly", in West African Psychology, London: Lutterworth Press, 1951, p. 7.

separate existence and operating in conflict against the benevolent creator god never existed in Ibo religious thought. *Ekwensu,* which literally means the deceiver is the Ibo word used to translate the Christian and biblical word "Satan". The concept the word *Ekwensu* represents is new and is borrowed from Christianity. In places like Awka there have been the cults of *Akalogeli* and *Ogbonuke* resembling remotely the concept of the Christian Satan; but *Akalogeli* or even *Ajommọ* is quite different, in that its existence is always associated with something else, like the sacred grove or the ancestor, rather than a self existent dynamic force with independent life and personality. [4] In support of this view it is interesting to note that there is no authentic traditional Ibo proverb that bears reference to *Ekwensu* and there is no Ibo name that alludes to it. [5]

The relationship between man and the spiritual world is maintained through many channels. Obedience to the codes of behaviour and the customs (*Omenani*) approved by the ancestors, and enforced by the earth goddess through priests and titled elders and heads of various extended families, is the most important channel. To the Ibo therefore the spiritual world is very real and intimate. Hence the belief in the existence of spirits in all aspects of nature and its various phenomena. *Chineke* the supreme and creator God is believed to be so important and so remote that he allows a great many minor gods and spirits to intervene in the daily affairs of men thereby providing the intimate relationship between the seen world of men and the unseen world of gods and spirits. A good many scholars have argued that in effect these minor gods are worshipped, prayed to and feared to the exclusion of the Supreme God, whilst a new crop of researchers and writers are saying that these minor gods are mere intermediaries. This they say, is like the concept of the pluralism in the Godhead which in the Christian faith is expressed in the doctrine of the Trinity. The Ibo world view and religious practices tend to confirm the latter view. Man cannot of his own powers approach the majesty of the great *Chineke,* and although a part of him is formed into the new born

---

[4] *Akalogeli* is supposed to originate from the spirit of a dead man who in his life time had no wife, no child and no property and died unnaturally. *Ogbonuke* refers to belief in misfortune caused by such evil spirits. *Ajommo* means evil spirit.

[5] Ibo proverbs and names contain in large measure aspects of Ibo world view, religious faith, hopes and fears as well as philosophical attitudes to life. See Appendix II for some names and Appendix III for some proverbs. See also names and proverbs used in illustrating Ibo moral concepts in Chapter VI.

babe through the *Chi* that *Chineke* himself gives, man is still other than the great God who in order to keep up his otherness observes the activities of men from afar, allowing his subordinates to have the more immediate relationship with man. [6]

There are parts of Iboland where public and private shrines of *Chineke* exist. At Ihiala I have discovered a public shrine called "*egbo Chukwu*" (the square of the Supreme God). The annual public sacrifice performed at this shrine and offered to the Supreme God, includes the offering of cocks by mothers who had given birth to male children, and hens by those who had given birth to female children, within the period between one annual celebration and another. Because it is believed that life comes from *Chukwu* or *Chineke,* this annual celebration before the *Chukwu* shrine is an acknowledgement of such life given to the newly born children in the village, and the dedication of the life of all the inhabitants to *Chukwu.* Prayers are also offered to *Chukwu* on behalf of all newly married women who are presented at the shrine with the ceremony of "*ihibe akwukwa*", the setting up of the hearth, the earthen tripod on which a wife cooks her meals. This is to symbolise that the newly married wife is now established in her new home into which *Chineke* will be pleased to send children to be fed with the food cooked on this hearth. All *Ọzọ* titled men at Ihiala erect household shrines to *Chukwu,* commonly called *Ihu-Chukwu.* Sacrifices are offered at these shrines annually during religious festivals like *Iro Muo* and *Ite Otite.* [7] Special sacrifices are also offered at these shrines when the diviner orders. Although this *egbo Chukwu* shrine is not widespread all over Iboland yet this evidence at least indicates that both in worship and in thought *Chukwu,* the Supreme God, is not completely neglected and that his relationship with man can in some places, be intimate and sacramentally enacted. [8]

Life is meant to be continuous but the evil of the unknowable

---

[6] For the view of those who say that the Supreme God is not really believed in nor worshipped see for example G. T. Basden, London: Seeley Service, p. 37, "As he is not honoured with an 'alusi' neither is sacrifice made to appease him"; M. Unegbu "Ibos and Christianity", *Missionary Annuals 2,* 1954, p. 12; C. K. Meek "The Religions of Nigeria", *Africa,* Vol. 3, 1943 pp. 112-113. For those who say that the Supreme God is the all important deity worshipped and sacrificed to through the minor gods see: Andrew Lang, The Making of Religion, London: Longmans 1898; E. Bolaji Idowu, Olodumare: God in Yoruba Belief; London: Longmans 1962; R. S. Rattray, Ashanti, London: Oxford University Press, 1923.

[7] See Glossary of Ibo words used in this study in Appendix I.

[8] Cf. G. Parrinder, West African Religion, London: The Epworth Press, 1961, p. 25.

forces in man and nature brings about death, which in the Ibo world view is regarded as a calamity any time it occurs; even when an old man of ninety dies it is regarded as due to the displeasure of some evil spirit, possibly of an ancestor, or of living enemies who have employed evil powers in the form of "death-invoking" medicine so as to put the old man out of the way, and bring poverty and weakness to his lineage. I have not come across any death that any Ibo accepts as natural and biological end, because man, like all organisms that have a beginning must also have an end. After many painstaking enquiries I realize that to the Ibo life is "eternal" and man, because of his share in the Supreme God, *Chineke,* through the *Chi* particle in him, is meant to be immortal. Man is more of the spiritual essence rather than the biological, and although man lives in the world of nature, he is not quite a part of it. When pressed further the Ibo gives the impression that it is not only man who possesses this spiritual nature. Even some animals, trees and streams are spoken of as also possessing essentially spiritual existence as well as biological. Hence in most villages and clans (as also in many parts of Africa), there are religious practices which point to a supposed relationship between the village or clan and some sacred animals and trees like the iroko tree. This relationship is even extended to snakes, especially the python family. [9] This is the background to "totem" animals and also to the numerous spirits which are feared and sometimes worshipped in the religious life of the Ibo. This belief or desire for immortality is part of the background to the cult of the ancestors through which the dead share in the life of the living. Furthermore children yet unborn receive the spirit genius of some dead ancestors through a kind of reincarnation. It is in this way that the Ibo believe in reincarnation. But it is only those who lived a good life that are believed to be capable of coming back in human form. Those who lived sinful and unprofitable or purposeless lives, by departing from the moral code of the clan, cannot find human bodies through which they can reincarnate. That is why they are forced to live unenviable and formless "spirit" lives, in which form of existence, their delight is mainly to harm their more fortunate members who live a human life. To protect oneself against these spirits "medicine", (which early writers

---

9 This extension of kinship terms to animals is discovered by M. Mead among the Arapesh of New Guinea. See her contribution "The Arapesh of New Guinea" in *Co-operation and Competition Among Primitive Peoples,* edited by M. Mead, New York: McGraw Hill, 1937, p. 20.

called magic or fetish) sacrifice and proper religious observances are prescribed. After death the spirit of the departed is believed to hover around the home for about seven native weeks or fifty six days. During this period, the correct burial rites befitting the dignity of the deceased as well as of his extended family, are performed. The spirit of a deceased elderly man who has taken a title takes about twelve months before it can join the ancestors. Second burial rites must therefore be performed about this time. This is believed to help the soul to rest in peace in the company of other ancestors. It is also believed that improper or negligent burial rites performed by children for their parents, or for any relatives within the lineage, would incur the displeasure of the deceased's spirit and bring curses and misfortune upon their offspring.

There is another type of "reincarnation" found among the Ibo. Some children are believed to be capable of reincarnating into various "life journeys" which last for very short time during each trip. This type of children form themselves into a group in the spirit world, and decide to be born into various homes, where they live for a very short while and die, all in a group, normally before reaching puberty. They form themselves into another spirit group and are reincarnated into another group of children, to be born sometimes by the same mothers that previously mothered them, or by their close relations. These various and often repeated comings and goings, are meant to punish these women, by tantalizing them into believing that they have got children. These *Ogbanje* children (*Ogbanje* means coming and going) can be detected and out-manoeuvred by the "medicine man" through various devices.

In the Ibo world view there are not many myths, especially those relating to the various origins either of man or of the universe or of death. There is one told by people at Agukwu Nri about the beginning of the world and the origin of yams and of their cult of priest kings. [10] Instead of myths of origin there are many folk stories, traditions and fables which teach philosophical truths by the use of animals instead of human characters. It is through these stories, traditions and fables that one comes to understand some of the unspoken thought patterns, beliefs and wisdom of the people. The use of proverbs and the significant way by which names are given to children also reveal religious faith, a world view, and the aspirations, hopes and fears of the

---

[10] See W. T. Northcote, Anthropological Report on the Ibo Speaking Peoples of Nigeria, Part I, London: Harrison & Sons, 1913, p. 50.

people.[11] There is no clear concept of life after death in some bodily form. Although there is the general idea of a form of continuity after death within and outside reincarnation, yet it remains true to say that another form of existence, just like the existence of spirits (*Muo*) in a form that looks like a replication of this present life, is more or less believed in without being carefully thought-out. Furthermore there is no concept of the end of the world, nor the hope that all mankind will be gathered together for a final stock taking before *Chineke*. There is the belief in an "afterlife" reward for the good man, especially through the quick reincarnation that he is allowed to make. Apart from this, goodness seems to be thought of entirely in terms of a man securing good fortune in this world for himself, his lineage, his family and his grand children yet unborn. This means that the afterlife of man does not seem to be within the jurisdiction of *Chineke*. The dead who join the spiritual world of *ndemuo* (spirits) seem to lead their own life independent of *Chineke*.[12]

Birth, Puberty, Marriage, Death

The religious beliefs and practices associated with these occasions relate to the more personal aspects of individual and family life, and could therefore be properly termed *rites de passage*, indicating movement from one stage of life to the other, symbolised in rites and religious ceremonies.

Birth

The birth of a child is accompanied by various rites. Before the child is born the mother must have offered various sacrifices to the *Ala* goddess, to the *Chi* symbol of her own mother and to *Ndebunze* (spirit of the ancestors of her husband). What is to be offered (yam, chicken or goat) is indicated by the diviner. The reason for offering these sacrifices is to secure the favour of these gods, so as to make

---

11 See Appendixes II and III for some of these names and proverbs.

12 Religions that have not developed absolute type of monotheism do not seem to have clear eschatology. Cf. R. H. Charles in Religious Development Between the Old and the New Testaments, London: Oxford University Press, 1948, p. 160, where he says "eschatological beliefs are universally the last of all beliefs to be influenced by the loftier conceptions of God". Prof. E. G. Parrinder in a private discussion seems to think that Charles was exaggerating as Hinduism and some bush polytheisms do have eschatology. John Mbiti in his New Testament Eschatology in an African Background, sketches the eschatological concepts of his Akamba people, London: Oxford University Press, 1971.

the childbirth easy and the child to be born blessed in advance by the gods. It is an abomination if the child is born with the feet coming out first, or with any teeth, or as twins. Such children were destroyed and the abomination against the earth goddess cleansed ritually by an Nri priest. Where the delivery is normal, the child is taken inside the house after it has cried fairly loudly, as an assurance that there is plenty of life in it. No child is to be born inside the house but rather at the back of the mother's own house. The navel cord is buried by the side of a newly germinated palm tree, pear tree (ube) (*dacryodes edulis*) or breadfruit tree. It is believed that this plant, which from then on is regarded as the child's natal plant, will become fruitful in proportion to the fame of the child's subsequent achievements as an adult (see page 23).

Various social and ritual ceremonies relate to the birth of a child. Circumcision, especially of males, may take place within three native weeks, that is about 24 days. Females usually are circumcised a bit later. In a few isolated Ibo areas like Aboh on the southernwest banks of the Niger, girls are circumcised about the time of their puberty with greater religious and social celebrations. Presentation to ancestors and the cleansing of the mother from the pollutions of childbirth may be performed after 24 days in one area, or after seven native weeks (56 days) in other areas. The following two childbirth ceremonies taken from Ihiala are like those from Enugu Ukwu within the Nri [13] clan. They illustrate the general pattern of childbirth ceremonies performed in various Ibo areas with more or less details.

Asa Nwa (naming of child and its presentation to the people). This is performed after seven native weeks (56 days). Parents and grandparents both from the father's and the mother's sides play prominent parts. The extended family and sometimes the minor sublineage members are expected to attend. At the *Obi, Iba* or *Obu* of the child's father (or grandfather where the father is still fairly young) where the ceremony takes place, the senior titled member, that is the *Okpara* of the lineage called the Umunna, presides. The child is placed by the *Ndebunze* (the cultus symbol of the ancestors) shrine. Names are given by the parents and sometimes by the grandparents, while the senior titled member holds the child in his hands and all present cheer

[13] Nri is the acknowledged original home of many Ibo villages and clans and the source of many religious rites among the Ibos of the Northern area or the Onitsha Ibo. The recent Shaw archeological finds at Igbo Ukwu may have belonged to former priest kings of Nri. See Chapter 1 footnote 5.

loudly as he gives these names to the child. Next he places a hoe and a matchet, the chief farm implements, in the child's hands and says this prayer:

> My son, with these farm implements your fathers lived well. We call upon you to acquaint yourself with them properly and be hard working. We wish you good fruits out of your labours. Live, grow and wax strong and may the gods of our land bless and guide you.

All present respond with the chorus of *Eha! Eha!* (so let it be) and cheer and exchange greetings, using mainly the salutation or the *Ọzọ* title praise name. Presents are given to the child and those present are feasted with palm wine, pounded yam meal and meat.

Three factors usually determine the name given to a child: (1) The day of the native week on which it is born. (2) The historical incident peculiar to the child's birth or to the circumstances of the parents. (3) The philosophical or religio-social faith which the child stimulates in the parents. For example there are four days in the native week bearing the names: *Eke, Oye, Afo, Nkwo.* A male child born on *Eke* day would probably be called Okeke. If a daughter were born to a father at the moment of his going on a journey to a distant place, she would probably be called Ijeoma (a journey that is already blessed); and if a son is born to parents who had long looked forward to getting a son, he would probably be called Tabugbo (Tagbo for short, meaning it is not yet too late).[14]

Igba Agu: This is the ceremony of finding out the ancestral archetype of the newborn child through divination. There is no fixed time for this. It is performed at the convenience of the father or when ordered by a diviner. The father invites a diviner who successfully manipulates his oracle so that it reveals to him which of the dead ancestors has been re-incarnated in the newborn child. When this is determined, a big dumbell-shaped piece of wood called *Okpensi* is prepared, to represent the presence of this dead ancestor who now lives again in this new little child. This little son can now be presented

---

14 See Appendix II for samples of Ibo names and their meanings. In more recent times many Ibo Christian parents give only Ibo names to their children at christening, instead of Biblical or European names because they say that these Ibo names are more meaningful to them. See also Chapter VI on Ibo names that have expressed ethical or theological significance.

with his own religious symbol, like the *Ọfọ* stick with which he offers prayers and meal offerings to the gods and ancestors.

Puberty

Puberty is the passing from boyhood or girlhood into adult life. Various religious and social ceremonies accompany this stage of development. We have noted already the ceremony of female circumcision done in Aboh area. It is not only the physical or surgical operation that is involved here. Deep religious convictions are brought into it in the form of sacrifices, the giving of part of the mother's *Chi* symbol to the now adult daughter who can then be given to marriage. A fattening period,[15] of varying lengths of time in different Ibo areas, follows the appearance of a girl's first menstruation period with the accompanying sacrifices of chickens to various gods according to the direction of the diviner. At Nri town the *Ufe Akwali,* a yearly festival for maidens, takes a special turn for all such maidens who have reached puberty and are about to go to their husband's homes. A goat is killed, put into a basket, and another basket is filled with yams and carried to the mothers of the maidens concerned. Sacrifices and prayers offered during this puberty rite observance are intended to secure the goodwill of the gods to grant happy home life to the young woman, especially through the gift of children. The market parades of young maidens at the end of various puberty rites and ceremonies are great social occasions in most areas; just as in many things, the religious is not far removed from the social.

There are no known cases of late circumcision of boys in Iboland as a puberty ceremony. The more familiar puberty rites for boys are initiation into the masquerade secret societies and the installation for the boys of their first shrines or personal gods. The *Amanwulu* ceremony from Enugu Ukwu is more or less a puberty rite. In Ihiala town most parents who can afford it install the *Agwunsi* cultus symbol for their sons as a puberty rite. *Agwunsi* is the introduction to the personal gods and shrines which a man acquires gradually in life. This therefore becomes the first shrine of the young adult, where he learns to offer his first prayers and sacrifices to the gods. The initiation into

[15] The fattening period is the time when girls go into seclusion, leave off all manner of work, including cooking, decorate their bodies with calm-wood-lotion, learn the lessons of motherhood. Psychologically such rest periods ranging from two to six months, help girls to get over the shock of the first menstruation experience, physically they fatten to prepare for childbearing.

the secret societies involves some ordeals and tests in manly endurance, expected of a villager who has through puberty passed from boyhood to adulthood. In some areas of Iboland both boys and girls mark their bodies with tattoos as puberty rites. Others cut spaces into their front upper teeth by thinning the four frontal upper teeth. Almost everywhere young men newly initiated into the *muo* (masquerade) society take new salutation or praise names by which people greet them formally in the homes and at social or ceremonial meetings.

Marriage

The religious aspects of marriage include the preliminary divination by which the young man who seeks a wife is enabled to find out from what clan or lineage his *Chi* (guardian spirit) permits him to take "a wife of fortune". When the diviner pronounces the clan and lineage from where the future wife will be found he also prescribes the sacrifices to be offered to the ancestors to prosper the young man and to help him find a "good" wife, which invariably, means a childbearing woman. When the girl is found, her own parents consult the diviner to make sure that her own ancestral spirits would permit her to marry the young man. When all the preliminaries are finished and bride-wealth is paid and the girl is ready to go and settle in her new husband's home, at that time the mother gives to her daughter *chi* cultus symbol. This consists of two small clay pots and four small wooden pieces in a wooden plate.

After the birth of her first child this *chi cultus* symbol is ceremoniously installed by the mother of the young wife. This religious custom is to ensure that the girl in going over to the family of her new husband retains some part of the spirit ancestry of her mother's lineage.

Death

The death of young people and children do not call for religious ceremonies of any magnitude. Such deaths are regarded as great calamities and the gods do not merit much consideration on such occasions. The death of elder women and *Ọzọ* titled men on the other hand entails very expensive and colourful rituals. At Ihiala when the news of the death of an elderly woman is announced to her relations, sacrifice of a chicken is offered by the extended family head before the young men and some not too old *Ọzọ* titled men together with wives of the lineage mournfully march to the late woman's home. After a long day of mourning in songs and dances, various articles are prescribed by the relatives of the dead woman, which are then brought forward one by one by husband and children of the dead woman. Goats, chickens, yards of cloth, some chalk and calm wood lotion are included. When the corpse is to be buried in the dead woman's family home sacrifices are again offered.

The death of a titled man involves all amount of religious observances. A cock is killed, its blood is mixed with some leaves, with which a specially invited titled man who is also a "medicine man" washes the hands of the dead man to cleanse him of evils committed with hands while still alive. A white plumed cock is then offered to the ancestral spirits to announce the death. All the shrines installed by him are encircled with the tendrils of palm leaves (*omu-nkwu*), whilst another white plumed cock is tied alive head downwards at the point where the dead man is laid in state. All this is done to ensure a peaceful passage of his soul to the land of the dead. Before his corpse is buried a goat and/or a cow, according to his children's or relation's financial means, is slaughtered and blood poured into the earth where he is to be buried. Soon after the burial the wives of the man wash their hands with shrubs known as *akoro* and *ujiji* for four times at the women's *uke* shrine so as to absolve themselves from their husband's death. None of his wives would eat until she had performed this ceremony. The *uhie* drum would then announce the putting down into the mother earth of the corpse and continue to be announced, by being played for seven native weeks. Prayers and incantations are said to the spirits of dead ancestors, to receive the dead man's soul, and to punish any human being who in one form or the other, might have caused the death of this titled man.

Arts and Technology

The erection of the earthen or wooden images of gods and goddesses constitutes the greatest works of art in Iboland. Examples include the *Igwe ka Ala* at Umunoha and the *Mbari* Houses both in the Owerri Division. It is believed among a good deal of Awka people that their skill in woodcarving and blacksmithery is not unconnected with their being special messengers of *Agbala,* the great oracle consulted by many in deciding cases. Expertly carved panel doors and stools constitute some of the paraphernalia of the *Ọzọ* titled man. The carved stools, masks and staffs as well as images of gods and goddesses and emblems of dead ancestors, are the bulk of works of art in traditional Iboland.

Art work and what could be termed techniques of any sort, are inspired by and express religious faith and practice.

Worship Private and Public

The following account taken from Ihiala is typical of Northern Ibo acts of worship. Cross checkings from towns like Agukwu Nri, Enugu Ukwu and Onitsha indicate close similarities.

Private Worship

This is divided into two parts: routine and occasional. Routine private worship includes the daily offerings made by the head of a household to the ancestors at the *Ndebunze* shrine in kola-nuts, lines of white chalk and prayers for protection, prosperity and well-being of the family, while holding up the *Ọfọ* stick. The *Igwọ Ọfọ* worship is also a routine, done once a year, as a prayer privately offered by the head of a household when the *Ọfọ* stick is ceremoniously cleansed with blood of a chicken sacrificed to the ancestors and wiped off with *akoro* leaves. Occasional private worship is done when ordered by a diviner as a result of his being consulted by the individual concerned. There are also cases of a diviner meeting an unknown person in the street to whom he gives a message, said to be received from the gods, requiring the unknown stranger to offer some sacrifices. This is, however, very rare. When the diviner prescribes what is to be done, the individual concerned goes to the priest of the special deity, and offers the prescribed sacrifice either of chicken, or eggs and kola nuts with alligator pepper or goats, palm wine and chalk, as the case may be. The special intention in this act of private worship performed for the individual by the priest, is usually one or more of such needs as:

(1) To seek favour from the ancestral spirits.
(2) To seek protection from evil spirits like those of witches or evil minded persons.
(3) To seek healing from an illness or cleansing from defilement in eating forbidden animal, or entry into "bad bush", or contact with menstruating women.
(4) To propitiate neglected ancestral spirits or angered gods.
(5) To seek the gift of children.

Public Worship

Public Worship is also divided into two kinds: the family and lineage worship, and clan or village worship. Both kinds involve annual or biannual celebrations bringing people together to enact aspects of the history of the family, lineage or clan; but more so to celebrate aspects of natural and agricultural manifestations of the local and family gods. This list is taken from Ihiala.

(1) *Ime Obi umuaka* (the spirit of children). A white chicken is slaughtered by the head of the lineage at the special shrine to ensure increased fertility and well being of children. Prayers are offered to the ancestral spirits and to *Ala* goddess, while the chicken sacrificed is used in communal meal, followed by ritual dancing around the Ala shrine of the lineage by the young unmarried maidens only, as this act of public worship belongs mainly to such young maidens of between 9 and 18 years.

(2) *Ime chi la agu* (the propitiation of the spirit of relationship and kindreds). Married daughters take eight pieces of yams, palm-wine, fish and sometimes cloth to their mother. Their mother's husband propitiates the woman's *chi* with the gifts from the daughters and blesses the daughters praying for their well being.

A young wife who has not had a married daughter, provides the sacrificial materials for herself and calls her husband to propitiate her *chi* for her and her young children. Part of the tribute and sacrificial materials from the women of a lineage are given to the oldest woman member who keeps the shrine of *Ara la Oma* (the collective spirit of all the extended family and lineage).

(3) *Ida ji* (the collection of yams). Young unmarried women of the village parade with songs to the homes of all the *Ọzọ* titled men collecting yams from them in the month of May when yams are so scarce, and collecting corn and pears (*ube na oka*) from elderly women and young men. These are heaped in the home of the leader of these young ladies, where after they have been offered to the *Ala* goddess, they become food for the young ladies who must stay together in their leader's home for seven native weeks communally feeding on such yams, corn and pears as they have collected. This is believed to ensure a plentiful harvest, communal well being and harmony for the village for the forthcoming harvest year.

(4) *Ite Nsi.* This is the propitiation of *Ife-jioku,* the god of farming before new yam is eaten. A cock offered by the wife is sacrificed at the shrine of *Ife-jioku* inside the barn and parts of the animal distributed to various members of the extended family

as prescribed by custom. All the young brothers must take tribute (*Ife-nru*) of eight yams, eight pieces of fire wood and a leg of the sacrificed chicken to their oldest brother who in turn takes the same kind of tribute to the oldest head of the extended family. The new yam is eaten seven native weeks after this public worship.

(5) *Iro Muo*. This is the biggest of the celebrations. It takes place during the period of agricultural plenty. It literally means "the feast of pleasing the gods". It is a kind of harvest thanksgiving.

All sons and married daughters take tribute (*ife-nru*) of eight yams, and kolanuts to the oldest surviving son of their father who offers them in sacrifice to the *Ndebunze*, the ancestral spirit, together with the goat which must be provided by the oldest married daughter of the household. Communal eating follows, culminating in ritual dance at the village square after the appropriate sacrifices have been offered at the shrine of the lineage god by the lineage priest. Both the young and the middle aged people take part in this ritual dance. The prayers offered at the shrine of the household ancestral spirit, and the one said at the public square to the lineage god, contain thanksgiving to *Chukwu*, *Ala* and *Ndebunze* for protection, for good harvest and increase in children, for deliverance from epidemics like small-pox and from abominations of any kind for which the wrath of both gods and ancestral spirits would have punished "the land".

Occasional public worship includes the sacrifice of atonement. After epidemics of any kind the diviners are consulted to know what had "spoiled the land". If no particular individual is accused as being responsible, all the village then becomes guilty. A sacrificial animal, sheep and sometimes a lamb or goat is bought with money collected from adult men. The priest of the lineage or a priest of a particular god mentioned by the diviner will tie the four legs of the animal, drag it about around some public places and then sacrifice the animal at the shrine of the clan earth goddess. Its meat is not eaten by the worshippers but rather it is given to the *Osu* people dedicated to the *Ala* goddess. Another example of occasional public worship is the *ichu-aro* (driving away of an old year). Sacrifice of chickens brought by each family head, as well as the breaking of old baskets and pots at the *Aho* shrine, feature in this act of worship together with the saying of incantations and prayers. This in some places, is an annual worship while in some places it is ordered occasionally by the diviner after plagues, floods and other calamities. The climax of public worship is the annual propitiation of lineage gods. Each lineage has its own public shrine dedicated to its own protector. I watched the annual propitiation of the lineage god of Umunwajiobi called *Ogwugwu* at Ihiala. This was in March before planting of yams. The men collected money to buy goats and women (wives of the men and not their sisters as in *Iromuo*) to buy hens. The animals are sacrificed at the shrine of *Ogwugwu,* whose cultus symbols contain a big earthen human seated figure with two young children by each side, an earthen pot in front, and outside the hut sheltering the figures stands the *ogirisi* tree in a central position. The eyes of the five figures are particularly open and awe inspiring. The blood of the animals is poured into the earthen pot, the plumes of the chickens are heaped inside the hut by the side of the pot, kola-nuts are broken and placed into the hands of the five human forms; lines of chalk are drawn according to the number of the sublineages of Umunwajiobi. Then the *Okpara* begins his prayer while the women start cooking the meat of the sacrificed animals and some yams. A big feast is prepared. First of all, pieces of appropriate parts of the animals, together with lumps of *foofoo* are thrown into the hut with the prayer that the *Ogwugwu* god should be pleased to share in the meal offerings of his children and bless them. All eat together out of the meal so prepared. Women bring white chalk and *akoro* to decorate the hut of the shrine and ritual dance is staged. The lineage ballad singer praises the ancestors of the lineage, tells the story of the brave deeds of past leaders of the clan, and all present respond with warm glee that as their forebears had triumphed in the past, so will the present and future generations triumph, *Ogwugwu* being their god and protector. Children are then particularly enjoined to remember that *Ogwugwu,* the ancestors and their spirits frown at deeds which spoil human relations. This worship is regarded as an annual covenant making between the members of the lineage both living and dead with their god *Ogwugwu.* The final act is the pouring of wine libation by the *Okpara,* the lineage head, and then by all the *Ọzọ* titled men while the women take the chalk from the shrine and mark their breasts and abdomens. This done, people begin to go home singing joyously as they go.

Priest, Medicinemen (Dibia) Oracle

The picture of Ibo religion is incomplete without some discussion about priests *dibia* and oracles. The Ibo believe in the priesthood of all heads of households, lineages and clans. Also all *Ọzọ* titled men are priests insofar as they offer sacrifices and perform ritual functions including praying to *Chukwu* and to the ancestors. In addition to this there is a class of special priests made up of two categories. One class comes from the *Osu* (people taken captive and dedicated to special gods). One of them is always chosen to be the special priest of that god and must live near that god's shrine.[16] The other class of priests is made up of men who become priests through "appointment" by ancestral spirits. Such men behave queerly and are noticed by those already priests who take them in and train them. Such people sometimes combine three functions: those of medicine men with the knowledge of healing herbs, secondly divination and thirdly sacrificing priests. They also have power at times to exorcise, prepare medicine for warding off evil, for protecting from harm like car accidents and charms that bring good fortune in trade or hunting. Such "medicines" are what people sometimes call charms or fetishes. In each village a priest is known to be specially related to one or more gods. When a diviner prescribes sacrifice he also names the proper priest that should perform the function. In this way priests exercise leadership among the people. In some circumstances there is a class of men greatly gifted in the knowledge of the use of herbs to cure various diseases. These men are commonly known as "*dibia*" and not priests. They cannot divine but work hand in hand with diviner-priests. In all cases no cure is carried out entirely by the *dibia* without consulting diviners. Divination in the case of illness, nearly always, leads to finding out what spirit had been wronged and what human relationship had been strained. Sacrifice and propitiation accompany whatever herbal medicine is given to ensure proper cure.

Divination in simple process is done by any diviner-priest. Major issues are referred to the principal oracles of Iboland of which there are four:

(1) The *Chukwu* Oracle *Ubinukpabi* of Arochukwu popularly known as the long juju.
(2) The *Agbala* of Awka.
(3) The *Igwe-ka-Ala* of Umunoha near Owerri.
(4) The *Onyili Ora* near Agu-Ukwu, Nri.

---

[16] At Ihiala the priests from *Osu Ulasi Ogboro* have now refused to be so styled. They do not continue to perform their priestly functions as described here. The Government of Eastern Nigeria had passed a law that these outcasts should be declared "free men". ...

Each of these has its highly organized system of priests and attendants and agents. In the absence of widely organized political central authority in Iboland, the oracles had united people from all corners, as people in search of well being and good health, or increased fortune, or those in search of "knowledge of the truth" from the gods, go to consult them.[17]

Holy Days

There are days which are holy to gods and to most adults in Iboland. There are four market days running in two parallels thereby forming one complete round of native week of eight days made up as follows: *Eke Nta, Orie Nta, Afo Nta, Nkwo Nta, Eke Ukwu, Orie Ukwu, Afo Ukwu* and *Nkwo Ukwu* (*Nta* means small, *Ukwu* means great). Certain gods must be worshipped on their holy days, for example, *Afo* and *Eke* are holy days to *Anyanwu* and *Agbala* at Awka. *Orie* is a holy day to *Ogwugwu* the clan god of Umunwajiobi in Ihiala. Most *Ọzọ* titled men keep *Eke Ukwu* as holy day, on which day they must not eat food cooked with palm oil, nor come into contact with women, nor go to any farm work. The *Ọzọ* titled man must "meditate" on such a day and keep "quiet time" with the ancestors and offer special prayers to them for the well-being of his "family". Some young men who have not taken any title could, through divination, be told which day they should observe as their holy day. Priests dedicated to special gods observe as their own holy day the day that is holy to their gods. At Ihiala *Afọ Ukwu* is the holy day to *Ulasi Ogboro* when all individual sacrifices ordered by a diviner are offered. Therefore the priest of *Ulasi Ogboro* on that day observes the ritual avoidances of the god including staying away from farm work so as to attend to the supplicants who might come to the shrine of *Ulasi Ogboro*.

This simple description of some aspects of Ibo religion suggests that there are characteristic features which can be discerned. (1) The impersonality of *Chukwu*, the Supreme God is emphasized through his diffused existence in godlings like *Anyanwu* the sun god, *Ala* the earth

[17] S. R. Smith in his study of the Ibo people notes four conditions requisite for the growth of these oracles: (1) Quiet remote place, (2) Some natural features like rocks, caves and steep valleys with running water or groves and dense bush to inspire awe, (3) A system of travelling agents to invite clients to the oracles, (4) An easy and secret method for the disposal of victims "eaten" by the gods of the oracle. See K. O. Dike, Trade and Politics in the Niger Delta, Oxford: The Clarendon Press, 1956, p. 39, fn. 1.

goddess or spirits like those of ancestors, or rivers (*Ulasi* for example) or other nature objects. Yet the Ibo sometimes speak as if *Chukwu* is distinctly and clearly living a separate existence from these other manifestations of his presence. This ambivalence in the Ibo concept of the Supreme Deity belongs to the perennial difficulty of man to describe explicitly the being of God. The Church still lives with the mystery of the three Persons in One! (2) It is a naturalistic religion as opposed to revealed religion but it is also an ethical religion. (3) It has elements that are local (*Anyanwu* is principally worshipped at Nsukka whilst *Amadi Oha* is prominent at Owerri), and yet in its interpretation of the justice of *Chukwu* it shows universalistic tendencies. (4) It has communalistic as well as individual emphases, but the personal elements of religious life derive from one's membership of the group's religious life. (5) On the surface, it does not seem to have carefully worked out philosophical unity, yet it still has the dimension of depth. It still seeks to supply answers to such questions as what is the meaning of life? Where do we come from? Where are we going? What shall we do and what shall we become in the time between birth and death? This is the Ibo world, its religion, culture and peoples, with which world religion—Christianity as well as the humanistic technology of the west, with its secularization tendencies, made their contact. We now proceed to examine the arrival of these influences. In doing so we hope to indicate the relevant ethos of Christianity in the way its dominant ethical values tend to agree with or be repugnant to Ibo values. This we hope, will help us to see more clearly in subsequent chapters, the nature of the interaction between Christianity and the culture it brings along with it and Ibo traditional culture and society. This will further help us in determining the possibilities of developing Christian ethics in an African background and what will be the nature of the ethics so developed.

CHAPTER FOUR

PATTERNS OF CHANGE IN IBO SOCIETY THROUGH CHRISTIANITY

THE ARRIVAL AND THE SPREAD OF CHRISTIANITY

The definitive date was 27th July, 1857 when an agreement was finally executed between a missionary group led by Samuel Crowther and Obi Akazua of Onitsha and his councillors to establish a Christian mission station at Onitsha, an Ibo town on the eastern bank of the river Niger. Earlier attempts had been made from England, through the joint efforts of publicly financed exploration companies and the Church Missionary Society (C.M.S.) founded in 1799, with the express aim of evangelising the heathen lands especially of Asia and Africa. Such earlier expeditions took place in 1841 when the C.M.S. sent two representatives J. F. Schön, a German missionary, and Samuel Adjai Crowther, a Yoruba ex-slave, educated and trained in Sierra Leone who later became the first African Bishop of the Anglican Church on June 29, 1864. During this expedition an agreement was made with Obi Ossai of Aboh on the one hand, and Captain Trotter leader of the expedition on the other hand to the effect that the Ibo people of Aboh would accept Christian missionaries. [1] This became the first recorded consent of an Ibo chief to accept missionaries. Another expedition of 1854 made further contact with the same area of Aboh, but for unknown reasons other than the death of Obi Ossai, no effective missionary work resulted.

It was left to Onitsha to have the pride of place in becoming the place of active beginning of the evangelization of Iboland. [2]

---

[1] Captain William Allen and T. R. H. Thomson, A Narrative of the Expedition to the Niger River, in 1841, London, 1848. Reprinted by Frank Cass, London 1965, Vol. 1, p. 223. It could also be mentioned here that Crowther's membership of this expedition and the part he played in this agreement with Obi Ossai was a tribute to him and to Sierra Leone that gave him his education and later became the cradle of West African Christianity. Most of the earliest missionaries in Iboland came from Sierra Leone.

[2] A large amount of literature exists on the subject of the planting of Christianity in Iboland and so we do not intend to detail the historical aspect here. See for example: F. D. Walker, The Romance of the Black River: The story of the C.M.S. Nigeria Mission, London, 1931; K. O. Dike, Origins of the Niger Mission 1841-1891, Ibadan, 1957; J. Jordan, Bishop Shanahan of Southern

Two Titled Men and Some Titled Women. The Men's title is *Ọzọ* while that of the women is *Nnyamala* (Obosi). The women are wearing very costly type of beads (*Erulu*) and wrist bangles made from Ivory. The *Ọzọ* men are holding their elephant tusks (Odunze or Odu-enyi), used in saluting the ancestors, in greeting a fellow *Ọzọ* man when passing through his homestead and for other *Ọzọ* music on ceremonial occasions. The man wearing tall cap is an *Ndichie* or *Okpara.*

Aniemeka Anene, the Idemili (Obosi) priest holding in his right hand the sword of the deity (*Mpama*) and in his left, the staff (*Oji Muo*). He dresses in white because the symbol of the deity is Purity. In front of the shrine is the *egbo* made of palm leaves and other things and hanging overhead to indicate that the place is sacred.

Before 1920 he was a reputed *Nwadibia*; today he is a well known Christian lay preacher.

SOME
IBO RELIGIOUS OBJECTS

1. *Ekwe-Ozi* (a small wooden drum); 2. *Ekwe* or *Uhie* (a large wooden drum
3. *Ogene* (metal gong); 4. *Okwa Muo* (sacred wooden saucer); 5. *Oche Ọz*
(traditional stood for *Ọzọ* titled men). The staff behind no. 4 is *Oji muo* used b
priests. The two long staffs are metal staffs called *Ogbala* used by *Ọzọ* titl
men. The two shorter wooden staffs are called *Osisi Ọzọ* also held by *Ọzọ* titl
men. The object at the foreground is called *Ekpili. Ekwe Ozi, Ekwe, Ogene* (no
1-3) and Ekpili are musical instruments.

Prominent in the actual establishment of the local church at Onitsha was John Christopher Taylor from Sierra Leone of Ibo parents to whom Crowther entrusted the work whilst he himself went back to the Niger Delta. Taylor was assisted by Simon Jonas another Sierra Leonian of Ibo origin who spoke the Ibo language well and became the interpreter to the missionary group. This led to the establishment of the evangelical wing of the Anglican Church which in course of time spread northwards to Enugu and southwards to Owerri covering groups of villages along its route like Nnewi, Ihiala, Nkwerre and basing its southwards headquarters at Egbu, very near Owerri. The spread of the gospel westwards from Onitsha across the Niger led to the establishment of the Anglican Church in Asaba and Agbor areas of Iboland. Further south-eastern parts of Iboland like Aba, Umuahia and Ndoki areas were evangelised by the Anglican missionaries from the Delta areas of Bonny, Brass and later from Port-Harcourt, the Ibo seaport on the Atlantic which grew up to become the centre of evangelization by other mission agencies which we will discuss briefly later.

The Roman Catholic thrust in the evangelization of Iboland started in 1885 under the leadership of the French-born Father Joseph Lutz who had some experience as a missionary in Sierra Leone. His party was again, as in the case of the C.M.S. party of 1857, well received by the King and Chiefs of Onitsha.

Before very long the Roman Catholic missionaries had penetrated into the interior of Iboland to found strong footholds in places like Igboriam and Aguleri, Ozubulu and Ihiala, Emekuku and Uruala. The Society of African Missions (S.M.A.) with headquarters at Lyons in France, directing the Holy Ghost Fathers mainly from Ireland, was responsible for this work.

A third missionary activity towards the evangelization of Iboland was started by the Primitive Methodist Society in 1892 in the area between the Qua Iboe River and Port-Harcourt. Earlier in 1879 the Rev. John Milum, leader of the Methodists in Lagos, had toured the Niger Delta areas and was cordially received by the famous King Jaja of Opobo who promised to support missionary work of the Wesleyans if it would be manned by Europeans. However it was the

---

Nigeria, Dublin; Clonmore and Reynolds Ltd., 1948; C. P. Groves, The Planting of Christianity in Africa, London: Lutterworth Press, 1958, Vols 2, 3 and 4; F. K. Ekechi, Missionary Enterprise and Rivalry in Igboland 1857-1914, London: Frank Cass, 1972.

opening up of the Railway from Port-Harcourt to Enugu which led to effective Methodist evangelization of Iboland, with Uzuakoli as headquarters, from which places like Umuahia, Ihube and Agbani were reached with financial support from the Methodist Society in London.

The Baptists under the leadership of William Hughes from Colwyn Bay Institution in North Wales started work in the Port-Harcourt area, which moved westwards into Iboland around places like Oloko and Obinze.

Another missionary activity towards the evangelization of Iboland was that started by what was later known as the Qua Iboe Mission. George Watts, a British trader, had started a school at Ibuno by the bank of the Qua Iboe River in the Ibibio country. Later this Church-school interest was taken over by an interdenominational missionary body by the name of Qua Iboe Mission with headquarters in Belfast, Ireland. This missionary body later moved into Iboland especially in the Ngwa areas around Aba.

Much earlier on, the Presbyterians through their establishment at Calabar in 1846 had penetrated into Iboland around places like Arochukwu, Uburu, Ohafia, Afikpo and Abriba. These Ibo areas along the regions of the Cross river became, as it were, the only missionary confines of the Presbyterians, through the United Free Church of Scotland, in Iboland until quite recently, when Churches have been built by them in places like Enugu and Abakaliki.

It is through the activities of these six European based missionary agencies that Iboland was evangelised to the extent that, by the time of the outbreak of the first world war in 1914, it could be said that Christianity had been planted in Iboland. For a quarter of a century, precisely between 1914 and 1939 when the second world war broke out Christianity in Iboland had acquired a definite foothold, not only in its numerical strength, but also in the social life as well as the economic life of the people. Many schools and colleges had been built by Churches for the education and training of children of their adherents, for example, in addition to the hundreds of elementary schools, the C.M.S. had built at Onitsha in 1925 the Dennis Memorial Grammar School. This is a very highly valued and systematically organised boarding secondary school through which a large number of the present day Ibo elite has passed. The Roman Catholics in 1933 built their own elitist secondary school—Christ the King College; the Methodists in 1923 their own—the Methodist Institute Uzuakoli. Teacher

Training Colleges were set up at St. Paul's Awka (C.M.S.), St. Charles' Onitsha (The Roman Catholic Mission, R.C.M.) and Uzuakoli Institute (The Methodist Mission). By the employment of a large number of people as preachers, teachers, clerks, salesmen in bookshops, nurses in hospitals and as odd jobsmen in mission houses, the means of livelihood of many people in Iboland depended on Churches and the employees' faithful membership in them.

Various factors must have contributed to the numerical growth of the Churches in Iboland at this time but, before we discuss this, let us carry forwards a bit the general historical survey. Within the twenty-five years period of 1914-1939, Iboland felt for the first time the influence of a separatist Church as well as of an American sect. In 1916 the Garrick Braide secession had taken place in the Delta area and entered Iboland through the Christ Army Church organised from the secession. Braide had been an influential member of the Anglican Church where at Saint Andrew's Bakana he was the Pastor's warden around 1914-1915. He later developed efficacy in divine prayer healing, and a prophetic attitude to religion which for some time he employed in the pastoral work of the St. Andrew's Bakana Church, but later he organised what he called Prophetic movement. This was declared heretical by the Anglican Bishop Johnson in charge of the Delta area. A large number of members of various Anglican Churches who sympathised with Garrick Braide joined him in forming the first "Prophet" Church as well as the first breakaway Church which eventually grew in Iboland. Today the Christ Army Church of Garrick Braide has divided into two: Christ Army Church and Christ Army Church Garrick Braide Connection, prayer and faith healing being the chief characteristics of these two.

The American sect that arrived within this period was the Faith Tabernacle "Church", another faith healing Church. We will at a later stage in the history of Christianity in Iboland discuss the emergence and role of the many prophet-prayer-healing Churches in Iboland. Suffice it now to indicate here how the first appearance of "prophet" Church in Iboland came in to "intrude", as it were, upon the "neat pattern" of the more orthodox missionary and Europe based Christianity, both of the Roman Catholics as well as of the Protestants.

Another historical period of twenty-five years can be identified from 1939 to 1964. The history of the Church in Iboland within this quarter of a century was characterised by signs and pains of growth. The second world war started in 1939 depleting the number of expatriate missionaries. Quick efforts were then made to find some trained Ibo Christians to hold educational and administrative posts hitherto occupied by European missionaries. Furthermore Ibo educated laymen were multiplying and some of them were becoming critical of the missionaries. The West African Pilot, a nationalistic newspaper founded in 1937 by Nnamdi Azikiwe, an Ibo trained in the United States and living in Lagos (Nigeria's Capital City), was becoming influential. It quickly became a ready medium for much critical opinion about the work of the missions. Acceleration of missionary effort in taking education to all the corners of Iboland was another feature of this period, especially the education of women. The Roman Catholic Mission opened secondary schools for girls at Onitsha, Awka, Umuoji, and the Church Missionary Society at Port-Harcourt, Ogidi, Enugu, Nkwerri. Close co-operation between the various non Roman missions, started in the previous historical period (1914-1939), became structured into the Christian Council of Nigeria. [3] Between 1955 and 1958 various regions of Nigeria achieved regional political autonomy in preparation for the country's independence in October 1960.

Iboland and the missions working in it also experienced both the nationalistic as well as the psychological stimulation that such political and economic dynamism brought to the country. Therefore quick efforts were made to turn the missions into national churches especially among the Anglican Churches which had all along trained and used natives as agents and pastors. The various districts of the various dioceses were staffed with Ibos since 1922 when the first diocesan synod was inaugurated, largely within Iboland, with the Rt. Rev. Bertram Lasbrey as its first diocesan bishop. The same was true of the Methodists and the Presbyterians who in due course organised their own type of self governing and self supporting Churches. The Roman Catholic Church had its own way of encouraging local government.

Another feature of the Church life in Iboland within this period of twenty-five years (1939-1964) was the growth of many Ibo-inspired healing homes and prophetic-type Churches. We had called attention

[3] As early as 1909 co-operative meetings were held at Calabar to agree on the areas of influence of four Protestant Mission Bodies working in Eastern Nigeria including Iboland. Other meetings were held in 1911 and 1917 without a great deal of success as missions continued to enter places within the areas of influence of other missions. See G. O. M. Tasie, "Denominational Co-operation and Rivalry in South East Nigeria 1880-1918", in the *Bulletin of the Society for African Church History*, United Kingdom, Vol. III, Nos 1-2, 1969-70, pp. 44-51.

to the start of the first of such Churches through the activities of one Garrick Braide in the Niger Delta area and its spread into Iboland. For many years the Christ Army Church remained the only Prophet-Healing Church in Iboland. But within the 1939-1964 period the Cherubin and Seraphin Church as well as the Christ Apostolic Church, both "Prayer-Healing-Prophetic" type of Churches, arrived in Iboland from Western Nigeria through Yoruba settlers in Iboland and had spread all over the place. The first Ibo founded "Prayer-Healing" Church was by Madam Nwokolo of Ufuma who in the early 40's started healing through prayer, fasting and the use of holy oil. She refused her members' pressure to inaugurate and register a separate Church. Rather she advised those she had "cured" to go back to their own denominations. This fine example of Madam Nwokolo was not followed by the more "institution-minded" prophets and prophetesses, with or without connections to her, who have dotted Iboland with over two hundred of this type of Church. Since after the Nigerian civil war the number has escalated by at least fifty percent, giving credence to the sociological theory that times of strain, stress and economic depression tend to induce more people to seek "salvation" from the promises of this sectarian type of Churches, whether their emphasis be prayer or healing or pentecostal prophetism.[4] There are two sources of inspiration to this group of churches in Iboland: American Pentecostalism and Ibo traditional religious experience. The genius for prophetism in the form of vision seeing and vision interpretation is like traditional divination. The combination of healing through herbs and oils with religious practices, and the desire for visible symbols of religious vitality in the form of spirit possession, ecstasy and the feeling of abandon and "carefree"-worship patterns have their counterpart in traditional religion also.

To complete the history of Christianity in Iboland at this period, we should mention the gradual disappearance of schools as the Churches' strong arm of evangelism. More and more schools especially in the secondary level, were opened by enterprising individuals, communities or governments—local or regional. Effective teaching of Christian doctrine in the schools started to disappear gradually until after the civil war (1967-70) when schools were completely taken over by the

[4] Cf. J. Milton Yinger, Sociology Looks at Religion, New York: Macmillan Paperback 1966, especially chapter 2 where he discusses Religion and Social Change—Functions and Dysfunctions of Sects and Cults Among the Disprivileged, pp. 39-63.

State Government in Iboland, halting almost completely such aspects of evangelistic work missions had done through school.[5]

Furthermore the Churches that have grown out of European based missionary work started acquiring features that would make them more indigenous for example in the hymn tunes, and to some extent, Church architecture. However the more militant nationalistic elements in the Churches started demanding greater adaptation to the environment of Ibo life, religious ethos and traditional practices. Many who failed to get what they had demanded tended to drift over to the Churches we have called prayer-healing-prophetic type of Churches, originated by Ibos or breakaways from the missionary founded Churches.

In summarising, we would say that looking at the history from the arrival of Christianity into Iboland to the present, three main periods could be identified. From 1857 to 1914, a fifty-seven year period of the planting and of the contact with Ibo traditional religion and Ibo way of life, Christianity appealed to the Ibos for various reasons. Its expansion seemed to have been supported by the historical factor of British acquisition of influence in the area, first of trade and later of political control. The second historical period 1914-1939 was marked by the competitive spirit of various missions in their scramble for membership and for areas of influence, earlier attempts at a gentleman's agreement on comity of missions between Protestant bodies notwithstanding. The third period of another twenty-five years from 1939-1964 saw the beginnings of the growth of national or indigenous Churches, the coming together of Protestant Churches in institutions like Trinity Theological College, Umuahia for the training of ministers, hospitals like Queen Elizabeth Hospital at Umuahia and joint rural training centre at Asaba. New enterprise between the missionary bodies in Europe and Churches in Iboland in partnership of the utilization of personnel from abroad also developed. "Churches" with more features of Ibo traditional religious "feelings" and "methods" appeared and Churches' influence in education through the ownership of schools was terminated as governments took over schools. More demand began to be made on the more orthodox Churches to indigenize the Churches by taking in greater features of Ibo culture like the *Ọzọ* title, polygamy and the significant aspects of the many ramifica-

[5] For an analysis of Church-State relationship in education from the early beginnings, see David B. Abernethy, Church and State in Nigerian Education, Ibadan: NISER Reprint Series No. 43, 1966, pp. 27 to 36 (on Iboland).

tions of the extended family, for example, the place of the ancestors and the symbols of their being reverenced in libation of wine and the sacrifice of food.

It is this situation which has given rise to the sharpened interaction between Christianity and Ibo traditional way of life including a sharp confrontation between Ibo moral life and Christian ethics, between the western norms associated with Christianity and Ibo concepts of norms and values learnt through the organised traditional community life and religion which we have discussed in chapters II and III. Christianity therefore becomes a force inducing change in Iboland. It is to some aspects of that change we now turn, starting from the general interaction with the earliest missionaries, and deepening the enquiry later with case studies of three Ibo localities as at present (see Chapter V).

Interaction between Early Missionaries and Ibo Values and Institutions

From chapters II and III it could be deduced that before the arrival of Christianity, Iboland was a place in which the traditional religion laid the basis of behaviour. Social and cultural identification, and the principles of socialization from the older to the younger generation were clearly understood. With the arrival of missionaries and traders from 1857 onwards the neat pattern became disturbed. Plurality of religious beliefs and value concepts appeared for the first time to start the rapid social change that has been going on in Iboland ever since then, although more rapid at some periods than others. Christianity challenged Ibo beliefs as well as social control methods like divination and consultation of oracles. It also challenged the place and authority of dead ancestors recognised in the cult of *Ndebunze* or *Ndichie* (ancestors). John Christopher Taylor, the first missionary and pastor in Onitsha 1857-1869, had hoped very confidently that the *Nwadibeas*, (diviner-priests and healers of Iboland), would soon disappear. In his Journal entry for 6th February 1863 he reported to the C.M.S. Headquarters in London: "Already the *dibeas* are ashamed in this district and they could not boldly show their nose, and are trying to rid themselves, as their craft is now in danger of being exposed before the pure light of Christianity and in the eyes of their long-trodden vassalage".[6] Hence the efforts to undermine the work of the *dibias*.

---

6 See C.M.S. CA 3/037, Journal, 6th February 1863.

In the same Journal, Taylor had also reported in the entry for 28th June, that he was very glad as he saw the converts throw away "with temerity" the traditions of their homeland. In "The Gospel on the Banks of the Niger" he had also indicated that the Ibo gods—"Their idols *Ikenga, Tshi* and *Ọfọ*, their country gods, are now tottering and I hope will be ere long for ever paralysed... The *Tshuku* (god) of ... the Ibos in general, shall fall down before the Gospel, as the Dragon fell before the Ark's".[7] To indicate the general pattern of the uneasiness the gospel naturally induced among the Ibos at this early period, we will point out the beliefs, values and institutions that first received shattering from Christianity.

Twin Killing

It was an Ibo old custom to destroy twins because it was considered unnatural for human beings to be born more than one at a time, only lower animals like hens, goats, dogs and the rest could give birth to more than one at a time. A woman giving birth to twins would therefore need a special cleansing sacrifice and the twin children would be destroyed, otherwise the land thus abominated would incur the wrath of the ancestral spirits, which would plague the community, because the "natural" harmony between man, the spirit world and the cosmos in general, had been destroyed. Taylor at Onitsha advised the newly converted Christians to disobey this custom and keep their twin children. This the converts found difficult. Then they came to Taylor with a request that he, Taylor, should provide them protection from the outrage of the populace, who no doubt, would forcibly destroy such twins of the Christians and punish their parents in addition. In a letter Taylor wrote to Venn at C.M.S. headquarters in London he confessed that he was helpless in the face of the demand of the converts for protection.[8] He hoped that the British Government would soon establish its authority over Iboland and be in a position to destroy "this antique custom". When the Rev. Solomon Samuel Perry from Sierra Leone, of Ibo parentage, had taken over the C.M.S. work at Onitsha, he made many entries in his Journal on the subject of twin killing, and the efforts he made to stop the practice. On

---

[7] S. Crowther and J. C. Taylor, The Gospel on the Banks of the Niger 1857-1859, London: 1859, p. 272.

[8] See C.M.S. CA 3/037 J. C. Taylor to Henry Venn 25th October, 1865. In the same block No. see Taylor's Report on the Political and Spiritual State of Onitsha for 1864.

January 21, 1876 he learnt that one of the wives of the *Odu,* an important chief of Onitsha, had delivered twins. Before he could do anything, the twins had been destroyed. Another entry was for July 31, 1879, about a convert whose wife had given birth to twin children a few days after the death of a son of this Christian couple. All the Christians agreed with Perry to save the twins. The following day all the Christians rejoiced openly and publicly that they had got twins. Archdeacon Crowther, Bishop Crowther's son, was visiting Onitsha and so gave moral courage to the Christians, although he left a day afterwards. For the second day running no one said a word against preserving the life of these twins. Later Chief Onya and a half dozen of the relatives of the King came to Perry to demand explanation why the twins were still kept alive. Perry answered that he had the impression that Christians, having been allowed to worship God in their own way, could preserve such life. Perry went further that he had understood from earlier meetings with the Onitsha chiefs, that if missionaries preserved such twins in their Church quarters and not in the town, that would be agreeable to the Onitsha people. Onya and his party went away, but a few hours later it became known that the people were in a war mood to destroy both the twins and the Christians. In the attack made upon the mission house, where the Christians had congregated to protect themselves and the twins, two men died of the shots received; several properties were looted from the mission house; doors and windows were carried off. The twins had however been taken to Lokoja with the assistance of the merchants, especially Mr. J. Pinnock, the Agent General to whom Archdeacon Crowther had appealed for help.[9] This was the first open stand taken in the name of Christianity against an unhealthy Ibo custom.

Of course it took the added efforts of other missionaries like Mary Slessor in the extreme south east of Ibo land at Aro-Chukwu, and the influence of British colonial masters to end this practice of twin killing.

Human Sacrifice

Three types of human sacrifice had existed in Iboland before the arrival of Christianity—the sacrifice of atonement when extreme abomination to the land had led to breach of harmony between the spirit

[9] C.M.S. CA 3/030/7, Perry to C.M.S. Headquarters, July 31, 1897.

world and the community. This was of course rare. The second was when chiefs and some noblemen holding the *Ọzọ* title were burried with their slaves partly to ensure a smooth passage to the land of the spirits where they join the restful bliss of the ancestors. It was believed that such slaves would also serve their masters in the life after death.[10] The third occasion was the use priests and manipulators of secret cults, oracles and shrines made of human sacrifice to appease the gods of such oracles, for example the water spirits at Onitsha. Missionaries in Iboland were naturally worried about this practice and at once did whatever they could to stop it. Crowther reported of a woman slave at Onitsha who should have been killed, but when he pleaded and convinced the people that it was wrong to sacrifice a human being in burying the nobles of the land, she was loosed from her bonds. Crowther on the first interview with King Akazua of Onitsha got him to promise to abolish human sacrifices.[11] Of course such promises were more easily made than kept! Sometimes the missionaries paid ransom in money or goods to redeem a slave about to be sacrificed. For example Perry at Onitsha on the 19th December 1874 had to rush to Oko on the other side of the Niger and redeem an Onitsha man from Umuasere captured by the Oko people after paying to them goods worth seven pounds sterling. An entry in Perry's journal for December 25th, 1875, revealed the continued distress at the encounter these early missionaries had with human sacrifice in Iboland. After preaching a Christmas sermon and feeling rather happy Perry went out on visit, and was astonished to find the body of a boy whose head had been chopped off. On enquiry he was told that it "was done by the King's orders, to implore the protection of the old dead kings, who used to have their dwellings about there".[12]

The missionaries' fight against this custom was continued at the turn of this century. The political officers of the British colonial administration joined in the effort, by destroying shrines like the *Kamalu* and *Nkuku* in the Bende District of Iboland.[13] The conten-

[10] See Francis A. Arinze, Sacrifice in Ibo Religion, Ibadan: University Press, 1970, pp. 85-91. His view that "such killings were not at all sacrificial" is not upheld by my findings. An element of sacrifice to the ancestors for easy passage and entry into the bliss of life after death existed, though it was not the most outstanding reason for burial of chiefs with slaves.

[11] S. Crowther and J. C. Taylor, The Gospel on the Banks of the Niger 1857-1859, London, 1859, pp. 34 ff.

[12] C.M.S. C.A. 3/030/5, S. S. Perry's Journal, December 17, 18, 19, 1874 and December 25, 1875.

[13] See Frank Hives and Gascoine Lumley, Ju-Ju and Justice in Nigeria, New

tion that the missionaries' success was not without association with colonial and commercial interests also from Britain, (a subject we shall discuss fully later,) could be sustained by incidents like this.

Burials

We have noted how the missionaries rightly frowned against the practice of burying with slaves some chiefs and important persons. In course of years Christians were taught to refrain from paying the extended family and village collections levied for various activities because part of the levy went to sacrifices to idols. Part also went to certain activities associated with burials, like the masquerades and payment of certain fees to some functionaries at burials, which were done on the communal level. Greater complications arose when many children of many family heads became Christians, and were forbidden by the teaching of the missionaries to perform the second burial of their fathers. The Ibo practice was to bury an elderly person soon after death, with preliminary ceremonies. Then after a year or less, sometimes more, the second burial would take place with a lot more elaborate ceremonies than the first. It was believed that this second burial, was the one that helped the spirit of such departed elderly persons to rest comfortably with the ancestors in the land of the ancestral bliss, from where they plead effectively with the gods for the well-being of their children on earth. If this second burial was not performed, the proper inheritance of the late father's property could not be finally settled. What was worse, the extended family would be harrassed by the hovering spirit of the dead person who had not properly settled down with the other ancestral spirits. For quite some time this presented a big problem to many converts who were ready to obey the teachings of the missionaries, and at the same time felt the compunction of filial duty to dead parents as well as respect to community opinion, as such converts were also members of the local non-Christian community. A meeting was called at Onitsha in May 1914 under the chairmanship of Archdeacon T. J. Dennis to discuss the whole question of the "Church and Native Customs" of which the burial question was one. After several sessions of "useful", "near useful" and "not quite so useful" views had been expressed on the subject-matter of second burial, it was resolved and adopted "that the

---

York: Ballantine Books Inc. 1963 for the adventures of Frank Hives, an Administrative Officer in Iboland in helping to exterminate the practice.

Government be asked to make it law that Christian heirs inherit the property, pay the debts of the deceased, (father or brother) and leave out the burial". In the discussions the chairman "held strongly that it is not right for a Christian to have anything to do with a second burial".[14] Thus a useful opportunity was lost in integrating this native custom into the Church officially. In more recent times Christians in many Ibo communities have started performing the second burial of their parents or older brothers with or without religious memorial services, recapturing as it were, the traditional practices of the past generations yet without official Church pronouncement!

Etiquette—Children's behavior patterns

Another Ibo value that the missionaries opposed through their teaching, especially to school children, was the ordinary attitude of deference to seniors—parents and natural rulers like kings and chiefs. An illustration can be taken from an incident at Onitsha in 1863 about which J. C. Taylor had made some comments. The King of Onitsha and his first son—the Prince—and heir apparent were sitting by the King's square when a group of the mission's pupils marched past through the town. As they drew near the square the son of the Prince by name Odita stood up and bowed his head before his father and the grandfather—the King. He was asked why he did not do the customary courtesy to the King which was to kneel down and bow the head to the ground in front of the King, he replied that he had been taught at school that kneeling down was only for prayer and bowing down was only to God. The King and the Prince were greatly surprised by the behaviour of Odita whilst Taylor was filled with satisfaction as shown in the entry in his Journal for December 29, 1863 that the actions of the children (including Odita's failure to salute the grandfather properly) resulted from their acting from higher principles which had been inculcated through the Christian religion.[15]

In different parts of Taylor's reports to the C.M.S. Headquarters in London it could be seen that he was completely disrespectful to most of the cultural aspects of the socialization of the young. The custom of the subjects of the King of Onitsha, falling down and

---

[14] Minutes of "the Church and Native Customs Conference", May 12, 1914, C.M.S. Ozala, Onitsha - Nigeria, typed script in the C.M.S. archives at Onitsha unpublished Mss, p. 16.

[15] C.M.S. CA 3/037 Taylor's Journal Entry for 29th December 1863.

bowing their heads to the ground before the king was described as a "source of deep mortification" and "a humiliating posture" which he hoped would very soon wane and be forever eclipsed. [16]

In general the children who went to school were unable to participate in the activities of their age sets like initiation into the masquerade societies, learning the social and cultic dances and the various acolyte duties associated with the various celebrations, sacrifices and the public worship of clan and family gods. Hence the emphasis of the missionaries was on the running of boarding schools in which the children would be socialized in different values and ethos far away from what was obtaining in Iboland. [17]

We will now look at a few of the Ibo institutions with which the early missionaries came into destructive contact, further illustrating how Christianity in Iboland inevitably brought about changes in the value concepts of the people, which again started disorganization in the normative quality of social as well as individual life style. We will discuss mainly three—some political and social control institutions, the *Ọzọ* title and polygamy.

Some political and social control institutions

As we indicated in chapter III Iboland used shrines (where oaths were sworn), oracles and taboos as means of social and political control. Christians were taught not to accept these any more as they were rightly regarded as unchristian practices. But in the absence of other forms, it was, no doubt, constituting the Christians into a "law-less" group, in the sociological sense. Such Christians would live under no enforceable code of behaviour against which community sanctions could be imposed. Ekechi, writing on this period, said: "The converts in turn became quite fanatical and threw caution to the wind. Induced, no doubt, by their teachers, the Christians began to cut down the trees in the various groves and religious shrines as a test of their earnestness in religious commitment". [18]

At the missionary conference held at Onitsha in May 1914 the question of swearing oath at a shrine as a means of adjudicating

16 Crowther and J. C. Taylor, The Gospel on the Banks of the Niger 1857-1859, London, 1859, p. 282.

17 See C.M.S. CA 3/037 Taylor's Journal dated 31st March, 1864 where he speaks of borrowing from a local woman to keep the boarding school going.

18 F. K. Ekechi, Missionary Enterprise and Rivalry in Igbo-land 1857-1914, London: Frank Cass, 1972, p. 36.

between two contending parties was raised. Should a Christian swear an oath to justify his claim to a property, rightly his own, which someone else was claiming falsely?

In the end the conference decided "that our C.M.S. authorities would approach the Government in connection with this difficult and most important subject, asking them to design a way—other than swearing a juju or idol—by which Christians in this country can prove their right to a claim or property. If the Government failed to find a way suitable, then a conference could be held for the final consideration of the subject".[19]

Of course Government found a way and Christians were required to swear in a British colonial court on the Bible to justify a claim or prove innocence when falsely accused. But Ibo system of control through oath, sacred shrines and sacred bushes had been shattered by the Christian teaching thereby influencing the tempo of social change. Again in the work of destroying the powerful oracles and shrines of Iboland, the British colonial administration in Nigeria played important part, justifying the general view that without the British Imperial might the progress of Christianity in penetrating Iboland would have been slower. The most important of the oracles with its shrine in Aro-Chukwu was the Long Juju, properly known as the *Ubiniukpabi* of the Aros. In 1901/02 the British carried out an expedition to Aro-Chukwu in pursuance of its opening up of the interior of the country but with the specific aim of destroying the shrine of the Long Juju. Historians have argued as to the part played by the Calabar Mission of the Presbyterian Church in inciting the British colonial authorities to carry out the expedition so as to facilitate that Mission's evangelization work in that part of Iboland.[20] Whether or not the Presbyterian missionaries were party to the decision to deal with the Aros militarily, the fact remains that it was the British military might which finally destroyed the shrine and the *Kamalu* as well as the *Nkuku* shrines already referred to (see page 66), so as

[19] Conference Report, C.M.S. Archives Onitsha, unpublished Mss, p. 9.

[20] Prof. E. A. Ayandele in his: The Missionary Impact on Modern Nigeria, 1842-1914, London: Longmans 1966 argued that the Presbyterian missionaries in Calabar were party to the decision to deal with the Aro and their Long Juju militarily. Prof. A. E. Afigbo in an article: "The Calabar Mission and the Aro Expedition 1901-1902", *West African Religion* Nsukka No. 9, 1971, pp. 14-27 and *Journal of Religion in Africa*, E. J. Brill, Leiden, Vol. 5 Fasc. 2, 1973, pp. 94-106 argued with convincing evidence from archives that the missionaries were not party to the decision to deal with the Aros militarily.

to enable the missionaries to apply more effectively their teaching, that Christians should ignore the social control and other uses made of the shrines. The continued existence of such shrines, with the many evils perpetrated in their names, would have remained visible artefacts of the religion against which Christianity preached; but that their destruction constituted dislocation in the social structure of the Ibo until the British administrative and judicial systems were fully introduced cannot be denied.

The Ọzọ Title

In chapter II we have indicated the religious and socio-political significance of the *Ọzọ* title in Iboland. A modern historian has described the *Ọzọ* title holder as occupying a position in Iboland comparable to the peerage in the English society, with the same social prestige of "Lord" in the society, as indicated in the new title name the man is given at the successful end of the title-taking. [21]

Whatever was its political, social and economic significance, because most of the *Ọzọ* rites of initiation were associated with many religious rites, the missionaries understandably educated their converts to have nothing to do with it. *Ọzọ* title holders at conversion must renounce their title and burn the insignia of the title as well as the cult objects associated with it. At the conference held at Onitsha on Tuesday the 12th of May 1914 to consider many aspects of the confrontation of Ibo customs with Christianity the *Ọzọ* title was fully discussed. It was classified as "political custom". The Onitsha conference had many arguments in favour and against Christians taking the title until the consensus reached seemed to be that: "*Ọzọ* is idolatrous and therefore no Christian man should have anything to do with it". To this Mr. Nzekwu, the Rev. G. Anyaegbunam, and some other members of the conference replied: "Scarcely is there any custom in this country that has nothing idolatrous or superstitious in it. But what and where shall we be if we reject and throw all these customs out as quite unfit". [22] Another member of the conference Mr. H. Nweje (later

---

[21] E. O. Egbo in "Conflicts Between Traditional Religion and Christianity in Igboland, South-Eastern Nigeria", *West African Religion* Nsukka, No. 10, July 1971, p. 13. Such title names as *Dim Nwakarame* (the noble lord whose son had done great honour) or *Ezeakukaria* (the king or lord whose wealth overflows) would suggest this. See also on title names at Onitsha R. N. Henderson, The King in Everyman—Evolutionary trends in Onitsha Ibo Society and Culture, New Haven and London: Yale University Press, 1972, p. 260.

[22] Conference Report, *op. cit.*, p. 4.

archdeacon Nweje) said that he was unable to see "in *Ọzọ* any evil so grievous as to warrant Christians totally rejecting it". He continued by requesting the conference to draw up plans to enable Christians take the *Ọzọ* title.

This was not done by the conference of 1914 and even in recent times conferences have been called from April of 1966 to as recently as April of 1973 and no solution has been given at least by the Anglican Church, as to what Christians should do with the *Ọzọ* title. The Roman Catholics on the other hand started with antagonism to *Ọzọ* but in more recent times seemed to have worked out some acceptable scheme of accomodation. Father Shanahan (later Bishop) of the Roman Catholic Mission at Onitsha in 1911 suggested that Christians should be organised to form their own kind of *Ọzọ* society as a counter and a way of ignoring the tradional one. [23]

In the past five years the Roman Catholic Archbishop of Onitsha had worked out a system whereby Roman Catholics could take the *Ọzọ* title in "a Christian way". [24]

Polygamy

From the earliest contact of Christianity with Ibo life and society, polygamy seemed one of the most difficult institutions of Ibo life to be easily thrown away by converts. Taylor was feeling pleased in the first few years of his missionary work when some of the converts apparently adopted monogamy by putting away all wives except one. Not long afterwards Taylor discovered to his great disappointment that the people were strongly attached to their heathenish practices and way of life including polygamy. [25] The classic example was the case of one John Samuel Okosi which Taylor reported on so fully in his Journal entry for November 21, 1864 and in November 1, 1865 as well as in May 30, 1866. Towards the end of 1862, Okosi brought all his idols in a big bag and handed them over to the missionaries, and confessed that he was fed up with the gods of sticks and wood and said that the word of God had entered into his heart, and that he wanted to forsake his past foolish way of worshipping those idols.

---

[23] C.S.E. Paris 192/A/11 Shanahan to the Directors, 15th September 1911. Quoted by F. K. Ekechi, *op. cit.*, p. 165.

[24] See: E. O. Egbo, Conflicts Between Traditional Religion and Christianity in Iboland, South Eastern Nigeria, *op. cit.*, p. 14.

[25] C.M.S. CA 3/037, Taylor's Journal for the quarter ending, September 30, 1864.

He was very gladly received by the missionaries and was among those baptised on 23rd November 1862 with forty-one others. He was given the names John Samuel Okosi. Three years afterwards—in 1865—Okosi was being drawn back into his old life, as he had lost his place in the Onitsha social life, and was unable to find enough meaning in the Christian society or in the monogamous life he had only three years ago adopted, when he drove away all his wives except one so as to accept baptism. Moreover he could not feel he was right to withdraw himself from the only society he knew—the Onitsha Society—as he had stopped paying his communal contributions to the people and king of Onitsha. Okosi therefore appealed to Crowther to permit him to return to polygamy and still remain Christian. This Crowther rejected; and thinking that Okosi's main reason in wishing to revert to polygamy was economic, offered him a job in the mission compound as a monitor at twelve shillings a month (about 11,700 cowries, Ibo native money at the time). Okosi rejected the offer and went ahead and reverted to polygamy. He furthermore apologised to the King of Onitsha for the "insulting attitude" of his Christian years when he paid no communal contributions, and as evidence of his sincerity to the King, presented a goat to him and pledged that from thence he would do everything that all Onitsha did, irrespective of the instructions of the missionaries. Taylor was so greatly disappointed by this incident that in the 30th May entry into his Journal about the Okosi incident he ended it with these words—"What a fall!" [26] The missionaries went further and acted uncharitably in sending out of the school, Okosi's son, Gilbert, which led to the withdrawal of all the other Okosi "family" children.

The Okosi incident is not only an illustration of the problem of a convert in the early history of Christianity in Iboland relapsing into polygamy, but contains also the problem of uprooting one from one's culture and environment which was involved. Furthermore the failure of the missionary leadership, in this case Bishop Crowther and Taylor, to understood the depth of the problem presented by polygamy, has continued to be a source of ethical embarrassment to the Church, not only in Iboland but all Africa. Solomon Perry in his Journal dated 16th September, 1872 has given the indication that he had understood the complex problem of polygamy for the African convert. Said he:

---

[26] C.M.S. CA 3/037, Taylor's Journal, 21st November, 1864; 1st November 1865 and 6th May, 1866.

"All admit that Christianity is good but the only impossible barrier to it is that it sets its face against polygamy and adultery of every description. My general answer to them is that we have never made it a plan to give strong meat to the children, neither have we ever expected to see effects where there are no causes, and therefore I would advise them to come as they are". Further in the same Journal he narrated his conversation with a near convert who told him (Perry) that the only loop-hole through which he (the near convert) could see the folly of the Christian religion was polygamy. [27]

This understanding was not shared by Bishop Crowther who strongly felt that "true religion can admit of no compromise with the world" and therefore the Church could not admit polygamists. In the notes he prepared on polygamy for the 1888 meeting of Anglican Bishops —the forerunner of what we now know as the Lambeth Conference— he spoke out clearly: "The heathens will affirm that the life of polygamy as practised by their forefathers was more suitable to them than that introduced by the new religion, and needs no change. The heathen young men would take advantage of the admission of their fathers into the Church, and wait till they have married many wives, and then apply to be received; if their father would be received as such, why should not they? The converts who had renounced polygamy before they were received into the Church, will be shaken in their faith". [28] This opinion of Crowther upheld by subsequent Bishops in Iboland, never did anything to solve the problem posed by polygamy to an Ibo convert whose social structure, links of association on the father's side as well on the mother's side, and the relationships of cousins, uncles and nephews or nieces have been built around the many wives of the family, nuclear or extended. The roots of the young Ibo's personality and the consciousness of his communal existence, which was the only existence he knew then, as now, went deep down into polygamous association. Hence Archdeacon Dobinson in one of his Niger letters of August 20, 1890 said: "one never realized till one got out here how serious and difficult a question it (polygamy) really is." [29] How serious and difficult the dislocation Christianity

---

[27] C.M.S. CA 3/030, Rev. Solomon Samuel Perry, Umedei Station, Onitsha Journal dated 16th September, 1872.

[28] C.M.S. G3/A3/o Crowther: Notes on the Life of Polygamy in West Africa, January 1887.

[29] Archdeacon Dobinson's Niger Letters, edited by his sister, London, Seeley & Co. Ltd., 1899, p. 63.

brought upon Ibo institution of family life built on polygamy is, can be seen from the fact that the problem is still with the Church after a century of the Church's existence in Iboland. Meanwhile we leave the subject hoping to return to it in a later chapter, believing that enough is said already to indicate the nature of the dislocation in normative, moral and ethical dimensions of Ibo life by the introduction of Christianity. This dislocation we must say straightaway, was inevitable in as long as two different value concepts confronted each other as did the Ibo traditional and religious life with Christianity. It is only with clearer understanding of Ibo traditional religion and culture, as well as with clearer understanding of the kernel of Christianity, as distinct from its cultural accretions, put on it by time and people and places, that this type of analysis is now possible with a view to heal, as far as possible, the dislocation. To this main interest of our study we will return in due course. Meanwhile we want to examine further other areas of initial contacts between Christianity and Ibo social, moral and cultural life.

Some Historical, Cultural, Racial and Moral Issues involved in the Planting of Christianity in Iboland

The planting of Christianity in Iboland involved a good many other factors of human nature, historical facilities or hinderances and the problems of racial and cultural misunderstandings. These non-religious factors will be briefly analysed so as to indicate the insight they give into the complexity of the interaction between Christianity and Ibo way of life.

The historical situation in Iboland at the time of the arrival of the missionaries was opportune. The activities of the Aro people (the Cross River Ibos who managed the *Ubiniukpabi* oracle) in harassing some villagers with their Abam mercenaries, and the hunting for slaves and the kidnapping of persons, had wearied the Ibo people to the point of their being ready to welcome something new. [30]

Furthermore the Ibos as a people have been enthusiastic about enlarging their views of the nature of reality, hence their adaptability about which some modern anthropologists write. A people of that frame of cultural adaptability do not close their minds to a new

---

30 See: J. C. Anene, Southern Nigeria in Transition 1885-1906, Cambridge University Press, 1966. See also: Equiano Olaudah, The Life of Olaudah Equiano or Gustavus Vassa, the African, 1789, reprinted London: Dawson of Pall Mall, 1969 in 2 vols.

teaching like that brought about by Christian missionaries.[31] Later at the turn of the century, the British colonial authority's efforts at opening up the country, together with the cordial relationship that seemed to prevail between the missionaries especially of the C.M.S. and the British officials, provided their own historical facilities that must have led to the increased number of persons adopting Christianity.[32] Furthermore the seductive approach of the missionaries in offering to the people, when ever they wanted to start missionary work, facilities for the education of their children and the manifest evidence of the benefit of education to such children when they were able to read and write, were attractive.[33]

Other forms of social services were provided especially by Father Lutz of the Roman Catholic Mission who used the supply of medicine to households as a regular means of winning "friends" whom to convert. What all these social welfare activities, including more developed educational systems later, added up to, was to overload the Christian message with western cultural values to the detriment of the Ibo traditional culture. This early in the history of Christianity in Iboland overloaded the Gospel message with foreign elements which have stayed on ever since. Nigerian historians have written quite a good deal on this topic, especially the indirect missionary influences in the creating of the Nigerian elite through schools and the growth of mission house "citizens" as well as other latent functions of the various missionary agencies. We do not therefore intend to repeat all that.[34] Rather we wish to call attention to some other historical and sociological factors that have created problems for the Church in Iboland, emanating as they did from the non religious aspects of the missionary enterprise.

The first of such factors was the close association between mission and commerce and European presence on the Niger coast. From the

---

31 S. Ottenberg, "Ibo Receptivity to Change" in Bascom, W.R. and Herskovits, M. J. (eds.), *Continuity and Change in African Culture*, Chicago: University of Chicago Press, 1959, p. 130 ff.

32 See F. K. Ekechi, *op. cit.*, pp. 147-150.

33 See West African Explorers edited by C. Howard, London: Oxford University Press, World Classic Edition where Crowther as early as 1854 offered to Chief Tshukuma (Chukwuma) of Abo to place a teacher to instruct the children. And that became the pattern all through Iboland.

34 See J. F. A. Ajayi, Christian Mission in Nigeria, 1841-1891; The Making of a New Elite, Longmans, 1964; E. A. Ayandele, The Missionary Impact on Modern Nigeria 1842-1914, London: Longmans, 1966; F. K. Ekechi, Missionary Enterprise and Rivalry in Igboland 1857-1914, London: Frank Cass, 1972.

earliest beginning of the Niger Mission in Iboland there was the closest form of relationship between the leadership of the Mission and of the European presence, mainly of commerce. Before Crowther left the Mission at Onitsha to move down to the Delta, he left for Taylor eleven point directive for the running of the new mission, one of which was: "If the cowries and goods I leave with you to pay salaries and to defray the expenses of the buildings, are not sufficient, you may take cowries or goods to the amount of £ 25 (25 l) more from the factory, an account of which you will have to render to J. M. Holl Esq. at the Church Missionary Society's House, London".[35]

This close association which was inevitable in the days before commercial banks, postal systems and transport facilities (all these were provided for the Mission by the trading company along the Niger) later became a source of embarrassment to the missionaries for three reasons: First, The immoral style of life of the commercial personnel, both European and Sierra Leonians; they kept concubines and slaves, employed sharp practices in trading and did not, generally, respect Church attendance and avoidance of work on Sundays.[36] A second reason was the speed with which converts started imitating the commercial people, both in adopting their greed for commercial gains, as well as sending slave girls and sometimes daughters to the factory for immoral hire by factory employees. Perry lamenting this in his report to C.M.S. Headquarters in London said: "Riches have come to Onitsha and have brought temptations which some of the native Christians are ill able to resist".[37] He was emphatic that the "unprincipled European Palm Oil Merchants" had brought these evils to Onitsha. With the complaints Crowther made to the C.M.S. Headquarters in London that the London Headquarters of these Commercial Organisations be prevailed upon to caution their men about hindering the Gospel, the C.M.S. in London did not seem disposed to do so. Rather they felt that "Europeans were well disposed towards the Africans and their human influence was bound to lead to social

---

35 S. A. Crowther and J. C. Taylor, The Gospel on the Banks of the Niger, *op. cit.*, p. 38.

36 C.M.S. CA 3/04 (a) Perry to Crowther letter dated 17th October, 1877 and Crowther to Wright at C.M.S. Headquarters dated 21st January, 1878 where Crowther complained "With the exception of a very few... the character of the few foreigners in this country is very detrimental to the cause of Christianity".

37 C.M.S. CA 3/030 Perry to Hutchinson received at C.M.S. London, 10th January, 1874.

improvement".[38] On the contrary, according to Crowther, the Africans were asking in the light of the behaviour of those Europeans if Christianity can be true "when those who are born, taught and brought up in the countries where it is said to be generally professed, live so indifferently of (sic) its teachings, laws and precepts?"[39]

A third source of embarrassment was the British bombardment of Onitsha in October 1879. Owing to the high handed action of the merchants at Onitsha the natives started reacting by plundering some of the goods from the merchants' factory and also shooting one Mr. Wallace. The British Consul decided to punish the Onitsha people by bombarding the place and H.M.S. Pioneer was employed to do this. Before the actual shelling and burning of Onitsha, the missionaries had taken shelter first of all in the factory quarters of the merchants, and later moved to Asaba on the other side of the Niger with some Christian converts. The Onitsha people, to show their resentment against the missionaries, looted the Church bell, benches, lectern and the reading desk. "They took the Bible too, tore a portion of it leaf by leaf and strewed the road leading into the town with them".[40]

For about two years there were no missionaries at Onitsha and the fate of the young Church hung by a thread. The Ibos blamed their calamities upon the introduction of Christianity in their land and yet men of faith remained and before too long the Church regrouped (the Onitsha people themselves having contributed money to rebuild the Church) but the feelings against the "European civilizers and their religion" remained strained. This close association of Christian mission and European civilising influence which started from the days of Thomas Fowell Buxton, the author of the "Bible and the Plough", and the inspirer of the ill doomed civilizing expedition of 1841 to the Niger, did not fare well even in the later history of the Church in Iboland.

During the heyday of the Royal Niger Company with its government over parts of Iboland, the Roman Catholic missionary Father Lutz had his troubles with "the civilizing merchants". His policy decision to be the champion of the natives against these groups of Europeans, seemed to have earned good dividends for the growth

[38] Ekechi, p. 51, referring to C.M.S. CA 3/L 1, Hutchinson to Crowther, 6th September, 1879.

[39] C.M.S. CA 3/04 (b) Crowther's Report of Visitation to the Niger Mission 1877.

[40] C.M.S. CA 3/030/8, Perry's Report about the bombardment forwarded to C.M.S. London.

of the Roman Church in Iboland. There was that insight among the Roman missionaries to separate the Church from commerce, British political manoeuvres and the like. It may be that the fact of their being French or the fact of wanting to oppose the C.M.S. and their cordial relationship with the trading companies was responsible for the position they took.[41] Further more after the British had established political control over all Nigeria including Iboland, the illusion of some missionaries that every white man in Iboland was a bringer of Christian civilization started to clear away but only very very gradually.[42]

A second factor of a non-religious nature that had created problems for the Church in Iboland, resulting from the history of the introduction of Christianity and its earliest interaction with Ibo life, was the ambivalent treatment of slavery by missionary leadership. Missionaries at Onitsha bought and kept domestic slaves especially young girls despite the policy of their London Headquarters to help abolish slave trade and slavery itself. In some instances the ransomed slaves, especially boys, became the leaders of the boarding schools; in any case a good number of earliest products of mission schools were either rescued slaves or children of slaves. When these took up salaried jobs they exercised leadership out of proportion to that due to them in traditional Ibo society. This led to the disdain with which some nobler families of Iboland regarded Christianity, which attitude, up to some measure is still held today against the Church, especially in the non Roman Catholic wing. The sociological problem created by this kind of situation, becomes clearer when a local Church makes serious attempts at being the means of the integration of the life of the community (where the greater part of the members of such community have become Christians). The effort could be vitiated by snobbish attitudes of the nobler sections of the community, mainly because their numerical strength in that local Church is weak. Going back to the treatment of domestic slaves kept by early missionaries in Iboland two classic examples of inhuman and absolutely unchristian treatment can be cited: the Father Lutz's slave girl scandal and the Johns' manslaughter case. The Johns' case was in connection with two slave

---

41 See Ekechi, *op. cit.*, pp. 103-104.

42 See Edmund Ilogu, "Some Hidden Influences of Christianity in Iboland", *West African Religion*, Nsukka, No. 7, April 1967, p. 16. See also W. R. Crocker, Nigeria — A critique of British Colonial Administration, London: George Allen and Unwin, 1936, p. 226.

girls of about thirteen and fourteen years old kept by Mr and Mrs. William F. John, a C.M.S. interpreter from Sierra Leone at the Onitsha mission. These two girls were said to have misbehaved in a most irritating manner so that Mr. John and his wife had these girls tied to a post, flogged them mercilessly and as if these were not enough, hot pepper was inserted into the young girls' anus and other private parts. Later Ame, one of the two girls, died and was buried secretly by Mr. John and his wife. Temper at Onitsha ran very high against Mr. John and his wife, as a crowd of people on hearing the story (the girls were punished at a spot where school-children in the boarding house could observe all that was done) pounced on the Johns and could have also beaten them to their own death were it not for the intervention of other missionaries. On 29th October, 1877 the Court of Equity at Onitsha tried Mr. and Mrs John but later exonerated both, and gave verdict that Ame "committed suicide by overmuch worrying herself". When John had been sent back home to Sierra Leone, the case was dug up once more as some members of the House of Lords in London had raised questions about the whole affair. A British Court in Freetown preferred charges of murder and contravention of the slave trade acts. Witnesses were sent for from Onitsha including Isaac Mba who was an eye witness to the whole activity. Mr. John was found guilty of manslaughter. This incident was regarded by the historian of the London Missionary Society as "a striking and instructive example of how great missionary enterprise ought not to be attempted". [43]

The Father Lutz slave girl scandal arose when in 1890 this great leader of the Roman Catholic Mission at Onitsha handcuffed for several weeks a slave girl he had ransomed, and furthermore flogged her severely. When he eventually released this girl from the handcuff and she was later married by someone, Father Lutz received the bridewealth paid on this girl and regarded that money as compensation to the mission for the money spent on the girl for ransom. The law enforcement officers regarded the slave girl episode as slave trading, and brought Father Lutz before the British Supreme Court sitting at Asaba where he was convicted, on technical points, of slave dealing and a small fine was imposed on him. Goldie, one of the outstanding leaders of the Royal Niger Company, who in all practical purposes

[43] Richard Lovett, The History of the London Missionary Society, London 1899, Vol. I, pp. 649-50, quoted by Ekechi, *op. cit.*, p. 52, to whom also I owe all of this story as well as the Father Lutz slave girl scandal.

was "the government" of Southern Nigeria at that time, described the Lutz incident as an evident offence against all Christianity and all morality.[44] When we put together, these two independent opinions about these two incidents concerning missionary treatment of slaves and the institution of domestic slavery itself, we begin to see some of the painful situations and the great moral problems created in Iboland by the presence and actions of those planting the Gospel in that land—problems which did not belong to the nature of the Gospel itself, but to the human weaknesses of its agents.

The third non-religious factor which created problems for the Church in Iboland and the most formidable of them all was racism. The C.M.S. Niger Mission in Iboland was largely an African mission, in the sense that from the earliest beginning almost all of its personnel was led by and consisted of peoples of African descent, especially from the colony of Freetown in Sierra Leone. Crowther the leader of this mission with Dr. J. F. Schön, the German missionary, had represented the C.M.S. in the ill fated "civilizing" expedition of 1841 to the Niger. They both made recommendations to the C.M.S. that the future missionary work on the Niger as well as in the interior of Africa, for health and psychological reasons, should be done by Africans; for Crowther native converts from Sierra Leone should be employed while for Schön West Indians should be preferred. The C.M.S. accepted the recommendation and resolved "that further measures should be adopted in order to train natives in Sierra Leone with a view to their being employed as teachers of their countrymen".[45] With this policy in view, Crowther recruited his missionary staff from Sierra Leone. Possibly due to problems of new beginnings, possibly due to inefficient leadership or difficulty of adjustment on the part of the missionaries, both the administration and the general quality of the mission showed signs of weakness.[46]

---

[44] Quoted by Ekechi, *op. cit.*, p. 100.

[45] See F. D. Walker, The Romance of the Black River: The Story of C.M.S. Nigeria Mission, London, 1931, p. 30.

[46] C.M.S. CA 3/L 1, Hutchinson's Letter to Crowther dated 25th November, 1880 although this letter resulted from the J. B. Wood Report against Crowther, which we consider racist document, views about weakness of the mission's administration can be deduced from facts like Crowther's failure to take firm stand on issues. Is this due to humility, Christian charity or indicision? Possibly all three? See also Peter Beyerhaus and Henry Lefever, The Responsible Church and the Foreign Mission, London: World Dominion Press, 1965, pp. 65-73. See also: To Apply the Gospel: Selections from the Writings of Henry Venn (ed.) by M. A. C. Warren, Grand Rapids Michigan: William B. Eerdmans, 1970, p. 30.

European missionaries in the Yoruba Mission based in Lagos especially Townsend of Abeokuta and Hinderer of Ibadan who had opposed Crowther's consecration as Bishop in 1864, as well as European merchants and visitors to the Niger, had all along discredited the Niger Mission's staff and their activities. Some of these activities were questionable, for example some C.M.S. agents in the Iboland (The Niger Mission) had paid more attention to trading than to evangelisation. Others had dealings with natives in a corrupt and morally bankrupt manner. Crowther himself in his Report of a visitation to the Niger Mission in 1875 said "To my pain and grief, it was found out that the formed habits of these men, uncultivated for mission work totally unfitted them for a connection with the mission, on which they would cast a lasting reproach in the country, instead of being helpful to its commendation".[47] Crowther was obliged to send these agents back to Sierra Leone. Having made this point, the lack of charity on the part of the Europeans (missionaries and travellers alike) towards the African personnel of the Niger Mission working in Iboland was abundantly evident. The climax of it was the J. B. Wood Commission. The Rev. J. B. Wood, who was appointed by the C.M.S. to look into the affairs of the Niger Mission, without checking his facts properly, issued a most damaging and critical report against the Niger Mission, its agents and the leadership of Bishop Crowther. When Wood was invited to a conference in Madeira in February of 1881 to discuss the report face to face with Bishop Crowther, he failed to attend, rather he blamed the C.M.S. for making the report available to the Bishop, arguing that he had written the report as a confidential document. In Anglican polity it was unusual for a person in priest's orders, which he received from a Bishop, to write a confidential report against a Bishop. But in those days in Africa many things could happen differently from the usual and the normal!

Some of the recommendations of the Wood Report were (1) that many African missionaries should be dismissed (2) that the Bishop henceforth should be confined to episcopal functions whilst the administration of the mission should be controlled by the Finance Committee over which the Bishop would preside. The African members of the Mission were quite clear in their mind that the "Report" was a mere ruse to facilitate handing over the mission to Europeans and reacted bitterly to this. In a letter addressed to Bishop Crowther by one

[47] C.M.S. CA 3/04 (a) + (b) with memo dated 2nd September, 1876.

Mr. Paul on 9th August, 1880 he said among other things: "Europeans, generally of British born [sic], sacrificing all morality, would not scruple to deliberately write anything false or misleading ... merely to obtain a certain object they have in view, good or bad". [48]

Archdeacon Johnson, a senior clergyman from Sierra Leone seconded to the Niger Mission, was forced to comment on the whole affair occasioned by the J. B. Wood Report: "It is the unconcealed contempt with which we are being treated that tries me so very much". [49] Despite the petition of the six ordained men and seven unordained agents of the mission against the report, the C.M.S. after a short period of hesitation, went ahead in implementing it. The C.M.S. secretary told Crowther that reforms were imperative. The Finance Committee became dominated by Europeans who then ruled the Mission, making Bishop Crowther mere figure-head. A large number of African agents were dismissed and others infuriated had to resign, therefore a good number of Ibo Church stations were left without agents and teachers. "The Oxford and Cambridge men"—young missionaries sent to the Niger Mission from England to replace the Sierra Leonians, adopted strict measures towards the Churches under the Mission. Mr. J. A. Robinson became the C.M.S. secretary at Onitsha to interpret and act on the mission's policy. The Sierra Leone missionaries having been disgraced, disappeared from the Ibo mission. European missionaries took their position and planned "a new era" of white domination which lasted from the death of Crowther in 1891 to the resignation of Archbishop Patterson from his see at Onitsha in 1969.

Dr. M. A. C. Warren, the General Secretary of the C.M.S. in London for over twenty years until 1963, in a recent private correspondence with the writer, gave the historical background of "the attitude of those missionaries who broke Crowther's heart and caused such tragic trouble in Eastern Nigeria". The first explanation he gave was political. After the "seventies" of the 19th century, the British Government decided to bring the Empire in to serve as a balancing force against the threat to British world leadership coming from German and American industrial growth. In all kinds of ways this had curious side effects. In almost every oversea's territory of the Empire, there was a perceptible increase in self-assertion on the part of British

---

48 C.M.S. CA 3/104 (a) Paul to Crowther. This is also a generalization, but it indicates the temper and "moral temperature" of the Mission at that time.

49 C.M.S. G3/A3/0, H. Johnson to Crowther 2nd May, 1882.

officials, traders *and* missionaries, a self-assertion which criticised the local population as being "not yet ready" for leadership. Venn's policy of training local leaders to take over from the missionaries was reversed, and it was not for another fifty years that the initiative in this direction was restored. The second explanation is more specifically religious. There was a movement in England about the same time (the 1870's and after) within Evangelical circles, and elsewhere in English Christian life, which emphasized "holiness". "Holiness" was defined on moralistic terms about the things a Christian might do and might not do. Many young missionaries coming into Iboland, like the Oxford and Cambridge graduates already referred to, were persons sharing this moralistic conviction. This moralistic attitude was unfortunately negative in the approach to problems existing in mission areas like the Ibo country. These missionaries therefore, made no allowance for any of the values of African society, assuming in fact that there were no such values. Furthermore, because their type of holiness was unknown in the Niger Mission Churches, this new breed of missionaries felt that there was great moral laxity in that Church. This they attributed to the weakness of Bishop Crowther and his clergy. Dr. Warren ended his observation with this remark: "They were, of course, utterly ignorant about Africa", adding that "their ignorance was shared by virtually every white man who visited Africa in the eighties and nineties".

This historical interpretation explains a great deal of the points we have made already and the subsequent conclusions we are reaching about the need to re-interpret Christianity to the Ibos. We will, for the present, continue the historical account of the clash between the new missionaries and the Ibo, by indicating some of the immediate actions the new European missionaries took to "clean up" the Niger Mission: the petition of two Ibo agents trained at the Lokoja Preparandi School for salary increase was rejected. This refusal was accompanied with the racially tinged, and condescending remarks of the Secretary at Onitsha, to the effect that in Ibo country, these two young men earning ten shillings a year, would have been considered very rich; but because they were employed by the C.M.S. and paid forty shillings a year, they had the impudence to ask for more. The official reply of the Finance Committee was more condescending. The young men were told that they were ungrateful to the Mission, that instead of being very appreciative of what the white man had done for them by raising them from heathenism to Christianity, they were asking for more money. The missionaries believed that if such increase in salary were to be granted, it would be used by the young men in buying foods and clothing to imitate white men's style. Secondly the Preparandi School at Lokoja was closed down the same year (1890), and all its Ibo students sent away because it did not give proper training to its Ibo students, who should be trained to live in the native style, even though these white missionaries knew nothing of Ibo style, its cultural and normative quality and dimension.

Thirdly strong demands were made by some missionaries for complete reform in the missionary work and in the Christianity preached and practised in Iboland. New rules were introduced that Christians must never marry according to native customs; they must stop paying the customary bridewealth and the naming ceremony of their children must no longer be performed in the Ibo traditional way. Catechumens who were found to have done any of these things, were never to be baptised. Of course the Roman Catholics took advantage of this and received such people quickly into their Church with immediate baptism.

Ibo Christians reacted to this state of affairs and openly said that the new white missionaries had come "to break down rather than to build up, to destroy rather than to help those that are dying". [50] The opinion of the Ibo Christians about some of the dismissed African agents, especially Archdeacon Henry Johnson, was picturesquely expressed in a letter of Isaac Mba, one of the most gifted of the early Ibo Church teachers: "The whole community (particularly the blacks) know that in your absence from the River they are deprived and in want, of a true Christian Friend, a lover of His Race, One that delights greatly in the happiness of others, a Guide to youth, a Father to his subordinates, a faithful minister of God, and the Pride of his countrymen and colour". [51]—things they knew that the white successors did not supply the young Church.

It could be asked why did these young British missionaries pumped into Iboland fail to show Christian charity for the work of their predecessors and regard for the feelings of the Ibos whom they had gone out to christianise? One of them, a more mature missionary,

---

[50] C.M.S. G3/A3/o Onitsha Church Members to European Teachers, 30th August, 1890, and from that date onwards the Church life in Iboland's Anglicanism had shown this "two fronts" existence: blacks the ruled, and whites the rulers. It was only the Nigerian civil war, 1967-1970 that ended it. Most of the facts contained in the last page are contained in this block of the C.M.S. archival material on the Niger Mission.

[51] C.M.S. G3/A3/o, Mba to Johnson, letter dated 9th April, 1890.

Archdeacon Dobinson, openly regretted his fellow countrymen's action "I burn with shame and horror now at the awful charges made against him (Archdeacon Johnson) in 1890—I grieve that such good men as Robinson and Brooke—should have been so completely misguided and lost to all sense of Christian fairness and charity as to make the horrible charges they thought it right to make".[52] This was part of a speech Archdeacon Dobinson made at the St. George's Cathedral in Freetown, Sierra Leone, and although he was rebuked by the C.M.S. secretary in London, because Dobinson was not authorised to speak on behalf of the Mission, it was evident from Dobinson's action that the Church still had men of real insight. But when racial prejudice blinds a few and they commit the Church or a Mission to painful non-religious problems, it takes generations to heal the wounds thus inflicted. In Iboland the wounds of racial intolerance on the part of some white missionaries have been healed by the labours of a few mature persons like Dobinson, but the scar still remains constituting the more thorny moral and ethical problems of the Church in Iboland.

When the first group of missionaries arrived it would have been a miracle for them to know Ibo life and thought, Ibo value concepts and their cultural expression so as to relate, as far as possible their Christian message to the people's way of life to reduce Christianity's foreignness. It was later from about 1890, that is after some three decades of missionary activity, that one would expect some insight and acquaintanceship with Ibo life and thought. That was the time the young reformist, racialist and overbearing proud British missionaries came upon the scene. They lacked the humility to learn, they condemned and hated what their black predecessors had done. This made it impossible for real, effective and understanding appreciation of Ibo people and their culture to be generated and utilized in the service of the Gospel. That problem is still unsolved—the problem of making the Gospel less foreign to Iboland than the Gospel's real nature suggests. For the Gospel, as the Good News of God's intervention in human affairs, is bound to be "foreign" in all lands inhabited and systematised into cultural patterns, influenced by time and place and peoples.

The pity is when, owing to racial bigotry, personal idiosyncrasy and lack of sympathetic approach to the peoples of a missionary area, the foreignness of the Gospel is added to by man-made features. We

---

52 C.M.S. G3/A3/o Dobinson to Baylis, letter dated 30th March, 1896.

illustrate this contention with a few incidents in the early missionary experience in Iboland which, with some better understanding later in the history of the Mission, could have been used in rooting more firmly the Christian Gospel into the soil of Iboland. The smallpox epidemic which raged in Onitsha in 1872 to 1873 had killed the King Ediari and his prince-son. Many attempts of the Ibo native-medicine-diviner priests (*dibia*) to avert the epidemic failed. This, according to the missionary Perry, seemed to have "shaken to its foundations every old established superstitious belief".[53] Furthermore a non Christian soothsayer told Onitsha people that he had seen a vision that unless people listened to the missionaries and went to Church, the whole of Onitsha would be wiped out by the smallpox epidemic. Losing faith in old superstition of the *dibia,* medicine and magic, and being impelled by a new one from a possibly demented soothsayer, many Onitsha people flocked to the Church. Already the leaders of the community including the *dibia,* were blaming the people for the smallpox epidemic because they had forsaken the traditions of the land, broken the taboos and angered the spirit of the ancestors, by paying heed to the teachings of the missionaries. The health of the community, which had depended on spiritual harmony between ancestral spirit and corporate religious vitality of the total community, was said to have started to suffer because such harmony and vitality had ceased to exist owing to the presence of Christianity. Instead of capitalising on this incident to teach the people from what they already knew to the new Christian doctrine of the wholeness of man, and man's healing through salvation in Jesus both in his body, soul and mind, Crowther felt that the success of the evangelistic work in Onitsha should not depend on such smallpox and the soothsayer's vision. He however believed, as God's opportunity could come from man's extremity, the incident might lead Onitsha people to the receiving of God's "solid word of truth". If he and the missionaries after him knew the people's emphasis on harmony between man, community and cosmos as the background to health and well-being, they would have capitalised on it to show how Jesus Christ is God's means of creating harmony between Himself, men and nature. Even now the orthodox Churches in Iboland do not capitalize on it; it is only the pentecostals and the Prayer-Healing-Aladura Churches who do so. Another incident resembling this was the report Crowther

---

[53] C.M.S. CA3/030/3 Perry's Journal received at the C.M.S. London on January 10, 1874.

made after his visit to Obotsi (Obosi) in 1886. He said that chiefs and others in Iboland were in the habit of requesting the missionaries to assure them that the acceptance of Christianity would mean "long life, multiplicity of children and fruitful productions of their land". To this request the missionaries would reply in the negative, the chiefs and others would then go away, unwilling to hear the Gospel anymore, telling the missionaries to go and "preach to the children".[54] Why reply in the negative as if the gospel was irrelevant to the people's daily existence and needs? Again today the Pentecostals etc. capitalise on this and "converts" flock to their Churches. The third incident was about a young man whom Perry asked why he stopped attending Church services. The young man said to Perry that "big men" of Onitsha were poisoning those who wanted to be Christians and requested him (Perry) to give him a charm which Christians used so that no amount of poisoning could do him any harm. Perry ended the report by saying "I told him that the charm we had was nothing more than absolute trust in God".[55]

If Perry knew the importance of visible symbols in the life of Ibos, he would have done more, he could for example have given him, after careful teaching, a consecrated crucifix to wear on his neck. But Perry and many missionaries after him, rigidly attached to extreme Evangelical dread of symbols and images in the Reformed Church, were not in a position to help the young man and the many like him. Roman Catholicism capitalised on this, but today, it is the Pentecostals and the Prayer-Healing-Aladura Churches who really appeal to the depth of Ibo sentiments and beliefs in the visible symbols of well-being as part of religious faith and practice.

We have in this chapter, used the history of the planting of Christianity in Iboland to show some aspects of the inevitable disorganisation in Ibo life and society, as well as in its value concepts and norms of social integration, resulting from the coming of the Christian Church. We have further pointed to some incidents in the initial encounter of Christianity with the traditional morality and life style of the Ibo which, if they had been handled with some measure of understanding, could have reduced the gap between Christianity and the people's

---

[54] C.M.S. G3/A3/o, Crowther's Journal of a Visit to Obotsi, entry for 25th September, 1886.

[55] C.M.S. CA 3/030/4 Perry's Journal received at the C.M.S. Headquarters in London 30th December, 1874.

inner consciousness. Thirdly we have indicated how the group of Churches which are sometimes called unorthodox Churches with pentecostal prayer healing, vision-seeing and prophetic emphases have appeared on the Ibo religious scene. They promise to bridge the gap between the Ibo unconscious (the product of the traditional religion and life) and the Christian faith, and it is this gap which all along had constituted the Christian faith into a foreign religion in Iboland. European missionaries who took over from the short-lived Sierra Leone missionaries, for various reasons, were unable to bridge this gap. Hence the more orthodox Churches they handed over to Ibo leadership remain heavily indebted to them and so continue the practice of the European missionaries, namely unwillingness to use Ibo cultural frame work to interpret the Christian Gospel message. All these form the data with which, we hope, to make further analyses and attempt some "prescriptions" or "hypotheses" which will indicate, as well as clarify, the thesis of this study. But before we do that, let us in the next chapter look at another aspect of dislocation in Ibo way of life, both in ethical as well as in normative dimensions, brought about by technological culture and modernization (which in Iboland was formerly called European culture). These, in the mind of the Ibo, as well as in that of most African peoples, are the twin brothers of Christianity.

CHAPTER FIVE

PATTERNS OF CHANGE IN IBO SOCIETY THROUGH TECHNOLOGY AND SCIENTIFIC MODERNIZATION

Christianity and Western Influences

From the earliest history of the European Christian Missions in all of Africa, there was a strong link between the desire to christianise and the desire to "civilize" the African. A classic example was in the forcefully argued case for combined action by British politicians, philantropists, commercial interests, agricultural and medical specialists, educators and missionaries which Thomas Fowell Buxton included in his book "The African Slave Trade and Its Remedy". His thesis was that through the use of the "Bible and the Plough" Africa's "dark continent" could be won to Christianity and to civilization. [1] This advocacy led to the expedition to the Niger, known as the Civilizing Mission of 1841, which had on it two C.M.S. Representatives—J. F. Schön and Samuel Adjai Crowther. In Iboland concrete steps were taken early in the history of the mission to use cotton as trade good with Britain as well as palm oil. This emphasis on genuine trade was to provide more acceptable substitute to slave trade. J. C. Taylor the first resident missionary in Iboland, jubilantly reported to the C.M.S. Secretary in London:

> With regard to trading affairs, I can assure you that there is plenty of oil, castor oil seeds growing luxuriantly, cotton in abundance as well as red pepper. I have sent you by Dr. Baikie a specimen of the Niger cotton, especially in the Ibo district to test it and see whether the Manchester manufacturers would open a trade upon the country for it. [2]

The Industrial Mission run by the C.M.S. had, as early as 3rd January, 1876 admitted boys at Onitsha to train in technical skills and trades like brickmaking and bricklaying, carpentry and the like. [3]

---

[1] T. F. Buxton, *op. cit.*, London 1839, 1840, and Reprinted in London: Frank Cass, 1967.

[2] C.M.S. CA 3/037/4 J. C. Taylor letter to Venn. dated Freetown, Sierra Leone, 17th December, 1858.

[3] C.M.S. CA 3/030/5 Perry's Journal 1875-1876 received at C.M.S. London 27th December, 1876.

This of course was the beginning of the training of the Ibo in skills of European technology. Before too long groups of skilled men were produced to build houses for the Mission and to print some of the literature the Mission needed. More importantly, through the various levels of educational facilities provided by the Missions, the desire for, and the facilities for the technological practices of Europe, were gradually introduced into Iboland.[4] Both by the use of the English language in schools, and by the influence of the British system of administration from 1900, as well as the importation of British manufactured goods from the middle of the 19th century, a preference for the European way of life was being indirectly built up in the minds of the Ibo, who already have had a cultural inclination towards adaptation to change by the enlargement of its "open society" system with variable new introductions.[5] When Buxton wrote his advocacy for a combined effort between Christian Missions and commercial, political and technological interests to work together towards the evangelization and the civilizing of the Africans, there was still some measure of common understanding between the Christian religion and European culture. But by the end of the 19th century all illusions about such connections had been dispelled.

Christianity became clearly separated from European civilization and such civilization with its science, its inventions and its organisation of life for material ends, became at variance with Christian beliefs, but yet sought to mould the future of the African continent.[6] From that time on, all Africa, including Iboland became confronted with two influences from Europe—Christianity and secular, technological scientific modernization. For some time, some missionaries in the Niger Mission behaved as if western technological and commercial interests, were still respecters of Christian values and life. Perry, a missionary at Onitsha, angered by the disregard of Christian values by the management of the West African Company wrote Mr. R. Cliff,

---

[4] For the influence of Missions in the modernization of Nigeria of which the Ibo is part see J. F. A. Ajayi, Christian Missions in Nigeria 1841-1891: The Making of a New Elite, Longmans, 1964; E. A. Ayandele, The Missionary Impact on Modern Nigeria, 1842-1914. A political and Social Analysis, London: Longmans Green 1966.

[5] S. Ottenberg, "Ibo Receptivity to Change" in *Continuity and Change in African Culture,* edited by W. R. Bascom and M. J. Herskovits, Chicago: Chicago University Press, 1958.

[6] J. H. Oldham and B. D. Gibson, The Remaking of Man in Africa, London: Oxford University Press, 1931, p. 17.

its resident manager in this vein: "The conduct of Europeans coming up this river has generally been such as to make the natives feel satisfied that Christianity is a fabrication of the blacks. (Perry was a black missionary from Sierra Leone)... It seems to me that you are determined to oppose Christianity in this country with all your might". Perry then catalogued Cliff's activities which led him to that conclusion. The interesting reply of Cliff brought out his resentment to Perry's "pretentions" that he, a commercial agent, should have been mindful of missionary that is, Christian concerns. Part of the reply reads: "I have received your letter. I should like to know who made you competent to judge as to whether I consider it necessary to work my men on Sunday or not. The object effected by your impertinent communication is, that if any of my men attend class in future they forfeit all claim on me. If instead of committing the workings of an unhealthy brain to paper and annoying other people with the same you would mind your own shop, your class would be more respected in this river". [7]

Analysis of Cliff's reply shows the offence he took at the missionary's suggestion that while carrying out his commercial activity he should be expected to respect Christian values. Furthermore Cliff insinuated that there was such a division of labour, between himself and Perry, as to imply that Christianity and Christian values belonged to Perry's (that is the missionary's) shop, whilst commerce and all its technology belonged to Cliff. The trend, started by men like Cliff in Iboland, has reached its climax when Ibo leaders of Government in recent years (1970) took over all schools arguing that education being the business of the State had nothing to do with the Church. [8] By this action, Ibo leaders in our government today, try to impress upon the people that training in technology must be seen as having nothing to do with religion; but rather, this and all other aspects of the training of the citizens, must be recognised as a secular undertaking. The Roman Catholic hierarchy reacted as if there still were the twin relationship between Western technological civilization and Christianity by dismissing one of their Priests who supported the schools take over by the State. [9]

---

[7] C.M.S.: CA 3/04 (a) Perry to Cliff and Cliff to Perry—both correspondences contained in Crowther's correspondence to Hemmingway at C.M.S. London, 19th September, 1875, See also Cliff to Crowther 27th October, 1875.

[8] See the East Central State "Public Education Edict 1970", Government Printer, Enugu.

[9] Father Bede Onuoha, who quickly changed his name to Enyeribe Onuoha

It is not only against the Christian religion and its values that secular technological and scientific modernization has opened a front. It also disrupts Ibo traditional religion and society. We will now attempt an analysis of some of the changes brought about by technology on Ibo life and society so as to indicate the magnitude of the work Christianity is faced with if it could ever be the means of integrating such a society through the new ethic it can develop in Iboland.

Economic Trends

In the old traditional Ibo way of life, in the absence of money economy and orientation of life along market system, economic life was largely directed by the simple necessities of the life of the extended family community, rather than of an individual. A man was considered wealthy if he could have many adherents or large extending relationships; if he could give feasts from time to time and give patronage to the arts in the form of music, either of the trumpeter or the ballad singer or the talking drum expert. He might add being the "father" of dances and masquerades. He would own large farms of food crops, palms to produce oil and wine, but what is more is that his large following made up of his children, members of the extended family and others, would ensure adequate labour force for the farms. His prestige, which would grow from these considerations as well as from nobility of birth, age, title, military or artistic role, gave him honour. If one had great possessions of farm crops, cattle and wives but failed to cushion these with large following, patronage and the other appurtenances of social acceptability, he was not regarded as "wealthy" and "honourable". An Ibo ballad singer would say:

Ude Dike na ude ogalanya
Bu n'otu,
Egbue Dike, ewelu Ogalanya
Gwo aka,
Nso adiro ya,

"The fame of the brave and the fame of the wealthy are identical. When the brave is conquered, the head of the wealthy could be used in burying him (in cleansing the hands of the brave). To do this, is not contrary to tradition (no abomination)".

---

after the expulsion and issued a pamphlet "What I Believe", published by Operation-Sociological, Owerri, Nigeria, n.d. (possibly December 1972).

Greater honour in this context lies with the brave and not with the owner of possessions. In contrast, technological emphasis on individual success through ownership of property, has altered this scale of values. Economic pursuit has become market oriented, concentrating on organization and on the search for things that multiply profit, in which followers become more of labour hands rather than persons and "children of the commune". Collective participation in meaningful labour and the exercise of skill is abandoned. For in the traditional society craftmanship was held in honour. A village basketmaker regarded his skill as a gift from the ancestral spirit for the well-being of the community of which the dead ancestors were still a part. No consideration of quantity would diminish the quality of the finished product. All forms of skills and craftmanship were means of looking beyond the temporal to the spiritual source of beauty. There was the fear that failure to execute skillfully in woodcarving or blacksmithery or building the walls of a house, could incur the wrath of the ancestors and bring calamity upon the community. With Christianity and school education, coupled with the influence of scientific technology, such fear was destroyed, but nothing was put in its place to create still the inner urge for good and dependable workmanship. Now people work mainly for money, sometimes for the absentee or faraway employer, to whom the workers can not relate personally, and the old sense of contribution to the common good learnt in traditional style of life is lost. So also the love of work as a means of welfare rather than a means of wealth is lost. Extended family's communal working together diminished the danger of class consciousness, but with the new emphasis of the market system of technological culture, individualism has been encouraged, and with it class consciousness has started to develop.

Growth of Towns

Development of industries and markets, centralization of administration and travel facilities in roads and railways, have led to the growth of towns. Ibos as a people lived in scattered agricultural villages and hamlets in the past, but in the last fifty years on account of the causes stated above, towns have grown, prominent among them being Enugu (coal industry and state or regional capital), Port-Harcourt (seaport, oil industry), Aba (beer brewing, soap making, textile factory and centrally located market), Onitsha (river port, textile industry and central market for agricultural products and food supply to other parts of Nigeria), Umuahia (beer brewing, ceramics industry).[10] The Church is fully established in these towns, the general technological and secular influences we associate with town life are evident, although such influences quickly travel to the more rural areas and clusters of villages very close to them.

Many people have been attracted away from the villages to the towns. The usual problems of town life have started to manifest themselves in shortage of housing, congestion in slum areas together with criminal facilities and the desire for anonymity. Coming away from villages, they had got used to the neat pattern of communal living and sharing in the large extended-family units, with its organised patterns of social control through customs, prohibitions and the use of religious systems of oath and authority, associated with the ancestors through the *Okparas* (heads of lineages or of extended families). Such controls and traditional religious sanctions do not operate in the towns, and if people are not full members of active Christian Churches and become somehow detribalised, they lack inner restraints for living meaningfully. Some people organise in the towns their various clan unions embracing people from the same group of villages, and try through these clan unions to bind themselves together by norms of their former village life, especially in matters of social welfare and cultural interest. It is some of these clan unions from the towns, who go back to the villages to demand that the Churches incorporate features of Ibo traditional culture into the Christian way of life, as a means of their recovering what they regard as their lost identity as Ibos and as Africans. Again it is through some of these clan and town unions, that attempts have been made to use the local village Church as centres of village development and competition or rivalry between adjacent villages or different missions.[11]

The moral problems of town life in Iboland, originate mainly from the fact that the change from village to town life, means a sudden

---

[10] Population figures are not readily available as Nigeria was organising census in October-November 1973. From past records a fair estimate is that Aba, Enugu and Onitsha each will be approximating 300.000. Port-Harcourt since after the Cival War 1967-1970 is made Rivers State Capital.

[11] A great deal has been written about these Town Unions in Nigeria in general and Iboland as well; See J. S. Coleman, Nigeria: Background to Nationalism, Los Angeles, University of California Press, 1958. Audrey C. Smock, Ibo Politics—The Role of Ethnic Unions in Eastern Nigeria, Cambridge, Mass.: Harvard University Press, 1971.

transition. It is a transition from a fairly neat pattern of community oriented life to another style of life where individualism, which requires inner-controlled and conscience-directed actions, as well as freedom of choice, make up the style of life. To a young couple rearing their children for the first time in the town, a great burden is thrown upon their shoulders; for whilst living in the village, the education of the young would have been the concern of the whole extended family or even the village.[12] This community concern for the proper moral upbringing of the young in village life, presupposed knowledge of the norms and values in which the children were to be socialised. In the towns such common norms and values do not yet exist, for people are brought together in the new town-community from different areas. The governing moral principles as well as acceptable social philosophy of town life, when towns first appeared in Iboland, could have derived from schools and Churches, which were the main agents of social change at that initial stage. But the failure to relate Christian social values to the cultural sentiments of the people created a gulf which has not been bridged as yet.

Prostitution which was said to be unknown in the pre-colonial, pre-Christian village life, has since appeared in the towns and also in some rural areas. The problem arose when young men who had migrated from the villages into the towns, left the young women in the villages without the men folk to pay attention to them. Some "enterprising" young women went up to the towns. Not having good enough education to secure jobs, prostitution became the easy way out. Now that female education has nearly caught up with that of the male, some other reasons still keep some women as prostitutes. We may add here that since money economy came into Iboland as part of the technological package, many young men do not easily save enough money to be able to marry. More marriageable women now stay unmarried more than was the case in the traditional pre-technological time. The emphasis of the Church on one man one wife, had also added to the number of women who remain unmarried. Some of these in despair would also go into the towns as prostitutes. A third group of women go out to the towns in search of adventure, because they have learnt that town life is happier and easier than village life.

---

[12] See C. K. Meek, Law and Authority in a Nigerian Tribe (Ibo), Oxford University Press 1937, p. 301, where he indicated that "for misbehaviour young children are generally threatened by their mother with a flogging from the father, or the father's elder brother or sister".

Part of the characteristics of technological culture is that there must be the consuming community able to buy the products of industry. In Iboland American and European goods are in great display. The ambition of young men and women who struggle to get education and join the elitists group, is to be well paid enough to buy cars, refrigerators, radios and fine expensive dresses. Young women from the villages, are attracted into towns, to see if they will be lucky enough to allure such car-owning young men into friendship of the prostituting type, or at best into marriage. A high-life song portrays the languishing desire of a young lady who is very desirous of securing the favours of a "been to":

What shall I do to get a man of that type?
One who is a "been to".
Car full and frigful, (refrigerator filled with food and drinks)
What shall I do to obtain a man like that? [13]

There is nothing new in a young woman's ambition to befriend or marry a wealthy man, what is new is the technological value centred on cars, refrigerators, radios and the like. What is also new is that if such a young man does not make advances, the village girl out for adventure would leave the integrated village life and look out for such a young man, attracted no more by the desire to have a good man, as was the case before, but concerned with securing a man who could provide the ease, comfort and enjoyments coming out of technological products. Dr. Oldham quotes Oliver Goldsmith's lines:

When lovely woman stoops to folly
And finds too late that men betray
What charm can soothe her melancholy,
What art can wash her guilt away?

Then in the 20th Century T. S. Eliot observing the same situation wrote:

When lovely woman stoops to folly and
Paces about her room again, alone,
She smooths her hair with automatic hand
and puts a record on the gramophone.

---

[13] Quoted by K. A. Busia in a lecture he gave at the Graduate School of Ecumenical Studies, Chateau de Bossey near Geneva. Summer of 1956/7. What was Ghana's high life applied to Iboland too. A "been to" is the local slang for one who had studied abroad and got elitist position.

To which Dr. Oldham adds:

> The difference is not due simply to a change in "lovely woman", but also in large measure to the fact that she has got a gramophone! [14]

This "lovely woman" can also be identified in Ibo towns today. The moral problems created by the attractions of technological products is no longer evident only in town life. It is fast spreading all over Iboland. Traditional society of Iboland, before the advent of the white man, either as missionary or colonial administrator, trader or industrialist, provided for people satisfactory living with only the necessities of life. Lustful desire and insatiable wanting of possessions, were not part of that society's vice. Today with the skillful manipulation of advertisements men and women, both in towns as well as in villages, but more so in towns, are daily being told about the many hundred and one things they "need". Desire and greed are in such ways multiplied in the appetites of people.

To reduce monotonous generalization, we now look at three Ibo localities studied in some detail and through such examples, we might be able to fit into proper perspective the effects of technical, Western and modernization culture upon Ibo society and religion. The three Ibo localities are Ihiala—a rural agricultural area of ten villages—all of related lineages, which is also the headquarters of an administrative Division of the State Government; Nsukka, a rural place fast developing into a University town since the University of Nigeria was started there in 1961; and Aba, an industrial town of some 300,000 people. The choice of these three places is influenced by the fact that from them we cover a good sample of places where technological influences reach in varying proportions.

A Study of three "Towns"

Ihiala

Agents of technological and modernization trends include the Anglican Church founded in 1905. It was built in one of the sacred bushes of Ihiala—sacred to a clan god known as *Ngwu* and so the spot was called *Ude-Ngwu* (the forest sacred to *Ngwu*). It was a place known to be dangerous to enter, where people who died "bad deaths"

---

[14] J. H. Oldham in "Church and the Disorder of Society"—an ecumenical study prepared for the Amsterdam Conference of the World Council of Churches in 1948, New York: Harper and Brothers, 1948, p. 40.

had been thrown, and where the evil spirits with which *Ngwu* punished evil doers were believed to roam about. The faith of the Christians to enter it, after prayers and dedication, and to clear the forest and build a Church and mission compound on it, without noticeable incidents and deaths, was the start of desacralization as far as the people of Ihiala were concerned. Later in 1911 the Roman Catholic Church was started. These two Churches opened schools as centres of modernization and moreover the Roman Catholic built a big mission house with European Reverend Fathers living and maintaining a large staff of mission boys. They also planted fruit orchards and built a bookshop and a clinic for the care of twins. A third agent of modernization was the opening of the Native Court by the Colonial Administration about 1906. The Court Clerk and his staff attracted their own kind of attention, with or without the visit of the Divisional Commissioner from Onitsha. The fact that a representative of the Colonial Administration with education was there, who also had a higher standard of living than that of the villagers, together with the compulsory labour quota that the chiefs must send up daily to the court, all this started its own chain of "modernization" of the natives, which later formed part of the social change under the impact of technological culture, which change we now examine.

When we look at the effects of this foreign contact on the home and family life of the people of Ihiala, we notice that Christianity insisted that every convert polygamist who was to receive baptism, must send away his wives and retain only one with whom he was admitted into the membership of the local Church. Secondly Christians started building houses of "four corner" shape with windows and doors made of carpenters' planed and joined panels, instead of the more usual oblong type of house with doors and windows (where they had windows) paneled with carved wood—the ordinary native style doors of the villages. These carved doors were as from then regarded as the mark of a heathen's compound. Flowers were planted in the courtyards of Christian homes instead of the cultus symbol plants non Christians grew as part of the domestic shrines to their gods and ancestral spirits. Children went to the schools opened by the two denominations, and with it, childrearing practice by which children learnt from adults through participation and by joining various children's age-groups' organisations like dancing, masquerading, tattooing and being apprenticed to *dibia*'s (medicine men) guild became disrupted. Many Christian parents clothed their children instead of the age-long practice of young children of less than ten years running around in the tropical heat without clothing. These were the initial changes that came into the family life of the villages of Ihiala. As time went on, other changes came about. Many young people from various homes went to towns and other rural areas to work, the first of such paid employments was teaching in mission schools. With the gradual movement away from the villages, some families were left mainly of old men and women unable to farm their food, until a stage was reached quite recently, especially after the Civil War (1967-1970), where many families became really poor, in the sense of not having a house to live in and not having food to eat, nor money to buy food-crops to grow. On the happier side, for some homes, their town-dwelling young people brought back some wealth, built modern houses, helped in cultivating food crops with paid labour, took away some younger members of the family to be educated in the towns, and sometimes abroad in Europe and America. Such homes developed into what are now the elitist group of Ihiala.

Effects of this changing situation on the youth of Ihiala have been varied. Some have lived in the towns but later settled in the villages that make up Ihiala. Some young women have gone out to work in towns and other areas and have got married to non natives of Ihiala, some have gone to swell the number of prostitutes in towns. Some young people who live in towns near to Ihiala come home most week-ends in the year, to generate new youth activities or reform or revitalise the old traditional ones like masquerading.

The effects on the local Churches have been various too. Many who have had education or worked as Church teachers or businessmen in towns have relapsed into polygamy, some have taken the *Ọzọ* title and a few have got disgusted with the Mission oriented and more orthodox Churches and started the pentecostal-prayer-healing Churches. At the moment of our survey we noted four such Churches: The Assemblies of God with about fifty members; Faith Tabernacle with about twenty members; Apostolic Church with about eighty members and Christ Apostolic Church (*Odozi Obodo*) with about forty members. The Jehova Witnesses, a strict non conformist sect, was also one of the Churches started by Ihiala youth who left the Anglican Church. Other effects on the Church include the healthy one of enlightened leadership, which the Ihiala people living in towns give to the established Churches, including giving more money towards improvements either in their new Church buildings or enlarging schools' facilities. This group, by one or two meetings in a year, agree on measures by which the Church is still used as agent of enlightenment for the area. Demands for Christian adaptation of Ibo institutions like *Ọzọ* title and polygamy are made sometimes, but not as loudly as people in the towns make them. Traditional religious beliefs and social patterns described in chapters II and III still remain attractive even to Christians although by Church regulations Christians are expected to turn completely away from them. Instances were encountered during field interviews where Christians join in masquerades, second burials of relations and in visiting non Christian friends or relations with gifts when they take the *Ọzọ* title. Polygamists retain their membership of their Churches with their many wives, only that the men are not allowed to receive the Holy Communion or be elected into the Parish Committees.

Nsukka

Like Ihiala Nsukka is a rural area but is unlike Ihiala in that a University exists in it. There are four groups of villages surrounding what is called Nsukka Urban which come within four miles radius of the University. This is the area we have surveyed. Again Nsukka is unlike Ihiala in that it is situated at the extreme north-eastern part of Iboland, at the boundary of Iboland and Northern Nigeria and has had no "trunk—A road" (a major highway) passing through it like the Onitsha to Aba and Port-Harcourt road which passes through Ihiala. On account of these geographical facts both missionaries and Colonial Administration were late in establishing themselves at Nsukka. The first group of Churches (Anglican and Roman) were started in 1928. Schools were opened as usual to start formal school education with its modernization influence. A divisional Headquarters was opened later by the Colonial Administration with "stranger" elements who introduced certain new technological artefacts like motorcycles, cars and trade centres for palm oil and European imported manufactured goods. The greatest influence on Nsukka was the opening of the University of Nigeria in 1961 by the then Government of Eastern Nigeria. A large concentration of faculty and students suddenly descended upon village peoples only very lightly touched by modern influence. The teaching staff at that initial stage was made up of about half, Americans and the other half, Nigerian and British. So it was an international group and in the Nigerian context, an intertribal group that started the major influence on Nsukka. The first noticeable moral problem was "child prostitution". The attraction of a large number of young men as undergraduates, concentrating in this area where there was not an identical number of educated young women to offer companionship, created a "market" for prostitutes, among whom were some girls under the age of eighteen, which under the traditional morality was unthinkable. The next feature of this large number of people of varied backgrounds in Nsukka, was the development of Churches. Before the coming of the University and its modernization influence, there were fifteen Roman Catholic Churches and some twelve of the Anglican Church in this place. After the University had been started, the Churches we characterised as Pentecostal-Prayer-Healing and sometimes Prophetic, began to appear in Nsukka, mainly influenced by people from the University: Eternal Sacred Order of Cherubin and Seraphin with two places of worship and a total membership of about one hundred including children; Assemblies of God; Christ Apostolic Church which has two places of worship and a total membership of about ninety and Church of Christ, started by an American generally called "Brother" Currier, in 1966. Apart from the last named, all the Churches have their counterparts outside Nsukka and in various parts of Iboland. Jehovah Witnesses also has a Kingdom Hall and a fairly strong group. But a few religious organisations also going by the name of "Churches" exist in Nsukka which are not known anywhere else in Iboland. One is called Morning Star, another is the Sabbath Church and a third is called Muyiary-El-Cherubin and Seraphin. The last one was started by one Apostle, Peter, in 1971 in a private house turned into a Church. It is one of the Nsukka examples of Churches started in Iboland by vision-seeing "Apostles" and "Prophets" since after the civil war in answer to the stress situations of suffering, poverty and disillusionment created by the war years and their aftermath. Within the University itself are young men among students and faculty, who propagate secularist and Marxist teachings, influenced either by science or by Marxist social ideology. There are among these so called secularists, the very vocal minority who hold that the days of religion, especially the imported ones, are numbered. To them only the cultural aspects of Ibo traditional religion will survive. They follow the usual Marxist line of regarding religion as a stage of human ignorance which will disappear naturally as soon as people get to know better. A good majority of the students and faculty criticise the mission oriented Churches for slowness in expressing the life of the Church through the cultural patterns of the Ibo people. Half of this group attend religious worship fairly irregularly. A core of the rest of the University people are great students of the Bible who believe in the infallibility of its contents and organise their life according to its teaching, especially in matters of sex, decency of dress habits, and modesty of living. The greater percentage of this class are women undergraduates. To them there is no conflict between their science courses and their Christian faith. All classes of students and faculty accept whole heartedly the conveniences of technological culture and adapt a good measure of their Ibo way of life to the Western way. In dress, in music, in food as well as in personal relationships they can move in one day from the one to the other. Contraceptives and birth control methods are valued as well as large families of up to seven children. Monogamy is favoured as against polygamy. *Ọzọ* title as well as one's duty in the extended family are preferred to the Western attitude about them.

The effects of the technological culture on the homes and family life of the people of Nsukka are nearly the same as at Ihiala. Strain on the extended-family which was building up, started easing off after the war. Many people forced back to the village from various towns of Nigeria started re-integrating once more with the stay-at-home members. Many aspects of the old traditional cultural activities like "the sending of the spirits home", a religious festival that has to do with the start of the agricultural year, have taken on a new lease of life as both Christian and non-Christian youth join in them. Early betrothal of young girls (sometimes as young as seven) is disappearing as these young girls go to school in increasing number.

Both at Ihiala and at Nsukka, all the more grotesque of Ibo traditional religious practices, have died out as a result of the influence of modernization brought about by school education, Christianity and Colonial Administration. Examples include the killing of twins, human sacrifice, burial of chiefs with slaves, domestic slavery, punishment of criminals by inhumane treatment like burning them alive or beating them to death. In both places Christians have come back to ask why they should not pour libation to the spirit of ancestors. They now rejoice in the freedom to give their children, at christening, Ibo names which they regard as more meaningful than what early missionaries called "Christian names", although most of them happened to be Italian or Anglo-Saxon names. In both places the number of people converted from heathenism into Christianity in 1973 is about 45% lower than the peak conversion period of 1935-1945, although the number of young people who come forward to take Christian weddings has remained on the increase. In both places, the Ibo custom of paying bride-wealth to the parents of a girl by the family of the young man wanting to marry her, has been retained by the Christians although at various stages some missionaries and some leaders of studies organised by World Council of Churches had opposed it. [15]

Furthermore in both places this bride-wealth has risen considerably due to the influence of education given to girls. Where in the past (see footnote 11 in Chapter II) some cattle, work on bride's father's farm and gifts of things like cocoa nuts, would have been enough bride-wealth, today it has become any amount between one hundred pounds to four hundred pounds. [16]

Widow inheritance, a traditional Ibo custom in which a man could marry the young wife of his late father or his late brother, was frowned upon by the authorities of the Anglican Church at their Conference on "The Church and Native Customs", May 1914. Since then the practice is dying out very gradually among the Christian people, mainly as a result of modernization which gives much liberty of choice to both man and woman as to their life partners.

In both places we discovered that Christians have generally adopted the traditional practice of newly delivered mothers staying fairly in quiet rest and comparative seclusion for some weeks after childbirth without attending to public places like the Church, women's meetings or the market till after the christening and the service of churching of women after childbirth (in churches where such services obtain). The customary giving of feast for a new born child has been taken over by Christians.

Aba

We now turn to the case study of the one town we have selected. As we had indicated already, Aba is an industrial town, a town at the

---

[15] I remember heated discussion I had with a European female personnel from the W.C.C. on this subject in 1955. The All Africa Seminar on the Christian Home and Family, Mindolo Northern Rhodesia (now Zambia) February to April 1963 however recommended that it be retained at least in "the form of some symbol". See their report, published by W.C.C., Geneva, 1963, pp. 16 and 17.

[16] No doubt European writers feel justified in speaking of it as "bride price" or "marriage payment". See E. W. Ardener: Divorce and Fertility, London, 1962, pp. 77-78 where he relates "marriage payment" to rising prosperity in Iboland and speaks of present marriage system in Iboland as being "demand sensitive".

road nerve-centre of the whole of Eastern Nigeria joining Iboland to the neighbouring peoples of Ibibio, Efik and the Kalabari. It has a market to which all these peoples come. Imported manufactured goods as well as the country's produce for export, food for home consumption as well as transport industry make the market important. The Eastern Line of the Nigerian Railway passes through it and at one time in the history of the town between 1939 and 1959 Aba almost alone supplied the *gari*[17] and palm oil consumed in Northern Nigeria especially by the people originally from the South. Port-Harcourt the seaport of Eastern Nigeria being only some forty miles from Aba easily provides for Aba easy water transportation. Aba therefore has all the facilities for growth. The population has grown tremendously in the last three years owing to the large number of Ibo businessmen who could no longer feel at home in Northern Nigeria since after the war in addition to the attitude of the new authorities of Port-Harcourt. It is here that we can see all the features of social change brought about by the influence of Christianity, technology, Western culture and modernization leading to urbanization with all its opportunities and problems. We have already discussed in general (pages 94-98) the effect of urbanization on Ibo life, what we intend to do now is to indicate a few particular aspects of Aba so as to sharpen and deepen the analysis of the changes brought about by technological way of life. Home life in Aba as of now, suffers a great deal from congestion owing to shortage of houses. I had seen during our survey early in 1973 a polygamous family of nine living in a two room accommodation. Here the man with his two wives and six children live and sleep. In the normal village life of Iboland, each of the two wives would have had her own house of at least two rooms in a separate unit of court-yard within the one walled compound of the husband. Each wife would then organise for the sleeping places of her children in her own house and the compound courtyard could have provided all the children of the two wives enough playing space. At Aba all the nine souls were crowded into two room space of not more than 480 square feet. Furthermore the two wives went out early in the morning to the market while the older ones among the children prepared for school and those children who were under six years of age were cared for by two young girls of not more than twelve years. Now these children would miss the attention of mother and father and of uncles,

---

17 A Nigerian food processed from Cassava, a tuberous food plant.

aunts and older cousins, who could have played their part in looking after them and socializing them into the village norms, if they had lived in the village, especially the "uncorrupted" village. The effects on the youth of Aba of congested accommodation include lack of play facilities, lack of opportunities in any type of privacy which is useful in personality development and the development of personal gifts and talents.

A survey of the youth life indicated the existence of two social welfare youth clubs, clubs associated with various Churches, boys scouts and girl guides, town-union dance groups, private evening schools for skills like shorthand writing and typing. A good deal of training in useful citizenship is undertaken through these organisations, and some more were being started, for example, the Young Men Christian Association (the Y.M.C.A.) were planning to build a hostel. Despite all the efforts of groups like these, juvenile delinquency was present. We counted seven brothels where half of the inmates were young girls of average age of eighteen, although the majority of them were not born in Aba and could not have been said to be spoilt by the inadequate "homes of Aba township". A large number of young people with secondary school leaving certificate were roaming the streets looking for work. We estimated there were then (April 1973) about three thousand, half of whom passed very creditably the West African School Certificate Examination—the highest qualification obtainable at the end of secondary school education. It was a very tempting situation for young ladies to fall into prostitution, no matter how enlightened! We also discovered that a large number of these unemployed youth, especially the girls, flocked into the daily evening pentecostal type of highly emotional worship service put up by the Pentecostal-Prayer-Healing-Prophetic Churches. We shall discuss the place of these churches in Aba later. We must add here that the Ibo lineage organization is the one saving grace in the whole situation of unemployed youth. Almost all of such young people would have a relation, no matter how far away the relationship might be, even to the "twentieth cousin", with whom to stay at Aba, and who in addition to feeding and accommodating, would help in searching for employment. It is not difficult to appreciate how this situation could lead to bribery, nepotism and other forms of curruption of public service personnel. Furthermore it is easy to deduce that with this large number of youth leaving the villages to flock to a town like Aba, there would be less people (mainly elderly people) to cultivate the land, therefore food supply to the towns would be scarce.

We can at this juncture look at the labour situation at Aba. With the existence of four fairly big industries (two soap making, one beer brewing, one textile) and some one dozen well established commercial houses, and a large number of public service employees, labour relationships could be exciting. The usual anonymity of town and city life, and the dehumanizing influences upon workers known only by their tally numbers rather than by their names as persons, was discovered. It was not as bad as one would notice in a city like Chicago, but for a people like the Ibo so trained in traditional way of life in which everybody participated in group activity as individuals, the distance between employers and employees in European type of organised industry was devastating enough. Trade unions existed and some workers organised Isusu Contributory Unions [18] for self help. Many workers participated in their own "Town-Unions" and through such avenues developed leadership qualities which could reduce anomie. Owing to large number of dependants whom a worker would house, feed and sometimes put through school with the exorbitant school fees, many of those we interviewed showed evidences of anxiety. The dignity of labour, the pride of carefully executed skill and the development of the inner resources of one's personality through the work one does, did not appear easily from interviews. It was on the higher levels of management that we discovered some sense of purpose through one's daily employment. We did not discover close association between one's job and his religion as would have been the case in the traditional society of last century or early this century. Some deeply fundamentalist evangelical Christians, would make references to their waiting for the Lord's will for them in the doing of their jobs, but there was not much evidence of their wanting to change the work ethos of Aba by the convictions of their Christian faith. Of course one can not hope in some research tours of a big town like Aba to be able to discover these more spiritual attitudes. It will certainly need many years of observation and documentation of evidence to be able to determine more accurately such religious influences. However, data already available, did not suggest that the "Protestant Ethic" theory of Weber was manifesting itself among the Christians at Aba, or that any "puritans"

---

[18] Isusu is an Ibo originated co-operative thrift society in which members contribute a certain sum of money which is given to a member to invest in some undertaking. When it has gone one round, another round is started.

or dedicated men of faith were using their Christian belief patterns to bring about new social and work habits.[19]

Another aspect of the work scene at Aba which we have observed was the growth of the management and executive and professional class as well as private businessmen who have succeeded. We noticed that they were fast constituting themselves into the wealthy class with a good deal of economic power. From discussions held with some members of this group, it would appear that some would not hesitate to employ sharp practice methods to accumulate more and more money. Quite a good number of this class still belonged to their Churches both in the town and in their village home areas, and gave quite a substantial part of their income to the work of the Church. A large number at the same time appeared indifferent to the claims of religion, having neglected the Christian Churches they attended as boys or girls. With money facilities to buy the technological goods now being poured into the country, a vague impression was created in our mind, that some members of this class were becoming materialistic, in a manner that our traditional values and ethos would not have allowed, namely, valuing money, wealth and properties more than human persons. But this again is an area where absolute certainty can not be established by mere questionnaires or interviews or statistics of properties owned, or how often the boss has been harsh to his employees or subordinates, only vague and general impression could be built. But what is certain is that this is a new phenomenon in Ibo society—the emergence of a wealthy and important leisured group who controls the livelihood of quite a number of people, without clear lines of relationship through which personal responsibility, care and concern are exercised. The "wealthy men" of Ibo traditional society were assisted by their kith and kin, slaves and children, wives and sons-in-law to build up their wealth; in return such "wealthy men" owed obligatory duties to all these in intimate personal way, including very often, their living together with him in his own compound under his personal protection. This was not the case with the group we observed at Aba. They would remind you that they owed their wealth to their education, industry

---

[19] Max Weber argued in "Protestant Ethic and the Spirit of Capitalism" that the beliefs and norms of Protestantism especially Pietistic Calvinism etc. were instrumental in bringing about capitalism which revolutionised Europe. Furthermore the doctrine of "The Calling" led to honesty and standards of excellence in people's work. See the translation by Talcott Parsons, New York: Scribners, 1958, p. 154; p. 180-183; 151.

and some good fortune and not necessarily to their employees or subordinate staff. The danger we see here is the possibility that this class of people may multiply, and destroy the fine links of brotherhood and fellowship which are central to the Ibo traditional concept of society. Pride can grow on such soil and with it envy, and then ill will between the haves and the have nots, with all the attendant evils of class struggles so well known in European history. Such excessive individualism which is made possible by the facilities from technology and modern market with its entrepreneural devices could destroy Ibo community consciousness. This kind of moral problems facing Iboland as a result of the advent of technological modernization is suggested here only to be noted for further discussion in a subsequent chapter.

We now look at the religious situation at Aba. The town grew out of a clan in Iboland known as Ngwa clan. Their traditional religion is patterned on the general Ibo traditional religion already described in chapter III. One particular feature of Ngwa traditional religious ceremony is the annual *Ọfọ* ceremony performed at Okpuala Ngwa, the traditional headquarters or the seat of the *Okpara* (priest elder) of the Ngwa people. At this ceremony the eight traditional *Ọfọ* (religious sacred wooden staves in which the spirit of the ancestors is believed to live) belonging to the eight ancestor-founders of the eight subclans of Ngwa, are presented and "washed", that is to say, cleansed and revitalised. It is a ceremony for re-enacting the solidarity of the people under the covenant of their unity through common ancestory and the protection of one clan god. This annual ceremony is continued even now and some Christians who, fifty years ago would not witness it, do so today as identification exercise with the rest of their fellow clansmen. A large number of people in Aba town would not even know that such ceremony takes place annually; having come from different parts of Nigeria, the special Ngwa clan traditional religious observance is not their business. Yet the more established Ibo elderly people from other places who have lived long in Aba could be invited to the ceremony. This is an example of what happens in most towns of Iboland today that whilst the villages who originally owned the land where the township exits can go on with their traditional religious life, the town remains unaware of what goes on around it. This further emphasises the dual nature of existence of most Ibo people—one traditional with little interruption from outside cultural influences and the other, mainly town life, manifesting the impact of outside cultural influences. This dual existence can also be detected in the people's religious life—one phase is Christian life, another phase is traditionally Ibo with its religious life. The Christian Church was organized in Ngwaland from about 1867. It has grown especially in the town of Aba and to that we now turn. We will identify four categories of "Churches" in Aba.

(1) The more orthodox Churches which have grown out of the missionary activities from the main stream of historic Christianity. Among this group are the Anglicans with six Churches in the town; the Roman Catholics with four Churches; the Methodists with four Churches also, and Qua-Iboe with two Churches.

(2) Non-conformist, world-denying and sect type of "Churches". This is made up of the Seventh Day Adventists with six Churches; Jehova's Witnesses with one large Kingdom Hall and other small meeting places in private houses.

(3) The Spiritualist or Healing, Pentecostal and Prophetic "Churches", made up of Sacred Cherubin and Seraphin, three Churches; Eternal Sacred Order of Cherubin and Seraphin with one Church; Christ Apostolic Church with one Church; Assemblies of God with one Church building; Faith Tabernacle (without pentecostal features) one Church building; St. Gabriels Christ Healing Church, one Church building; Onu-Uzo-Ndu Christ Apostolic Church (The Gate of Life Christ Apostolic Church) one Church building; Christ Army Church, one Church building.

(4) The fourth category is made up of questionable organizations that go by the name of "healing Church" or "healing homes" started by individuals of more occult persuasion than Christian faith. They are dotted all over the streets of Aba. The number has multiplied by about three hundred percent since after the civil war. They do not attract as many devotees as the third group and because of their extreme borderline existence between Christianity and occult divinatory practices, not much attention is given to them here. We wish however to point out that their existence owes much to town life and the impact of foreign culture. Talismans from India and other occult artefacts from the Eastern World are part of their religious features. Another observation is that some of the founders of this category of "Churches" are mere charlatans who play on the people's religious credulity and "prophesy for bread and butter". In a town like Aba, and faced with the problems of existence like unemployment, lack of certainty as to what values people live by, and the loosening of the bonds of extended family and lineage relationships, there is not dearth of people to fall victims of false prophets of Iboland!

An analysis of what class of people in Aba attend what kind of Churches out of these four categories we have identified, and what class of people ignore Christianity in preference to the Ibo traditional religion, or profess agnosticism, is quite revealing. The Anglican Church as well as the Roman Catholic and the Methodist attract both the poor and the rich, both the well educated and the less or even the uneducated. Many people remain in these more orthodox Churches as a result of loyalty to parents, teachers and their own associational tie to these Churches. All the three attract people originating from different parts of the country and of Iboland, only the Methodist Church appears to have majority of members mainly from contiguous areas of Iboland possibly due to the comity of missions agreement of 1911 already mentioned in chapter IV which restricted missions to areas of influence, although this was not strictly obeyed. Many members of these three Churches also belong to or only attend the worship service of one of the Pentecostal Prayer Healing Prophetic Churches which from henceforth we will designate by the phrase "Aladura Churches".[20] The basic recruiting channel of the Aladura Churches is sickness, anxiety about needs like employment, children, success and promotion in employment, business or trade. The use of visible symbols of well being like holy oil, holy water and sometimes incense and well known cases of spiritual healing are among the main attractions. Highly emotional forms of public worship with drumming, impromptu forms of prayer, "soulful music" that sometimes recalls folk dance tunes, and falling into trance and speaking in tongues, attract a large number who say that such worship patterns are more agreeable with their Ibo background and with the unconscious levels of their personality. Some highly placed people go to these Churches as a result of success-prophecies given them by the leader or the Visioner attached to the Church. Some four professional men told me at interview why they found the Aladura Churches satisfactory: one person said that it was as a result of a prophecy given him about the success he would make in some business venture; another told of fears he was having about certain prospects of failure in his practice until the Apostle of one of the Aladura Churches started praying for him when the fear feeling stopped. A third reason by another person was his need of

---

20 Aladura is a Yoruba word meaning "Prayer People". It is used as a classificatory name for the type of Church utilising Pentecostal features as well as African Healing and Prophetic Divinatory practices both as worship pattern as well as problem solving devices.

assurance that no evil minded persons would do him evil that could deprive him of the high government post he was occupying. Two of these persons have been members of the Anglican Church and the other two have been members of the Methodist and the Roman Catholic Churches respectively. When questioned why they could not get such assurances of divine protection, help and revelation by remaining only in their respective Churches, their various answers boiled down to the "fact" that the priests or ministers in their respective Churches did not seem to possess such "power" as the Aladura Prophets and Apostles had manifested. There is no doubt that all religious organisations, either of Christians or of devotees of traditional Ibo religion, make some provisions for the solution of the problems of members especially through the use made of services related to the rites of passage—birth puberty, marriage, death. It appears, however, that the Aladura Churches are believed by a good number of people interviewed, to help more effectively people's perplexities about work, success, health and well being and deliverance from the inadequacies of individuals, brought about by social change and the demands of modernization. Whether this is mere belief resulting from a psychological conditioning in which these Aladura Churches are adepts, through their fundamentalist approach to the Bible, for example the positive and affirmative repetition of Biblical words of assurance, and the inducement of trance and hypnotic condition during public worship, we can not say for certain as we can only go by the answers devotees give. There is however a possibility, that with clearer Biblical and theological education, many people in the various Aladura Churches may not continue to hold to many of the beliefs and practices which they now hold.

The membership of the Jehovah's Witnesses was drawn from the less educated and trader group of Aba. They were approximating the classical sect tendencies of opposition to the power structure, reluctance in accepting some ordinary decencies of life in clothing and other possessions. All native customs must be avoided, for to them they all represent idol worship including the use of native drums, dancing to native tunes or associating with any form of festivals of the people. They do not even celebrate Christian festivals like Easter and Christmas as these celebrations are not expressly commanded to be kept in the Bible, which they accept word for word, letter for letter, and memorise its verses for argument in street corners and in people's homes which they visit, welcome or not welcome. Their dogmatism no doubt makes it difficult for them to bear any noticeable social influence upon the town. Theirs is an example of responding to the problems of social change due to the impact of Western technological culture through withdrawal. They tend to regard the ordinary Ibo people struggling to adapt their traditional culture to the accommodation of both Christianity and modernization as people doomed to hopelessness and corruption, whilst they themselves belong to a very highly selected and exclusive association of those who would inherit the bliss of the Kingdom to come. Hence the name of their "Church building" is "Kingdom Hall". The Seventh Day Adventists are not as world denying as the Jehovah's Witnesses.

There is one Church which does not fit into any of the four categories we have mentioned. It is the United Native African Church which originated in Lagos in 1891 as a protest movement against white missionary dominated rule in the Anglican Church. Its branch in Aba maintains its doctrines, part of which is that only Bishops and other ministers are obliged to be husbands of one wife in accordance with the injunction in Titus Chapter 1 verses 5-10, and 1 Timothy 3 verses 1-10. The rest of the members of the Church are free to be polygamists in accordance with the social custom of Africans. This Church is known as the Ethiopian type of Church. It used religion as the means of fighting for self government, and for the overthrow of colonial rule and the giving of dignity and leadership to Africans in their own country. It is a spent force now that most African countries are independent. Apart from permitting polygamy it is like the Anglican Church, from which it seceded, both in polity as well as in administrative structure.[21]

We now discuss two more issues—one is how have the Churches in Aba reacted to the demands of technological modernization and the other is how have they reacted to Ibo customs and cultural institutions especially the three we have been studying in particular, namely, *Ọzọ* title, polygamy and extended-family relationships and duties. About the responses of the Churches as communities to modernization with its technology and westernising influences, we have already analysed the response of the sect group like the Jehovah's Witnesses. In the more orthodox Churches like the Anglican, Roman Catholic or Methodist there are two classes of people—the conservatives who insist on the Church being run, and its teachings kept the same as the missionaries

---

21 See J. B. Webster, The African Churches Among the Yoruba 1888-1922, London: Oxford University Press, 1964.

taught them over a century ago. Technology and modernization they say will soon pass away as mere fads. Although most of this group would ride in cars and enjoy other forms of technological conveniences, they do not seem to regard such comfort, ease and "cause and effect" scientism that brings these things into being so seriously as to require adaptation in religious teaching and practices. They would condemn as Satan's work such things as contraceptives, alcohol, ballroom dancing and youth culture of outspokeness and of seeking different values. The other class—the progressives would insist on the Church adapting its teaching, its organization and methods to meet the demands of changed times. To them, if people query the Virgin Mary's birth of Jesus, remove it from the doctrine; if monogamy is not absolutely necessary and people challenge it, permit polygamy. To them the Church should be more responsive to the needs of the unemployed and to the leisure needs of young peoples by organising for them in Church halls dances, youth clubs, and the like. In the Aladura Churches people tend more towards conservatism and biblical rigidity and yet more problem solving as we had already indicated. Technology and the civilization it brings are to them forms of temptation against which a Christian should build up a measure of self control and withdrawal through faith. The culture and society must be changed until its values become the values of the twice born child of God. [22]

On the second question: attitude to Ibo customs and cultural institutions, we have already given some indications. The sects would have nothing to do with them; the Aladura Churches are ambivalent, adopting the more artistic, divinatory and personal problem-solving techniques of Ibo traditional religion and culture, and making no definite pronouncements on the major institutions like *Ọzọ*, masquerades and polygamy. Some of them accept polygamy, taking of the *Ọzọ* title but have no theology or explanation to back their inclinations. The more orthodox Churches are again divided into conservatives who cry that youth "have spoilt the Church" by wanting to have these institutions incorporated into the life and structure of the Church and those who are impatient that they are not already fully taken into the life of the Church.

What religion has meant to the individuals set in the rapid social change noticeable in Aba, is not easy to analyse. We have already

---

[22] Cf. the Analysis of John Cogley about America's religious responses to modernity in John Cogley, Religion in a Secular Age: The Search for Final Meaning, New York: Frederick A. Praeger, 1968, pp. 117-122.

indicated (p. 112) what the four members, who in addition to being registered communicants of the more orthodox Churches, also went to the Aladura type of Churches, said about how their personal needs were satisfied by going to the Aladura.

Personal faith, strength to find courage enough for the demands of the time as well as being where one's "group" or "mates" or "associates" belong, constitute some of the satisfactions people seem to find, personally, through their membership of these Churches. We have already indicated through the study we made of Ihiala how people in the towns who are serious minded Christians register also in their home village Churches. We noticed at Aba that quite a good number of people felt that their personal fulfilment as members of the Church was realised through their home village attachment rather than through their membership in Aba Church. Some do not even seek membership in any of the Aba Churches, being content with the registration already made at their village home churches, where if they die they would be taken home for full Christian burial rites which means much to an Ibo man. Furthermore those Christians who wish to take the *Ọzọ* title whether approved by their Church or not, go home to their villages to take it. So to quite a good number of people in Aba town their home villages serve as the reference point of social belonging in many things involving native traditions and customs whilst Aba remains as their economic reference point. This feature of living in the two worlds of village and town, is an important aspect of the way many Ibos respond to technological modernity. They take in what they consider the best from each of the two worlds, so as not to be snowed down under the weight of the demands of either. When the attractions of modernity are too unbearable for one not having the financial means to cope with them in the town, there is an escape to the village; and when the conservatism and unattractiveness of village life is overwhelming, there is the town to escape to.[23] This state of affairs can either lead to persons exposed to them being cultural hybrids, not at home in either place, and therefore divided personalities or else it can lead to a new synthesis of adaptation of the old and the new, to the greater enrichment of life. It is the thesis of this study that

[23] See Josef Gugler, "Life in a Dual System: Eastern Nigeria in Towns 1961" in *Cahiers d'Etudes Africaines*, Vol. XI, 1971, No. 43, Mouton & Co., Paris, pp. 400-421, where he observes that throughout Subsaharan Africa "urban dwellers regularly visit their rural homes where they make gifts ... and want to be buried" (p. 401).

the Christian Church in Iboland can pioneer a new value orientation, a new ethos or social norm or ethics, by which this can be achieved.

But to this we shall return later, meanwhile let us summarise the main features of the interaction between traditionalism and modernity in Iboland which we have been analysing in this chapter.

(1) Technological influence is pervasive, it is present in villages as well as in towns, only that villagers are more "deprived" of it due to ignorance, poverty and lack of money-earning opportunities, whilst people in the towns have more of such facilities through industries, markets, education and foreign contact.

(2) Traditional religion as well as Christianity is being corroded by technology and modernity. The moral foundations built by both Christianity and traditional religion are being questioned by the system of modernity, especially in its emphasis on markets, profits, consumption and possessions, business and technological expertise. All these tend towards destroying the traditional values of consideration of the individual as a human person, and society as a community of fellows, linked together by bonds of long stretch of kinship. Instead of these, individualism and new concepts of wealth and values, are building up, and there is not yet enough moral foundation for them to stand on. Furthermore the Christian values being taught to the Ibo in terms of modesty, justice, regard even for the humblest as the neighbour to be loved as one's self, are being undermined by the competitive spirit in which the Ibo delight very much as a means of upholding the achievement motivation already present in their culture before the advent of Western technological culture.[24]

(3) Villages are being deserted for the towns and real poverty is growing where people, especially the elderly ones, can no longer find enough food to eat and huts to dwell in. Costs are soaring high for them to be able to build huts and voluntary extended-family communal labour, which could have been used in the past to put up such buildings without much cost, is no longer available. Equally too in some areas of village life new wealth has come in together with its possibilities and dangers.

(4) Ibo traditional religion as a system of beliefs, practices and social as well as cultural values is falling apart, the only centre that is still holding on in the face of modernity consists of the cultural

[24] See footnote 31 in Chapter IV, referring to Ottenberg's analysis of this achievement motivation.

institutions, relationships and some of the structures of human interaction, but none of these remains as neatly as before the impact of Western technology and Christianity. The belief in the spirit reality of existence and the necessity for man to be harmoniously related to this spirit reality especially through the ancestors, the use of charms and visible symbols of religious faith is still held. Hence the attractiveness of religious organizations that promise these things, for example the Aladura Churches, and in other direction, the Roman Catholic Church in its sacramental form of worship, the use of symbols and images and the place of the Blessed Virgin Mary and other saints in popular faith and doctrine.

(5) The Christian Church which in some places is less, and in others more, than a century old is neither acclimatised to Ibo surroundings nor is it still seen by all, as a European importation pure and simple. Those who do not have much attachment to it, still brand it as a hangover of Colonialism's technique for subjugating the people. The majority of those having attachment to it still ask questions as to how best the Churches can serve their human as well as their spiritual needs by being more related to their own cultural environment.

(6) All sections of Iboland want increased technology for the ease it gives to life and because their cultural tradition admits reception of the new into the old. But no one seems to be able to "prophesy" about the end it will lead the people to, nor be able to indicate what are its features to beware of, so as to give a sense of direction to its development. Whether the Ibo using their sense of the spirit world's reality, could avoid complete desacralization of life which technology brings in its wake, will yet be seen. Such desacralization had already been started by Christianity and technology. Some Ibo resist this and so live a kind of ambivalent life with one foot in the technological world of the scientific cause and effect and another foot in the Ibo traditional world where certain misfortunes including death sometimes are interpreted as the result of the displeasure of ancestors from the spirit world.

It is for people from this kind of background and in this kind of environment, living within religious belief patterns that sometimes conflict with the realities of the struggle to find their daily bread in a fairly materialistic society, it is to them that we want to give guidance through new normative values, and we want such values or such ethic to be Christian though the background is Ibo, and therefore "non-Christian".

CHAPTER SIX

URBAN-INDUSTRIAL VALUES, IBO TRADITIONAL MORALITY AND CHRISTIAN ETHICS

Definitions

This study so far, has indicated that Ibo society today is faced with three sources of value orientation struggling for primacy. These are: Christian ethics, Ibo traditional morality, and urban-industrial values resulting from technology and modernizatoin. None of these three can be said to be the dominant normative force throughout the area or in all aspects of life. In most cultural activities of the traditional nature, Ibo traditional morality would seem to be the normative force; while at the same time and with the same group of village people, Christian as well as non Christian, the influences of technological culture would appear to be the guiding norm of action. Furthermore it is easy to encounter several individuals, who show so much ambivalence in being strongly influenced by traditional values on one issue, and on another issue exhibiting the internalised influence of Christian ethics, only to give strong impression on a third issue that they are mere positivists obeying the law of the survival of the fittest without regard to the "neighbour-concern" of both Christianity and traditional morality. We will now analyse these three kinds of ethics mainly as they manifest themselves in Iboland, with a little discussion of their general framework in concept as well as in historical manifestations which will facilitate some comparative study later. But before we do so, we will attempt the definition of the principal terms being employed in this chapter such as "ethics", "morality", "moral law", "moral code", "ethical reflection", "value". We do this, starting with the simple dictionary meanings, because these words sometimes appear synonymous with one another, and yet they have their particular meanings which could create unnecessary debate, where such meanings are not defined, to indicate clearly what is implied by the writer.

"Ethics" is the study of the standards of conduct and moral judgment, a reflection on morality as well as a body or system of morals of a particular group like the Ibo or a religion like Christianity. [1]

---

[1] Cf. Paul Tillich's definition: "Ethics is the science of man's moral existence asking for the roots of the moral imperative, the criteria of its validity, the

"Morality" implies "rightness or wrongness as of an action", "moral principles", "right or moral conduct". As used in this study sometimes we mean "prevalent social customs" of the Ibo or problems of diverse kind, like different ways of making money or of chastity and marriage. "Moral" means "dealing with or capable of distinguishing between right and wrong" and "moral law" is used to refer to the law of nature or of the ultimate source of being which gives to morality an ultimate sanction; this is not normally, in this study, applied to mean the same thing as "natural law" prominent in Roman Catholic moral theology. "Moral Code" refers to the social sanctions by which a community like the Ibo organise and regulate their social behaviour. [2] "Ethical reflection" is the attempt to clarify the logic and adequacy of the values that shape the "lived" world of our daily experience. Part of the concern of this study is to apply ethical reflection on Ibo traditional morality, as well as on Christian ethics as it is practised now in Ibo society, and see how adequate or inadequate both are, and further to see whether some new insight can be brought upon both. "Value" in simple dictionary meaning is "the quality of a thing which makes it more or less desirable, useful and so on". Value expresses the significance, whether great or small, whether higher or lower, which we ascribe to particular experience, activity or life in general. This significance gives us some guidance in our behaviour as we live our daily life and make the many decisions involved in such daily life. Value is both subjective as well as objective; it is subjective in as much as it is by personal participation in deciding that we put value upon an object, it is objective in that values possess foundation independent of us hence our value judgment can be wrong or right. We now give brief analyses of the sources of normative influence on Iboland starting with Urban-industrial values.

Urban-Industrial Values or Ethics of Modernism

Of all the three value systems influencing Iboland which we have identified in this study, this seems the least structured. It has neither priests to propagate its code nor time-honoured usage and antiquity to conjure the aura of respectability, and yet its influence can be

---

sources of its contents, the forces of its realization", Love, Power and Justice, New York: Oxford University Press, 1969, p. 72.

[2] See Paul Roubiczek, Ethical Values in the Age of Science, Cambridge: The University Press, 1969, pp. 3 and 4. See also Webster's New World Dictionary of the American Language.

strong. It is an off-spring of Western technological market dominated value, whose influence and problems in Ibo society we have discussed briefly in chapter V.

Until about 1950 it was regarded as part of Christian value, but now with the greater impact of secularizing influence and the attractiveness of modernization through technology, it has come to be regarded as a different influence altogether. It contradicts in some issues both Christian values as well as the values of Ibo traditional religion. What then are the main features and characteristics of this secularistic ethic? Before analysing such main features and characteristics we might gain some insight from a quick look at the history of the development in Western culture of secularistic way of valuing.

The earliest appearance of the mentality that sought for change through reason and discussion, through intelligent enquiry and tentative consensus, was in the sixteenth and the seventeenth centuries. Through the activities of small groups of enlightened spirit, some form of the institutionalization of this mentality took place early in Holland and England. The Protestant milieu in England together with its concept of the "priesthood of all believers" enabled the Puritan Revolution to develop basic concepts of secular ideology of liberalism in politics, in religion and in social thought. When this was added to the new science that had already started with men like Francis Bacon, and to the growth of the new middle class in cities, who also actively participated in politics through the parliament, the foundations of secular and technological modernism were already being laid. [3]

It was however in the period of the Enlightment that these tendencies gained momentum in such a way that all areas of culture and society were deeply influenced by this secular temper. Its basic philosophy was the questioning of any fixed or given authority, which had to be summoned to the tribunal of reason, and the belief that conscious directional change was a primary human responsibility. Institutionalized Christianity was caught unprepared by this development and was forced into the defensive. Although one can say that Christian ideas of freedom, humanity, the nature of man and of nature itself, which had been neglected or suppressed, were taken up by the Enlightment.

---

[3] See Robert Bellah, Beyond Belief: Essays in a Post-Traditional World, New York: Harper and Row, 1970, pp. 64-72, to which I am indebted for this historical survey. Dietrich Bonhoeffer in his well-known "Letters from Prison" carries the beginnings of the development to "a world come of age" even back to the thirteenth century.

However Christianity on the whole failed to react properly to the challenge. Incidentally, in England as well as in Anglo-Saxon-influenced areas this new secular ideology did not involve a repudiation of religion. Rather some new forms of Protestantism such as Methodism could to a certain extent go with it. In France owing to the strong influence of Roman Catholicism the liberal movement assumed an antireligious stance especially through the revolution of 1789. This fermentation in the world of ideas was mightly reinforced by the rapid development of science, technology, industrialization and urbanization, which continued ever accelerating throughout the nineteenth and twentieth centuries. Looking back one must say that in the long history of Europe, many convulsions of rapid social change as well in religious, philosophical and ethical ideas as in science and technology, and the interplay of economic, social and political exigencies have been active together in generating the secularistic way of life. In course of time all that history started repeating itself (though in mild form) outside of Europe in which Iboland shares in some measure.

When we look at the general features of secularization which help to shape its ethics we find the following facts:

(1) Through technology, secularization and modernization man has achieved a greater control over nature, over his social environment as well as over his own life. Man now has an image of himself as a "self-realising and self-controlling" being. He has "come of age" and therefore is responsible for his "use" of this world, therefore the ethical inclination with which he faces the evaluation of his activities, decisions and achievements is "this worldly".

(2) Aware of the freedom of the redeemed children of God which Christianity has taught to western culture, technology has given western man the additional freedom from fear of the evil spirits, fear of abject poverty and from all the psychological inhibitions that go with tyranny and oppression. But because technical and secularised value orientation had divorced itself from the freedom which relates to the authority of God (whom to serve is perfect freedom), an ambiguous situation is created in the secular experience of man: the freedom brought about by technological modernization is accompanied by increased enslavement to the forces of mass culture. [4]

---

[4] I have been influenced in this analysis by the reports of the working groups at the Geneva World conference on Church and Society. See the official report, World Conference on Church and Society, Geneva, July 12-26, 1966. W.C.C. Geneva, 1967, pp. 188-203.

(3) The attractiveness of scientific technology and its modernization possibilities has world-wide appeal. Hence one of the presumptions of scientific culture is its ability to break barriers between races of mankind and constitute mankind into a global-world community. Whilst mass-communications-media and air travel facilities tend towards doing this unification work for mankind, the lack of basic spirit content and common reference point generates too many ideologies, view points and interest groups. This world that seemingly appears to be drawn into a global community, finds itself faced with pluralism of great dimension in religions, politics, economic pursuits and in the living of simple family life; "simple" in the context of "elementary", "primary" and therefore "basic" but now complicated by father, mother and children not having anymore a common understanding as to the meaning and method of living together as a real family.

From the foregoing brief analysis of some of the characteristic features of technical culture, we can deduce the ethics of urban-technological modernization as it manifests itself in Iboland. In the first place it is still not quite a well defined type of ethic. It is by nature provisional and pragmatic in the sense that it offers attractive behaviour pattern for groups, who regard themselves as "modern", and who get "satisfaction" in doing certain things by behaving in a way they feel serves their end of getting on in their "new world". The basic principle of the ethic of modernization as some Ibo "moderns" see it is freedom from the ethics of authority either of the Church or of the tribal code of morality. The goal as we have stated earlier on, is success and achievement through the utilization of the new powers technology has provided, such as: organization, market, communication, expertise and efficiency added on to some form of self discipline, knowledge and skill. No concern seems to be shown about the relevant effects of such success and organization to human beings nor to the community both present and future, nor to the individual character of the human personality, who through the spirit reality of existence in himself, as well as in other individuals, is related to the Ultimate Spirit. Stated in this way it can be seen straight away how different this ethic is from both Ibo traditional morality as well as from Christian ethics, especially in its lack of reference to any "Supernatural" value centre. We have indicated in the short historical survey of the origin and growth of secular liberalism that led to technological culture, some form of minor relationship that existed between it and Christianity. Such relationship could be identified even though in less defined terms, in the thoughts and actions of some Ibo who claim to have rejected Ibo morality and Christian ethics in preference for this "ethic of modernization". When talking with a contractor at Aba, one could sense from his emphasis on honesty in the use of building materials, that he was indirectly drawing from some New Testament concept of the meaning of "neighbour-love". He argued that his reason for using a six-inch-nail to join two pieces of wood (where the less scrupulous contractor could use the cheaper four-inch nail and save more money and make more profit for himself) was his belief in the trust the owner of the house reposed on him by giving him that job of house building. Furthermore he said that his own honour and consideration of future contracts could not permit him to do otherwise. An element of enlightened self-interest is contained in this explanation, yet the "neighbour-love" principle, which is best expressed in Christian ethical teaching, is also present. It does appear then that in theory as well as in philosophical conceptualization, urban-technological ethics of modernization can be naturalistic and opposed to religious ethics which it regards as theonomous and therefore supernaturalistic; in practice there is a possibility of a combination of influences from all three—Ibo traditional morality, Christian ethics and the values of technological modernism. We will take up this consideration later when we discuss the best way of advising the Ibo, caught in this interaction of rapid social change, through the comparative study of the three strands of ethical values with which he is faced at present. We now proceed to analyse Ibo traditional morality.

Ibo Traditional Morality

In chapter III, especially pages 36-42 we have discussed Ibo world view and Ibo understanding of man and nature. From such previous discussion we can deduce salient points about Ibo traditional morality. Key points to be noted are the existence of a moral code built up from the injunctions of the earth goddess (*Ala*) through the ancestors (*Ndichie* or *Ndebunze*). These injunctions, made up of approved observances and prohibitions, constitute what the Ibo call *omenani* (the "doings" or "ways" of the "land", that is the people, the community, the clan or the village). Those prohibitions are referred to as *Nso Ala* (the actions that are abominable to *Ala*, the land or the earth goddess). The second point, following on the existence of a moral code, is that emphasis is on group morality rather than on individual cultivation of goodness itself. The third point is that *ndu* (life) is the *summum bonum.* We will now discuss these three factors in Ibo traditional morality.

The moral code of Iboland commonly spoken of as *omenani* defines the various aspects of behaviour and social activities that are approved while at the same time indicating those aspects that are prohibited. Before we discuss these two aspects of the moral code, it will be helpful to try to see what the Ibos themselves understand about the nature of morality itself. The words used to express the concept of morality are mainly words that relate to the activities that could be moral or amoral. A man is described as *onye uru-ala,* literally the phrase means one that pollutes or abominates the land, but in effect it is used to describe a person of wicked intentions. *Ajo madu* is another phrase used to describe a bad man where the word "*ajo*" means "bad", the opposite of good. But the word "*ajo*" is scarcely used in its noun form, it is often associated with a being or an act like in the statement *igba ajo-ihe* (being very wicked). Furthermore, when things regarded as great offence or evil do take place, they are spoken of in terms of *iru-ala,* (desecration of the land) *ime-aru* or *ime nso-ala* —doing the abominable or acting in pollution of the basic earth.

The death of a young man can be received with the exclamation "*aru-eme o*" literally meaning "pollution" or "abomination" has happened, in the sense that a great evil has befallen the community. This way of describing "evil" as if it were a ritual avoidance in the sense of what destroys peaceful existence, is an aspect of tying the moral concept closely to the harmony between the spirit world, man and nature. (Here nature is typified more concretely by the "land"—the abode of man, plants, animals and all other living creatures as well as the earth, which is the abode of the spirit of ancestors and the place where all dead members of the community are buried.)

From this short verbal study it could be suggested that the Ibo do not seem to speak of evil or badness in its intrinsic abstract nature, but rather speak of its meaning in conjunction with actions and ritual avoidances "commanded" by the earth goddess through the ancestral spirits.

"Good" is expressed by the word *nma,* which sometimes takes on independent existence more so than its opposite word "bad" does in Ibo expressions. A child can be named *Nmakasi* (goodness is the superior virtue) Obioma (kindly heart), Ifeoma (a child of beauty or the good one). However the bulk of expressions in which *nma* is used show it more as adjective qualifying actions, decisions, state in life as well as hopes rather than as substantives expressing "goodness" as having "ontological" existence.

Turning to the moral code of Ibo land (*Omenani*), which is believed to be handed down from the earth goddess from time immemorial, the prohibitions (*nso ala*) seem to predominate. Like all theonomous social and religious injunctions, the Ibo code with its many "thou shalt nots" includes both purely moral demands of the religious nature as well as the purely social, political and economic considerations. There are variations in various parts of Iboland, but in general any list drawn up from any part will include the major and the minor prohibitions (*nso ala*). The major ones to which one could prefix "Thou shalt not" are:

(1) Stealing yams either from the barn or from the farm.
(2) Homicide.
(3) Incest.
(4) A freeman having sexual relationship with *Osu* (slaves of a shrine) or spending the night especially with the *Osu* in her house.
(5) Suicide especially by hanging.
(6) Poisoning someone else to take his life secretly.
(7) Theft of domestic fowls especially a hen in her hatching pot where it can easily be taken away with the eggs.
(8) A woman climbing palm tree or a kolanut tree especially if in addition she attempts doing so with the special palmtree climbing rope.
(9) Theft of any kind by an *Ọzọ*-titled person.

The minor ones are:

(10) Adultery by the wife.
(11) A wife throwing the husband on the ground during a fight.
(12) Killing or eating any "totem" animal on purpose; if accidently (which will be committing an abomination all the same) the guilt of the offender is viewed a little more lightly.
(13) Anyone deliberately cutting the tendrils of young growing yams in somebody's farm.
(14) Anyone altering land boundaries in secret especially in the night.
(15) Burning another person's thatch house maliciously.

(16) Disclosing the identity of the masquerade in public especially by a woman.

(17) A woman in her menstrual period cooking and serving her husband such food especially if the husband is *Ọzọ*-titled person.

(18) A widow having sexual relationship while still "wearing" for her late husband mourning clothes. She is considered to be in ritual danger until she had performed the "cleansing rite" normally after one year, such sex relation is regarded as spreading pollution.

(19) Someone dying a "bad death" (deaths resulting from leprosy, small pox, etc.) or after swearing an oath and then dying from the enlargement of the stomach.

(20) A husband deliberately breaking or throwing away the wife's earthen-ware cooking pot.

In addition to this list of twenty "abominations" that can be said to have some moral guilt attached to them in addition to being things prohibited by Ibo moral code, there are a few other "abominations" always listed with the above as causes for the "pollution" or desecration of the land which in fact relate to unusual occurrences in nature. These are:

(21) A cock crowing in the night (from about 8 p.m. to 3 a.m.).

(22) A woman giving birth to twins.

(23) A baby coming out of the womb with the feet instead of the head.

(24) A growing child cutting the upper tooth first. [5]

These last three, and no. 19 above referring to bad death, cannot be prefixed with "Thou shalt not", because the woman giving birth

---

[5] These twenty-four "abominations" or ritual avoidances or moral prohibitions by the earth goddess although regarded as the Ibo moral code could be subdivided into five. a) Those which regulate domestic life to ensure harmony at home and in the community (examples nos. 11 + 20), b) Those which control man's powerful sex urge (nos. 4 + 18), c) Those designed to protect the vital bases of the economic life of the community (nos. 13 + 14), d) Those which emphasise the "normal" rhythm of nature (nos. 8, 22 + 23), e) Those that protect the spirit relationship between man, nature and the ancestors (nos. 4 + 16). See M. S. O. Olisah, "Taboos in Ibo Religion and Society: Social and Religious Values of Abominations Among the Ibo" in *West African Religion*, no. 11, Nsukka, Jan. 1972, pages 1-18.

to twins cannot, by "moral" decisions and proper motivation, control the formation of the twins in her womb. These could therefore be described as metaphysical evil for which the individuals to whom they are attributed cannot be "morally" responsible. The Ibo in their effort to explain this aspect of life's experience, namely, natural evil and calamity, argue that these things result from "pollution" of the land somewhere along the line by which the harmony between man, nature and the spirit world became broken, hence the "abnormalities" like giving birth to twins, or a cock crowing when it ought not to do so. The sanction, of course, is the destruction of the beings in which the abnormality occurred, not because of any guilt attributed to them, but because their continued existence would further enlarge the gulf between man, nature and the spirit world. In addition to destroying the beings in whom the abnormality appeared the community, especially the immediate relations, must provide the necessary animals and things for the elaborate sacrifices necessary for cleansing the land so as to restore the harmony. If the *epieikeia,* the sweet reasonableness is re-established, the Ibos believe such abnormalities would not occur unless someone again committed unconfessed, and therefore unatoned, evil.

Sanction against any of the above prohibitions varies according to the gravity of the offence for example, theft of yam as we had already indicated in chapter II, would be followed by elaborate sacrificial cleansing of the land and the selling of the offender to slavers. Incest would receive as sanction in some places the tying of the two culprits' hands and feet and being dragged on the ground around the place of the incest and around the central village square, and then the cleansing sacrifice by the Nri priests and dwarfs whose priestly function it was to offer such sacrifices in many parts of Iboland. In Owerri areas another elaborate ritual purification is undertaken. The thoroughness with which the community see to the proper methods of imposing the sanctions, is due not to sadism or the urge to torture their fellow human being, but to the genuine belief that unless proper ritual and punishments are enforced, all the people would suffer as unbearable evil would befall the community. Hence morality in Ibo traditional society like all sacral or ontocratic communities (to use Van Leeuwen's phrase, see Chapter VII) was first and foremost the concern of the community. The essence was primarily to keep the harmony, well being and effective co-existence of the members of the "community" made up of dead ancestors, the present generation and the children yet unborn. Hence the great amount of vigilance exercised by all the members of the community in helping everybody to know of the contents of the moral code and observe them scrupulously.

On the positive side there is not much contained in the Ibo moral code except in so far as the *Omenani* includes semi religious duties, observances and rites of relationships which have moral flavour, and which must be properly observed for the enhancement of the "good life" which the Ibo regard as the most supreme value. In conclusion we will observe that the Ibo moral code, which could be identified in some outward forms with the Old Testament code, especially of the pre-prophetic days in its community emphasis (compare the story of Achan at Ai, Joshua 7), or in its ritual cleansing and strictness of sanctions, or in the existence of special category of priests to offer atonement sacrifices, had a casuistry. It was with this casuistry that it was able to inflict all sorts of severe penalties upon "offenders" without any qualms, just like the mediaeval Church used its casuistry and burnt "heretics" at the stake thereby forgetting the "agape principle" of its ethics and condoning the most barbarous punishments priests and prelates cared to impose.

Turning to the second point in Ibo morality deducible from Ibo world view (and we have already touched on this in passing) we see how communalistic Ibo morality could be. Because of the emphasis on the community, its well being and its ordered existence, the maintenance of the proper links of relationships in human kinship as well as in the relationship between man, nature and the ancestral spirit, most Ibo do not readily see the value of goodness for the exercise of personal responsibility. Goodness is seen primarily as a means of realising the social morality of the group, and this is capable of removing from moral life the joy of its inner motivation which is of the essence of morality itself resulting from choice, personal decision and responsibility. [6]

It is proper to mention here however that the Ibo have another social pattern by which individual growth in moral quality of a personal nature can be achieved. This we will elaborate when we discuss Ibo "good life". Another question that is often raised in connection with group oriented code of morality, is how far is such code capable of developing in the people concerned, the personal prick of conscience

[6] Writers like Paul Roubiczek argue that "to subordinate the good to another purpose, such as usefulness for society, falsifies its nature and thus falsifies morality". Paul Roubiczek, Ethical Values in the age of science, Cambridge: At the University Press, 1969, p. 57/58.

through guilt by which action related to motive and conviction is made possible? This raises the old debate between guilt-oriented culture and shame-oriented culture. The recent study of Gerhart Piers and Milton B. Singer has removed the sharp cutting edge from the debate. There is no scientifically demonstrable reason why in group-related morality, heavily influenced by community's rigorous enforcement mechanism including shame and taunting improvised denigrating songs, members of such group could not develop inner remorse or guilt. [7] It is our experience in Iboland to see a woman, who because of difficult labour she had, openly admitted having sexual relationship with someone else. As we watched her we felt there definitely was in her the prick of conscience as well as the fear of the spirit of ancestors punishing her at the hour of her physical and emotional weakness. We can conclude that although the shame element is evidently present in the way Ibo society enforces obedience to their moral code, the individual prick of conscience is also present. [8] We will now turn to the analysis of Ibo society's concept of the good life—their *summum bonum.*

As we stated in chapter III (page 41) life to the Ibo is the highest value. The Ibo word for "life" is "*ndu*" which appears in proverbs and personal names. Ndubisi, (*Ndu* is the prime necessity) Ndukaku (*Ndu* is superior to wealth) Ndulue (if *Ndu* stretches out). The opposite of *ndu* is *onwu* (death). Names given to children expressing the fear that death might ruin this supreme good "life" are many too. A few examples are: Onwudiwe (death is full of anger), Onwuchuruba (it is only death that stops me from being wealthy), Onwuatuegwu (death does not yield to any type of fear), Onwumbiko (a prayer to death to please spare).

Through names like these and a good deal of proverbs, the Ibo give expression to their belief that life is the very important value to be conserved. Hence all the rigorous ways by which the moral code is observed, because breach of the harmony between man, nature and spirit of ancestors would lead to a possible destruction of much life in the community. Therefore religious rituals, moral provisions and social network of kinship relations are channeled towards the preservation of *Ndu,* When a man goes to the diviner with a wreathed

[7] See Gerhart Piers and Milton B. Singer, Shame and Guilt: A psyco-analytic and a cultural study, New York: W. H. Norton & Comp., 1971, p. 99.

[8] A good deal has been written on Ibo morality, see footnote 4 in chapter II add Major Arthur Glyn Leonard, The Lower Niger and its Tribes, London: Frank Cass, reprint 1968, pp. 458-463.

tendril of the palm tree to enquire about anything, the *nwadibia* (diviner) lifts up his *ofo* stick and says to the client "*juru ndu*" (touch the *ofo* for life). This precedes all other parts of the divination techniques and procedures. Again early in the morning when a titled man offers the kolanut pieces in prayer to the ancestors, he starts by saying "*Nna ha-tanu oji, ihe ayi nacho bu ndu*", (Ancestors eat kola, the good we ask from your hands is *ndu*). These instances, few as they are, help to establish the value of *ndu* to the Ibo. But this *ndu* is not just to exist and be counted at the next census. It is the full dynamic existence in which other things—all the good things of life will come. *Ndu* is not only for individual persons; communities like the lineage, the clan and even the nuclear family have their own spirit existence—their own *ndu*. When the Ibo speak the proverb "*onye di ndu odikwute ihe*" (he who is alive will definitely stumble on properties or good fortune one day!) they seem to give out the philosophy on which all else in their ethical value-making and endeavours to achieve success in life depends. The belief held about *ndu* is that it is "endless", even after it has been terminated by death. Continuation is sought for in the male line of children to succeed the father, so as to keep the family tree growing strong and branching forth into many lineage subdivisions. Hence the importance of children especially males. Women's life is also continued both in the male as well as in the female children. This is one of the major reasons childlessness is regarded as one of the greatest "curses" to a family, hence polygamy in which even wives take the initiative to provide their husbands with a second, third or even fourth wife so as to get children by whom the dead parents' *ndu* is continued. Again ancestor cult, one of the most important of all the Ibo cults, must have arisen from the value attached to *ndu*. Reincarnation is another belief associated with this value, *ndu*. We have indicated in chapter III the part a man's individual *chi* plays in his role as a struggling and achieving member of his community. It is through the moral effort which each person makes to satisfy the value the Ibo society puts on worthwhile existence that one's *chi* is discovered, either as very auspicious or less so. There is great emotional as well as sociological rejection of the type of *ndu* which the Ibo speak of as "*Onye di ndu onwu ka nma*" (the life to which death is far better). This is the kind of life weaklings and idiots may be forced to live—no healthy person would ever permit himself to lead such a life, because he does believe that his *chi* could never lead him to lead such *ndu*, therefore he must labour to achieve. Suffering, poverty and all forms of disability must be combated through good life, hard work and religious duties that ensure walking colsely with one's *chi*, the ancestral spirits and through charms and "medicine", when necessary, keep close to the general life-force of the spirit world. It is in this active participation for *ndu* that Ibo positive moral values manifest themselves. For analytical purposes we will divide such values into two: those that stress life in the community or what one can call principles of social ethics and secondly those that stress individual virtuous life.

Community's social values include: respect for age and its seniority order; acceptance that the community is more important than the individual; justice; social harmony together with order and unity; hospitality; lack of duplicity; honesty; co-operation. Through socialization practices in which a child is brought up, the home, the various levels of extended family and the lineage, through the various age sets and initiation rites, he is taught these social values. Most religious celebrations are meant to strengthen these social values and the memorials of founding ancestors together with duties associated with the various ranks of lineage heads (the *Okpara*) are avenues for indoctrinating members with these values.

A brief discussion of three of these virtues will throw more light on their moral importance to the Ibo: Justice, co-operation and hospitality. Justice: The Ibo religious symbol for justice is *Ọfọ*, which we have already discussed in chapter III. As the embodiment of the spirit of ancestors it is spoken of in Ibo proverbs as the means by which the community is ever reminded that *ndu*, the supreme value, requires justice so as to even this *ndu* out to all members of the community. A popular song in Ibo says *Ejim ogu ejim Ofo, Ofo ka ideyi ji awa ala*—I hold *ogu* [9] in one hand and *Ọfọ* in another, it is through the power of *Ọfọ* that the soft rain water furrows the hard ground. This reminds the community of the power of justice which in its nature is believed to involve transparent honesty, innocence and fair play; the rain like justice may seem weak, but it is capable of leaving its mark on the hard ground. So can a man who observes justice succeed in the difficult job of pursuing *ndu*. An overused proverb among the Ibo is "*Egbe bere, ugo bere, nke si ibe ya ebena, nku akwapu ya*!"—let the kite perch and let the eagle perch, which ever says the other will not perch, let its wings break off! This again emphasizes the

---

[9] *Ogu* is a special stick or bundle of such sticks symbolising one's innocence.

people's concern for the principle of justice. In the living of *ndu* there is enough room for all to "perch" and achieve fully the supreme value. Greed, jealousy, destruction of other people's chances for making success of life and the lack of the spirit of give and take by which the community could live harmoniously and grow are greatly deprecated by the Ibo.[10] Hence the importance of the other virtue, co-operation. The ontological background from which the Ibo see co-operation is the emphasis on the "one blood" that flows in all members of a lineage, a clan, a town and even the human community, although it is easier to see it more clearly as it flows in the members of one unit of the lineage. In chapter II we described Ibo community in terms of *Umunna* "the children of one father" meaning the people in whom the one "blood" of the founder ancestor flows. From this background the virtue of co-operation can be understood. Many names, sayings and proverbs again portray its importance in Ibo language, life and literature. Azubike—back (meaning one with whom to co-operate) is strength; Onyeabo—I have got the second (that is one with whom to co-operate); Ibuadinma—two together ensure the good. Proverbs and sayings include: *Aka iri kwo aka ekpe, aka ekpe akwo aka iri, ha abuo adi ocha*—when the right hand washes the left hand and the left hand washes the right hand, the two will be clean; *Aku na nwanne-ya yi, keduzi ka ha si were ichara gba*—the two palm kernels in one husk are together like brothers; why did they separate themselves with a small shell? It is not the appearance or mere evidence of co-operation

---

[10] Many non Ibos even in Nigeria do not understand the Ibo man's passion for justice and fairplay. The recent civil war in Nigeria was mainly due to Ibo conviction that justice has not been done to them especially in the massacres of 1966, hence the complete despair that pushed them to secession. Prof. J. F. Ade Ajayi in his contribution on "Recent History of Nigeria" in *Africa South of the Sahara*, London: Europa Publications Ltd., third edition 1973, pages 611-612 said that "the eastern leaders were alienated by the killings of May-October 1966 and lured by the vision of the oil revenues" became the first group in Nigeria to carry out the threat of secession. If the allurement of the oil revenue influenced the Ibos who were among the eastern leaders, it was absolutely negligible. The real last straw was the killings by which the Ibo believed that no justice was done to them hence the sacrifice of life and all to secure jusitce through the war, unmindful of the reality of might in modern power politics. This again raises one of the perennial ethical problems: the balance between the claims of justice and the realities of power. But we cannot enter into that discussion in this study.

I am indebted to T. Uzo. Nwala of the Department of Philosophy and Classics at Nsukka for the ideas in his privately circulated paper entitled: *Igbo Traditional Moral Philosophy* with which I have compared information I had collected on the same topics.

that is desired, but rather real unity-inducing and service-rendering co-operation. This is the moral philosophy behind the practice of town or village improvement and clan unions which we had already discussed in chapter V. This is also the background to the endless "relatives" a man with some little substance is expected to maintain. It is a regular feature of Ibo lineage structure for a man to educate up to University level overseas sixth and seventh cousins or ordinary fellow-villagers. Care of the aged: parents, uncles, aunts and others, is undertaken from such moral and philosophical background. The virtue of self denial is developed by such co-operation which involves all the community. The man without money or property can offer willingly his time, labour and skill without any charge because it is expected of everyone to co-operate with whatever resources he has.

One who has spent all his earnings in these days of money income to educate relatives, does not expect any special "thank you" for after all he has done no more than his routine community duty.[11] It is the person who fails to live by this expectation and for whom the social values of the community in spreading *ndu* to others mean nothing that earns for himself a bad name. Such persons (and they were few in traditional society and there are still few today, although they are steadily increasing in the wake of social change facing the Ibo) could be shunned, and their children after their death exposed to difficulties, which of course they can overcome by not behaving like their fathers.

Hospitality is another of the three virtues of Ibo social life which we wish to discuss. The philosophical idea of it relates to the common blood flowing in humanity. The main emphasis is hospitality to those without kinship units in the area they find themselves for the time being, although hospitality to fellow clansmen is also stressed. Sayings like "*Onye ije neje odika onwero be*"—a traveller in a strange land is like one who had never owned a home, indicate the appropriate response expected of an Iboman to such a person—make him share in the comfort of one's home. "*Obia ije amaro ebe ala ruru*"—a traveller does not know where an abomination has happened on the land, therefore treat him with generous and tolerant attitude. When an Ibo has undergone some travelling where he had received hospitality from his host communities, he is likely to name his next child *Uzoamaka*—the road through which I have passed had been made good. This is his

11 The quick spread of education in Iboland through building of secondary schools by communities, as well as the award of scholarships which we mentioned in chapter IV, is due to this sense of co-operation.

way of appreciating the virtue of hospitality extended to him. The importance of the kolanut ceremony among the Ibo is an index of the significance of this virtue.[12] Except in times of war, strangers from any part of the world are protected; to kill them is a sacrilege. There is something like the Abraham concept in the Old Testament where by entertaining strangers one might unknowingly entertain angels who would later give him some blessings.[13]

This discussion on only three out of the eight "virtues" we have identified, is enough to suggest the general trend of the Ibo social morality's philosophical background, as well as the application of their social ethical values. As these have been practised in Iboland, much room exists for criticism to show how a very good system built upon pure intention can in practice degenerate into something less virtuous. In emphasizing justice people can become intolerant and impatient, although if co-operation is equally internalized and applied, it does reduce intolerance and increase patience. It is in co-operation that we detect so much room for the vice of one's virtue. Primarily co-operation is with the unit in whom the "closest blood" of relationship flows, for example uncles, aunts, cousins and fellow-townsmen. Furthermore the ease with which relatives expect such endless amount of aid, reduces the chances of building up capital for modern businesses which might be necessary for greater development and more employment facilities for a lot more people. Nepotism and bribery can be encouraged especially where people in charge of employment feel that to help someone outside the blood-community, is a special favour for which one pays in bribes and gifts. We voice these criticisms as part of the basis of discussion when we come to compare Ibo morality with Christian ethics. To point to these criticisms however is not to suggest that it is only in Ibo morality that practice falls short of the philosophical ideal. It could also be identified in other moral systems including the Christian. Taking notice of them however places Ibo morality in more proper perspective. We will now discuss values that for the Ibo emphasize more the personal or individual virtues.

The emphasis of the social values which we have just discussed is

---

[12] The Kolanut Ceremony is an elaborate introductory covenant-enactment between a host and his guests when kolanuts, ordinary edible fruit having cotyledons, are served, broken with prayers by the eldest person serving as a priest, and eaten as a sacrament shared among all present. See V. Uchendu, "Kola Hospitality and Igbo Lineage Structure", *MAN* 49 (March/April 1944) pp. 47-50.

[13] See Genesis, chapter 18, verses 1-15.

more on norms of ethical realities, that is, virtues in themselves. The individual virtues which we are going to enumerate and discuss now, are mainly qualities of individual life acquired through training and socialization in the social values of the community. They relate partly to personal endowments by one's *chi* or *Chi-ukwu* (the Oversoul) and partly to what one, in the pursuit of the supreme value *ndu,* finds necessary as "tools" of success. The "virtues" are: bravery; wit (what the Ibo call *ako* or *ako n'uche*) which includes intelligence, oratory, wisdom, common sense and the subtle carriage of one's personality so as to be able to dine with kings and at the same time walk with the common people, the *hoi polloi* and still keep one's balance; strength of character made up of truth, honesty, humility and patience. The summary given in these three blocks of virtues gives the picture of the Ibo gentleman. Salutation names and *Ọzọ* title names, which we have already referred to in various chapters, portray the community's respect for these personal virtues. A good wrestler could be given the salutation name *Ogbaji,* meaning one that bends even iron, by which his bravery, courage and skill in wrestling are recognised. We met at Ihiala a young lady popularly called *Ogene*; *Ogene* is the Ibo musical instrument cast of light iron in a conical shape with a hole which gives melodious but far reaching sound. This was a salutation name given to this young lady by the village for her great singing ability. The moral advantage of such names is the impetus they give to people to try and discover what gifts and abilities they latently have by which *ndu* can be enriched.

Proverbs and sayings that indicate the importance of these virtues include the following: "*Ako bu ije*"—wit and circumspection are the tools for walking, that is, taking any steps in life; *Di na nwunye di nizu ofu ibe ji ezuelu ha ugani*—When husband and wife are in patient accord, a slice of yam can last them the four months of scarcity (April, May, June, July); *Nwata elugh ogo juba ihe mere nnaya, ihe mere nna ya eme ya*—The child who does not wait to grow old enough before enquiring into the cause of his father's disappearance (possibly death by some underhand action of some malicious person) the fate that befell his father will be his also, meaning that patience and proper calculation before action are virtues to be inculcated; *Inagba oso aracha npisi-aka igekobe ya nenu uko*—Why lick the fingers so hurriedly, are you going to hang them up on the rafters? The moral this proverb teaches is that in the affairs of *ndu,* the supreme good, you have all life time to accomplish what can be accomplished, so make haste slowly, for "when an old woman has fallen down in two consecutive times, the whole contents of her headbasket can be counted by onlookers".

The general use into which virtues within this category are employed, is the achievement race in which the supreme value *ndu* places average Iboman. Not to possess them in good measure reduces a man's chances of *ndu*, they are the means of virtuous life by which the ancestors continue their life in the life and achievements of their offspring, and by which the community knows itself to share in the harmony that must always exist between the people, nature and the spirit world. Sacrifice, the use of "medicine" and the installation of personal deities like the ram headed Ikenga (a young man's individual god of achievement) are some of the avenues through which a young man ensures his possession of such virtues. When he has grown older and has been initiated into the *Ọzọ* title he uses his bravery, his wit, his strength of character to ensure that the moral code, the good life and the well being of the community are upheld. Ibo society rewards its sons and daughters (although more so the sons) with a good deal of status symbols for virtuous living.

When one looks at Ibo morality in its overall picture especially as it has come to confront Christian ethics and modern technical culture with its value orientation it becomes clear what its weaknesses and strengths are. We will spotlight these in detail when comparing all the three ethical systems—Christian, Modernization and Ibo Traditional. No one discussing Ibo traditional morality can forget the educative influence of fables, riddles and folktales, the principal actor in the tales being Tortoise. In the truly traditional informal education, boys and girls sit round some young men or women as well as some elderly persons to hear the fables, riddles and folktales and learn the morals from them. When Tortoise says to the Ibo: "anyone going to adjudicate between two persons must have in his pocket 'if it were myself' ", the biblical injunction "do unto others as you would be done to by them" rings a familiar note. But all of such children's time must not be taken up in hearing fables and riddles and folktales because one of their riddles has already given them a moral lesson to that effect: "Give me up and down"? "up and down" means that the bush rat climbed up the anthill and quickly climbed down saying that if his parents had been alive, that play of running up and down, would have been all he would be doing. Unfortunately his parents had disappeared and so he must do other important things like finding his food rather than running up and down the anthill! And so the children learn the need to employ their time in useful pursuits.

In conclusion we can summarise the characteristics of Ibo morality as follows:

(1) It has a code that is religiously oriented and like all such moral codes it developed a casuistry that accommodates some harsh and barbarous applications and sanctions.

(2) It is a utilitarian morality that aims at the preservation of the community and the encouragement of the emergence of "successful" gentlemen with personal moral qualities, to whom *ndu* is of great value.

(3) Because it provides a way of life that aims at achievement and success, it is elastic and can admit of the new through the quality of the life of the members of the community even when the traditional social structures remain less malleable.

(4) The principle of norm acceptance is authority and social order maintenance orientation rather than individual conscience or principled orientation.[14]

(5) It is not "other-worldly" type of ethics nor fatalistic, but an element of the unknowable intrusion of some life chance and spirits, including the ancestral spirit, emphasizes the need for man, while being as moral and virtuous as he could, to exercise faith and walk closely towards the spirit world by obedience to the demands of his religious practices.

(6) Sin is not therefore seen directly and primarily as rebellion against the Deity or deities, but more often as departure from the norm, the prescribed "laws" or falling foul of *omenani,* over which the earth goddess presides who is thereby indirectly rebelled against. Sacrificial atonement or removal of *aru* (pollution) restores the "sinner" (more often the offender) to a state of "grace".

(7) Personal responsibility through guilt, conviction and conscience is present especially through the values by which the individual aims to succeed, although what the community as a group emphasizes is societal values enforced through shame, conformity and codes.

---

[14] Lawrence Kohlberg in a Ph.D. Thesis entitled "The Development of Modes of Moral Thinking and Choice in the years Ten to Sixteen", University of Chicago, 1958 developed the theory of six stages of cognitive moral development in which "authority and social order maintenance orientation" and "conscience or principled orientation" are stages 4 and 6 respectively. We shall make further use of this model. See also J. J. Bacmeyer's "Ethics and the Psychology of Moral Judgment" in *ZYGON* no. 2, July 1973, pp. 82-95 on the same theme.

Christian Ethics

Christian ethics, generally speaking grew out of the Bible both as a guide for individual life, as well as for living as a believer in Christ, in the fellowship of the Church and of the community in the world. In the course of the history of the Church various doctrinal interpretations were developed from the summarised ethical teaching of our Lord namely love of God and love of neighbour [15] and also from the decalogue and other emphases of the Old Testament as well as from Saint Paul and other teachings of the New Testament. In the pre-reformation Church obedience to the Church, its teachings deduced from the Gospel and Natural Law as well as obedience to Church leaders were emphasized as the major ethical concerns. In the Reformation Churches the emphases were on repentance and faith in the Saviour through whom one could lead the regenerated life of the redeemed, pious and accountable to God whom one was free to approach directly in covenant relationship uninhibited by priests and prelates (as all believers have been constituted into a priesthood). Now there are so many approaches, emphases and slants on Christian ethics, either personal or social, that it is very difficult to speak precisely on what Christian ethics is. There is a debate going on as to what is the most effective way of expressing and practicing Christian ethics: should it be in a contextual setting (Paul Lehmann) or in a situation (Joseph Fletcher) or simply by being honest to God (J. A. T. Robinson) even to the extent of expressing Christianity and its demands of love in a religionless frame-work (Dietrich Bonhoeffer), always being conscious of the neighbour's needs in an agapist attitutde (Paul Ramsey) or being directly obedient to Christ as Creator and Redeemer (Karl Barth) or simply obeying the Gospel (Bultmann) and at the same time recognizing God's various "Orders of Creation" (Emil Brunner). [16]

---

[15] St. Mark's Gospel 12 verses 29-31.

[16] The literature of this debate is enormous. Attention can be drawn to a few.
Paul Lehmann, Ethics in a Christian Context, New York: Harpert Row 1963.
Joseph Fletcher, Situation Ethics: The New Morality, London: S.C.M. Press, 1966.
J. A. T. Robinson, Honest to God, London: S.C.M. Press, 1963.
——, Christian Morals Today, London: S.C.M. Press, 1964.
Dietrich Bonhoeffer, Ethics, translated Neville Horton Smith, London: S.C.M. Press, 1955.
——, Letters and Papers from Prison, translated, Reginald Fuller, New York: MacMillan, 1962.
Paul Ramsey, Basic Christian Ethics, New York: Charles Scribner's Sons, 1950.

Additional "insight" comes from the ecumenical thinking of the World Council of Churches and Vatican II. (There is also a new general trend in the Roman Catholic Church seeking to re-interpret Natural-Law to make it more responsive to the realities of today). [17]

The additional ethical insight of the World Council and the Vatican referred to, is the emphasis on the nature of man and his existence in the world of created nature, about which more and more is known through science-natural, physical and social. This twentieth century man has been described by John Macquarrie in five characteristics: he is a man or a being on the move, changing and becoming; he is an embodied man, right in the world or in the popular phrase of the existentialists "a-being-in-the-world" partaking of its nature (although self transcendent through self consciousness) but he lives without reference to otherworldly spirituality unless he happens to be also a convinced Christian; thirdly he is a social man sharing existence with other beings, influencing them as well as being influenced by them; fourthly he is an agent who acts and gets things done, *homo faber*, changing the world and being "perfected" in the world by the interplay of the realities and opportunities of his being a "creator"; and finally the "new man" is a man "come of age" who accepts responsibility for this world in which he lives; his "tomorrow", his comfort and his well being are all his responsibility and not that of some forces outside of himself. [18] This "new man" finds all existing ethical thinking unhelpful and seeks some other moral guide. [19] This situation therefore makes the analysis of Christian ethics more complicated, for there seems to be no body of consistent teaching that can now be spoken of

---

Karl Barth, Community State and Church: Three Essays, New York: Doubleday Anchor, 1960; Dogmatics, Vol. 3, Section 4.

Emil Brunner, The Divine Imperative, London: Lutterworth Press, 1937.

[17] Emphasis is on charity rather than law, conscience rather than authority of the Church. Barnard Häring is one of the leaders of this new Roman Catholic approach. See his "The Law of Christ" in 3 vols., Westminster, Maryland: Newman Press, 1963-66. (The English Trans.)

[18] John Macquarrie, Three Issues in Ethics, New York: Harper and Row, 1970, pp. 46-81. For World Council of Churches thinking on the "new man" in his new experience and understanding of nature and history, see New Directions in Faith and Order, Bristol 1967, Geneva: W.C.C. 1968, pages 1-31. For the Vatican see Gaudium et Spes, Constitution on the Church in Modern World, Vatican II, Rome, 1966.

[19] Harold Hatt in his "Cybernetics and the Image of Man", Nashville: Abingdon Press, 1968, says: "Guides for the conduct of life in the horse-and-buggy age are not adequate in the age of high-horsepower cars and space vehicles", *op. cit.*, p. 95.

as the authentic Christian ethics. We will however analyse what was understood as the Christian ethics with which missionaries presented the Gospel to the Ibo; and knowing that that ethic is not quite relevant today unless re-interpreted, as Iboland is part of the "new man" faced with the problems and realities of life today, we will at the end suggest the more relevant Christian ethics with which to hold dialogue with Ibo traditional morality and the urban ethics of modernization.

The theological background to the Protestant Christian ethics of the early missionaries in Iboland as well as the later ones is biblical. God is holy and righteous, he has given man the commandments especially the ten commandments through Moses and its meanings as of "love to God and to our neighbours" (or fellowmen) through Christ. This God who has redeemed man through Christ, has entered into covenant relation of love with him and has given him the power of The Holy Spirit to respond to this covenant relationship, through dutiful obedience to his righteous will. It is this Holy Spirit who therefore gives the believer grace, and enables him to have reconciliation with God through faith, and so live the good and moral life. In practice this good life is expressed as avoidance of stealing, not committing adultery, not showing manifest envy or malice to others, not showing interest or participation in things or practices or ceremonies associated with idols but rather showing active membership of the Church by observing its rules and regulations. Positive virtues like charity should be shown by one's contribution to Church dues, visiting those who mourn and those in hospitals. Another ethical influence taught to the converts comes from the beatitudes, where the picture of the Christian gentleman is drawn as one that lives peaceably with others, and in addition makes peace between contending factions and groups or individuals; lowly of heart and therefore not covetuous or overambitious; thirsting after righteousness and so being otherworldly and pure in heart. If need be he accepts persecution from his heathen neighbours hoping to be rewarded in heaven (although sometimes the things for which he would be persecuted resulted from indiscretion on his part); he is merciful and helps those in need. Sanctions are imposed for breach of any of the rules. Adultery which is easily recognised in a man taking another wife or wives than the first one he had already "married in church", is "punished" by excommunication from communicant-membership of the church. Stealing does not seem to earn sanction other than the one meted by society through the community punishment-structures (we have already discussed the traditional forms above in this chapter. With the modernization arrangements prisons serve for the punishment of court-convicted thieves). Earlier in the history of the Church in Iboland, the Roman Catholic Church imposed various forms of penance on "notorious evil-livers". Such evil-living was determined from the prescriptions of the Parish Priests expressing the well known views of their Superior and the teachings of the Church in general. Penance had been inflicted for such harmless "sin" as fraternising with members of the Anglican Church![20]

By way of a general comment on the manner in which Christian ethics works out in the practical life of the Christians in Iboland, we wish to call attention to what was said in chapter IV about the moral attitude of some missionaries and some nominal Christian traders from Europe and Britain living at Onitsha and other areas. In general, the pietistic Evangelical moralistic approach to life, was adopted and in most sermons vivid pictures of the tortures of hell and the joys of paradise were given. There was no attempt made to interpret ethical principles in terms of the Ibo social life situation. Rather the general belief among Evangelicals of the Victorian era and later, that the sum total of the good moral life of the redeemed (who in their fear of hell will abjure evil) will produce a just society, was evident. Furthermore the cultural and racial differences that tended to divide the missionaries away from the local congregations (see discussion on this in chapter IV) made it difficult for clear community-oriented Christian ethics to appear clearly in such local congregations.[21]

Old Testament ethics with its emphasis on "the people of the covenant" which could have easily agreed with Ibo traditional morality, at least in its communal framework, could not have been systematically integrated into the Christian ethics taught by missionaries who had been brought up in the "individualistic salvation-ethic" of Protestan-

---

20 The reconstruction of ethical teachings and practices of the Churches in Iboland given in this paragraph is a result of the writer's participant observation. I have lived through some of it in hearing sermons and bible class teaching, and have seen the one given penance for fraternising with non-Roman Christians in a village I lived as a boy.

21 Elizabeth Isichei in an article entitled "Seven Varieties of Ambiguity: Some Patterns of Igbo Response to Christian Missions" in *Journal of Religion in Africa*, Vol. III fasc. 3, 1970, p. 211, speaks of the severity of the policy of missionaries towards Ibo converts which formed a central theme in their correspondences in the archives of the Holy Ghost Fathers in Paris and the Society of African Missions in Rome which indicates lack of cordiality between converts and missionaries.

tism; nor was the Natural-law universalism of Roman Catholicism, interpreted through authoritarian dogma, in a position to help the Ibo convert better. Christian ethics in Iboland therefore became simply a system of some moralistic rigid code centred on excommunication from Holy Communion for the offence of polygamy (and sometimes for taking the *Ọzọ title*) and castigation for the minor offence of not fulfilling Christian duty of paying Church dues and levies. Refusal to accord Christian burial to a late offender is sometimes used as a sanction for these offences. The theological dynamics for Christian ethical reflection through insightful understanding of the nature of man, his place in society especially the traditional Ibo society, the responsibility of duty, and the deep agonising examination of motives before deciding on an issue, together with the devastating reality of sin as rebellion to man's true nature as revealed in Christ, the One True Man, could not, therefore be developed in that kind of moral teaching and practice.

When we look at the ethical responses of the Ibo to Christian ethics, we realise the difficulties of reaching deep down into the personal moral reflections (if any) of the early Ibo converts. The records of the missionaries do not discuss Ibo converts' moral attitudes and responses to Christianity and its moral demands. Lapsing into traditional ways of life especially into polygamy was the big worry of missionaries, as we had noted in the case of Taylor's remarks about Okosi's relapse into polygamy (see chapter IV, page 73). Bishop Shanahan, one of the great Roman Catholic missionaries at Onitsha was reported as telling his supporters in Europe that it would take six generations to produce a genuine Ibo Christian: "After some half dozen generations, our neophytes will have developed a truly Christian character. By that time the taint of paganism will have left their soul". [22] Around Ihiala area it was reported that the Anglican clergymen, some Ibo but under British missionary supervisors, demanded very high standard of moral life from their catechumenites before baptism, to the extent that many left that Church to get easier baptism in another Church. [23] Early converts, from oral information collected, tended towards living highly disciplined Christian life. There was in a village we lived as boys a convert known, even by the District Com-

---

[22] Annals of the Propagation of the Faith, 1919 quoted by Elizabeth Isichei, *op. cit.*, p. 219.

[23] Information given the writer by Venerable Archdeacon B. N. C. Nwosu, a retired, senior clergyman of over 70 years, himself an Anglican.

missioner in the Colonial Administration, as "Mr. Eziokwu" literally it means "one known for speaking the truth". The case of chief Idigo of Aguleri was widely reported in the Roman Catholic Missionary literature: a dibia (diviner-priest) and head of a fairly large village group and a member of the highest *Ọzọ* title of his place became converted, dismissed all his many wives but one, "and lived a life of extraordinary fervour until his death".[24] It was among the second generation Christians that a good deal of ambivalence to Christian ethics and moral life started appearing. The western money and market economy had appeared, and many of these second generation Christians in their eagerness to acquire as much wealth, power and influence as possible (which the new technological facilities brought along) tended to neglect the moral demands of Christianity. Converts into Christianity from the end of the nineteenth and early in this century had their inner struggles in adapting themselves to the more abstract and theological demands of the new teachings, but did not seem to have difficulties with its ethical demands. Already Ibo traditional morality demanded the virtues of truthfulness, peaceful co-existence, hospitality and the avoidance of sex laxity. Adultery as such was frowned upon as strongly as stealing, and in pre-Christian traditional Ibo society those with one wife were expected to confine their sexual demands to their one wife except in areas where the institution of concubinage existed.[25] These converts therefore found greater ease (due to their conversion, zeal and faith) and joy in transferring the traditional Ibo image of a "gentleman" into the Christian "gentleman", the difference between them "physically" (that is, in their outward visible structuring in a concrete, social group) being very little. The fear of the punishment from the earth goddess, and from the strictures of the community, which they had developed in their traditional moral upbringing, was easily transferred by the converts into the fear of the punishment in hell fire as well as fear of strictures from the missionary, the Church Community (which was more closely bound together then than now) and of excommunication from such Church Community.[26] Excommunication which was often employed by the Church

[24] Father Lutz, "Les Agouleris", Holy Ghost Fathre's Archives, Paris 191/A/1, 3. Quoted by Isichei in "Ibo and Christian Belief" *African Affairs*, Vol. 68, no. 271, April 1969, p. 131.

[25] See Victor C. Uchendu, "Concubinage Among Ngwa Igbo of Southern Nigeria" in *Africa*, Vol. XXXV, No. 2, April 1965, pp. 187-197.

[26] Information collected from the venerable B. N. C. Nwosu. The worry of early pioneers in Christian education in Iboland, of which venerable B. Nwosu

was dreaded as strongly as leprosy by the converts; both meant exclusion from one's intimate reference groups of communal life, which the Ibo value greatly. It can be argued that such "fear" does not suggest real conversion-moral life of grace and of the freedom of sonship before "our Father who art in heaven". This of course raises the bigger issue of how moral is man without the social demands made on him by the groups he belongs to. We cannot, of course, enter into the discussion of this in our present study, as it properly belongs to moral philosophy in its boundary with theology and sociology. Nevertheless the practical organisational means of "making" Christians moral in the early Church life in Iboland did not differ much from what obtained in the traditional society. It is with the gradual decay of the moral code of that society, and the advent of western technical culture, that the second generation Christians found themselves without any moral models, along which to build their ethical life. The Christian ethical teachings have not crystalized into adoptable models for a people torn apart by three competing values—Ibo traditional, Christian and technological values. To say this does not mean, of course, that there were not in Iboland the few devout Christians living the moral life of faith in Christ through the power of the Spirit.

We will now attempt an analysis of what we consider more helpful patterns of Christian ethics for Iboland. The key notes of this pattern of Christian ethics are mainly three: the need to relate Christian morals to non-Christian morals in a world that is no longer a Christendom, and also because we believe in some form of continuity between Christian morals and what can be called "the general moral striving of mankind".[27] Secondly there is the need to recognise that an appropriate starting point for the exposition of Christian ethics is an investigation into the nature of man—a consideration of the meaning of humanity as well as the common factors making up that humanity. Thirdly there is the need to appreciate the place of faith in moral life, "the problem known traditionally as that of the relation of religion and morality".[28]

The methodological procedure we will adopt in presenting this ethical

---

is one, is about the seeming absence of any sense of direction in the value concepts of many educated Ibo young men who had grown up through the church schools.

[27] The phrase is from John Macquarrie, to whom I am indebted for the clarification of my thinking in this section. See his: Three Issues in Ethics, New York: Harper, 1970, p. 15.

[28] Macquarrie, *op. cit.*, p. 21.

pattern is as follows: a start is made into ethical reflection by analysing the nature of man, especially the self image the twentieth century man has of himself. This is characterised in the five "images" which we have mentioned already (page 139). From this we move on to the understanding of the world in which man lives especially nature and its general law [29] and ordered sequence as it applies to the "general moral striving of mankind". This general law found in nature becomes basic to the understanding of the general action of man and some of the general principles of his behaviour, his desires, capabilities and tendencies irrespective of his religious faith. From this stage we move on to investigate further why man is unable to decide *always* in the appropriate moral manner that accords with the normal growth towards the fulfilment of his true nature, and we find that the reason is in the fact of sin, (no matter how sin is conceived of—as rebellion or as pollution). However, the existence of common grace (which Macquarrie defines as that element of the good in God's creation which was tarnished by the Fall but not completely obliterated by it by which man still recognises "the good" even when he cannot fully approximate it by his unaided effort) makes ethical living possible. This "grace" common to all mankind is what Macquarrie regards as the giftlike "possession" of man (the proof of "original righteousness" matching the theological concept of "original sin"). This is prior to particular experiences of grace within a community or a religious faith, the Christian special grace through the Holy Spirit, for example. Here the special influence of the Christian's ethical potentiality through his faith in the risen Christ, who works in him through the Holy Spirit, is to be recognised after taking note that all mankind, Christian as well as non-Christian, shares in a moral potentiality through this "common grace" of their humanity. The final stage in the methodological procedure of this pattern of ethic is to indicate the relationship between religion and morals. Christians and non-Christians alike have one form of religion or another and, if there is in such religion a belief in ultimate reality that has brought forth human life, it becomes the common basis or context of meaning and value prior to the meaning

---

29 We have refrained from using the term "Natural Law" because of the very wide theological and moral construction put on that concept especially in Roman Catholic Moral Theology. Part of what the "Natural Law" concept is trying to say, that is the common humanity of man, is included in what we prefer to call "the general law found in nature" to indicate precisely that man's understanding of himself and of the very world around him is a common ground for the different ethical traditions found in various cultures.

and values that we humans create in our ethical activities. All Ibos, Christian as well as non-Christian can be educated in this pattern of ethics. To the Christian of course there is something additional, namely that his religion starts with faith in God's creation (Lutheran moral theology connects the concept of natural law with the order of creation) [30] and passes through faith in the risen Christ as the initiator of the "new creation", making it possible for him to believe in the meaningfulness of life. The Christian strives in transforming his life and its social setting through self-giving devotion which is love. We see in this procedure how finally the links between the Christian's religion and morality appear in the activities of faith, hope and love, in other words, in the theological insight from the biblical themes. [31]

The features of this pattern of ethic useful for our study are three: the avoidance of strict lines of separation between Christian and Ibo traditional morality by starting our ethical reflection from the nature of man as man, especially the self image the modern man has of himself and not from dividing him into pagan, Christian and secular. Secondly from this first step we move on to an understanding of the world and nature from which the materials for moral decision-making are drawn and in which faith, hope and love as moral activities are executed. [32] This again is common to all mankind including the Ibo. Thirdly we can, by showing the relationship between morality and religion through faith (which means "acceptance of and commitment to Being or however we may name the ultimate reality that has brought forth human life" [33]) indicate how the Ibo man, even in his traditional religious background, or caught up in the modern-urban technological way of life, can accept morality that is Christian in orientation. This becomes possible because he, the non-Christian, has been taken along some of the way, through our common humanity, and our sharing of existence in this common world, in which all struggle alike to live meaningful life, which means a life of moral virtue and harmony among peoples.

The advantage of this model of Christian ethics (which we hope to develop and expand) especially for the African background of Iboland, is that in addition to providing us with a clear theoretical (as well as

[30] See Regin Prenter, Creation and Redemption, translated by Theodore I. Jensen, as quoted by J. Macquarrie, *op. cit.*, p. 136.

[31] Macquarrie, *op. cit.*, pp. 120-122, 131-135.

[32] Compare the new emphasis of the World Council of Churches in Faith and Order Studies on Nature in New Direction in Faith and Order, Bristol 1967, published by W.C.C., Geneva, 1968 especially pp. 7-31.

[33] Macquarrie, *op. cit.*, p. 135.

theological) frame work, it gives more manageable empirical basis in the realities of anthropology from which to start our new ethical reflection. In an era when many Christian writers are trying to interpret Christology anthropologically [34] and the scientific study of human experience has become the more acceptable means of acquiring authentic knowledge, this procedure is bound to be generally more satisfactory. Its opposite procedure of starting Christian ethics from what is distinctively Christian, from which the experience of the majority of mankind is excluded, because they are non-Christians, is bound to be less satisfying. Reference to authority whether human or supernatural as the proof of authentic knowledge especially in ethical matters, is no longer attractive; and if moral responsibility must proceed from knowledge of the nature and the demands of the ethical norm, this empirical introduction into ethical reflection affords us great advantage. Furthermore in an age of plurality of religions, plurality of experiences built on varying philosophical, ideological and cultural backgrounds, any possible common approach to the moral life of a total community made up of Christians and-non-Christians (like common humanity or common sharing of existence in this world) is highly commendable. Another advantage our study gains from this model of ethics, is that despite its anthropological and ecological dimensions, it is rooted in the biblical insight of the meaning of religion as faith and of man's involvement in the moral decisions of life as hope and love. If the demands of ethics include the inclination to attain the good (the *summum bonum*) by the emphasis upon "the ought", in the avoidance of the "ought not" (duty), and in knowing and internalising whatever moral power is necessary to attain such end and to accomplish life's duty, [35] (which is virtue) the discussion of the relationship of religion and morality becomes inevitably a

---

[34] Karl Rahner who in his book has argued that, from one point of view Christology can be considered as a kind of transcendent anthropology. See Karl Rahner, Theological Investigations, Vol. I, translated by Cornelis Ernst, O.P., London: Darton, Longman & Todd, 1961, p. 184. David Jenkins, The glory of Man, London: S.C.M. Press, 1967, where he interprets Christ as the "glory of man". Neither of these two writers would wish to reduce Theology or even Christology to Anthropology but only to indicate that Christ's Godhead can be best understood in terms of his being the one who precisely by being man in the fullest sense (which we can never attain) is God's existence into the world (see Macquarrie, *op. cit.*, p. 86).

[35] See article "Ethics and Morality (Christian)" in James Hastings (ed.), *Encyclopaedia of Religion and Ethics*, by Donald Mackenzie, Edinburgh: T. T. Clark, 1912, Vol. 5, pp. 468-474.

theological discussion, especially in this model of ethics. Someone may raise the objection that this ethical model which starts with the nature of man, will not have much theological roots because the self image man has of himself changes so often. Such changes, the argument contends, will keep on altering the theological construct put on the nature of man, and of the world in which he lives, which in turn reduces the value of such theology. This is the kind of conclusion made from a wrong premise that theology must remain an "unchanging doctrine". Vital theology, as the reflection upon the world, man and his activities through the Word of God, is at its best when it becomes living theology by being relevant to the age and time and the men living in them. Theology therefore must change from epoch to epoch and even from place and time to place and time. The facts of God's activities in creation and redemption through Christ, and in the sanctification of man through the Holy Spirit, do not change, but their interpretation and their application to man's situation do change.[36]

Some Comparative Examination of Christian Ethics and Ibo Traditional Morality

This comparative study will be done in two parts: in the first part Ibo morality is compared with Christian ethics as it now manifests itself in Iboland and secondly Ibo morality is compared with Christian ethics as reconstructed in this study. Ibo morality has been a code with which people have lived in practical activities of daily life. From that point of view, it has been a pragmatic reality existing operatively and not an ideal overlaid with philosophical systematization. Christian ethics in its ideal form either from the Bible or from the teachings of Church Fathers, theologians or philosophers, or even from the reconstruction we have modelled from Professor Macquarrie, is in the realm of the ideal, existing mainly as a theological construct, and there will always be the problem of comparing two things on two different levels of "existence". Practised Christian ethics in Iboland and practised Ibo morality, as we have already indicated, have common features. Both have operated as codes with sanctions which would include deprivation of fellowship with one's respective reference group of Church and/or community. Despite the emphasis of the New Testament, especially on

---

36 See Humanism and Christianity (Concilium) Claude Geffre (ed.), New York: Herder and Herder, 1973, p. 10, where the task of theologians is defined as "to restate in the present situation what Christianity has inherited from revelation".

the inwardness of a Christian man's moral behaviour, Christian moral life in Iboland seems to share with Ibo traditional morality in making moral life depend on social pressure from the group life. The problem of institutionalizing the Church and providing it with structures of administrative machinery, had turned the Church in Iboland into a law making body, with chains of command along the line who sometimes require to be obeyed, thereby constituting themselves unknowingly into lawgivers. [37] The circumstances of missionary work and the organizational necessities of the Church, turned some of the early missionaries into setters of standards which must be obeyed, thereby turning themselves into the equivalents of *Ọzọ* titled elders and *Nwadibias* (the diviner medicine man) of Ibo traditional society. After these few general remarks we can still indicate a few areas where Ibo traditional morality differs from Christian Ethics as practised in Iboland.

In its value orientation Ibo morality did not give much consideration to the worth of the individual person, hence the existence of *Osu* (the slaves of divinities), destruction of twins, and the burying of important personalities with slaves or other captives. Christianity in Iboland showed the value of the human person and helped in abolishing these practices from the Ibo way of life. In the quality of family and home life, the practice of monogamy by Christians theoretically was believed to have the quality or improving the place of womanhood in the society. In the experience of the writer and from data collected during research related to this study, liberal school education has definitely given greater personal confidence to both men and women, thereby enabling Christian mothers (who got more formal education than their counterparts in the traditional society) to help their children better than non Christian mothers. That the quality of home and family life was better in Christian than in non-Christian homes, resulting from the latter's practice of monogamy, was not supported by the data at our disposal. Christian ethics however, together with

---

[37] Karl Barth had warned that Christian ethics is not the following of a guide or the obeying of authorities, but obeying to the command of God which is not a code, but rather a day to day waiting and confronting life with what God shows us to do as mirrored in the life of Christ. See his Dogmatics III/4. Trimingham laments that Christian values are not being expressed in West-African Christian Communities, for such values are not integrated in African lives because Christianity is not related to African ways. See J. S. Trimingham, The Christian Church and Islam in West-Africa, I.M.C. Research Pamphlets No. 3, London: S.C.M. Press, 1956, p. 36.

technological, secular and modernistic influences, has started to induce more queries in the minds of the Ibo non-Christians as well as Christians about the proper meaning of love and sexuality between man and woman who are husband and wife. Compared with the ideal Christian ethics, as we shall indicate later in a further discussion, the Ibo norm in this regard is cold and almost unimpressive. In the moral attitude to unavoidable suffering the Christians accept this with greater relaxation than the non-Christian, the former with some measure of resignation heaps it on "the will of God" while the latter, being greatly perturbed as to the cause of his troubles, would run round many diviners to find out the cause and the remedy without any rest of mind, the kind the Christian finds in the faith he has in God through Christ. (It is true though, that some Christians would go to diviners like their non-Christian fellow villager.) We will discuss this further because the problem of suffering to the Ibo is far reaching in his value concepts.

We now come to the comparative analysis of Ibo traditional morality and ideal Christian ethics.[38] The word "ideal" suggests of course that such Christian ethics is not yet a practical reality in Iboland. Part of the concern of this study, is to indicate possible ways of such ethics becoming real, practiced and made part of the social as well as the individual life of the people, by creating more natural relationship between the African way of life and the Christian Gospel in Iboland. We will use six topics in conducting this comparison, namely: concept of various freedoms in personal and group relationships; meaning of love and sexuality; the acceptance of unavoidable suffering; law and grace; sharing of material resources and power; the will of God.

(1) *Freedoms and reciprocal relations of individuals and groups*

When we speak of "various freedoms" in this context, we mean that element in the self-conscious and self-transcendent nature of man which exhibits itself in the various activities of man in which he exercises choice. Choice within alternative courses of action, ability to distinguish the "good" from the "bad" aspects of daily existence, are all necessary in the exercise of any form of freedom. In Christian ethics as well as in Ibo traditional morality, choice or freedom of action, is controlled by the moral values approved by the societies;

---

[38] We have already indicated the theological reconstruction of such "ideal" or adequate Christian ethics in this chapter and will develop it in Chapter VIII.

so that freedom as choice is not absolute but rather it is controlled by many factors such as time, place, conscience and religious beliefs.[39] In Ibo traditional society, as we had already indicated, the demands of the community curtailed the freedom within which an individual could act. Customary usages, demands of the gods, spiritual forces and the fear they generated, provided narrow confines within which one could choose. For example a freeborn young man was not allowed to marry a girl from an *Osu* family; different kinds of taboos and ritual avoidances prescribed the animals to be eaten and indicated what places a man might or might not visit especially if he were an *Ọzọ* title holder. On the level of interpersonal relationship the group identity was more easily taken into consideration than the relative worth of the individual as a person, thereby restricting freedom of relationship that could have been developed between two persons. A simple illustration might help to clarify this. In a village where we did some interviews, a young man admitted that owing to the land dispute between his own lineage and another lineage living close by, he had not been able to visit some friends of his in that other lineage. If he did visit, his own lineage people could punish him as he would be suspected of being an "informant" to their "enemies". To this kind of situation the Christian ethics of freedom in a man's personal relationship with God, who is also the Father of all mankind, if properly internalised in the young man referred to above, who incidentally was a Christian, could speak very meaningfully. Litigations, if absolutely necessary for establishing right ownership, ought not to impair personal human relationship. Although one of the essential values of Ibo religion as well as of all African traditional religions is the integral union of personality and community. Yet the too close identification of the individual person with the community, to the extent that could destroy the individual's freedom of decision-making, and the maintenance of personal relationships, must be challenged with the broader view of Christian ethics. Freedom also implies clear understanding of what obligation means in an individual's life, through the personal sense of responsibility, rather than in the fear of punishment whether divine or human. Ideal Christian ethics emphasizes this kind of inner compulsive motive-driven sense of obligation, as a means of fulfilling

---

[39] Cf. Tillich's "Both freedom and relatedness, as well as awareness and self-transcendence, are rooted in the spiritual creations of faith and love—and they determine the process of sanctification". Paul Tillich, Systematic Theology, Vol. III, Chicago: The University of Chicago Press, 1963, p. 233.

one's personal relationship with God whom the Christian has come to accept as Friend, Master, Judge and Abba! Father! (Rom. 8:15).

Ibo traditional morality again tends to regard duty as "imposition" from the routine of lineage links of relationships—a kind of necessity imposed by the rigid codes of reciprocity. The biblical idea of duty as service of 'love' by which one confers divinity upon the neighbour—fellow men needing the services that such duty alone can offer—could be used to correct the rigidity of Ibo concept of duty thereby allowing the element of freedom, as a personal quality that should be present in duty, to manifest itself. It is with such freedom even in the performance of duty that duty itself acquires the element of self-sacrifice, a very desirable Christian quality, by which individual character and personality is enriched.

(2) *Meaning of love and sexuality*

The focus of comparison here is interpersonal relationship which is expressed by the word and the concept of love and self fulfilment between husband and wife in a home. Ibo traditional morality with its permissive polygamous norm, immediately suggests weakness in enriched exercise of love and self fulfilling sexuality. We have already argued that Christian ethics as practiced now in Iboland, since the introduction of Christianity, has no edge whatsoever over Ibo traditional morality in this matter of love and family life.[40] It is even doubtful if Saint Paul's teaching about marriage as a means of avoiding sin on the part of those too weak to avoid such sin without marrying, could support the ideal self fulfilling aspect of love and sexuality as Christians now try to understand it.[41] However the self image which modern man has of himself as "man come of age", has grown out of the scientific study as well as out of the biblical insight about the nature of man and the selfgiving dimension of marriage about which Saint Paul also spoke (Eph. 5:22-33). This has ripened into a fuller understanding of the meaning of love and sexuality in marriage. Therefore Ibo traditional morality developed several cen-

[40] Trimingham's judgment was that "Protestant Christianity ... has no social morality for Africa". See J. S. Trimingham, The Christian Church and Islam in West-Africa, I.M.C. Research Pamphlets No. 3, London: S.C.M. Press 1956, p. 30.

[41] See I Cor. 7: 32-38 ... "Thus he who marries his partner does well, and he who does not will do better". It could be argued however that St. Paul was influenced here by the supposed imminent second coming of Christ and the suffering which was to precede it. See 1 Cor. 7: 26, 29.

turies ago, could not have contained this new insight. Ideal Christian ethics with clear emphasis on the significance of individual personality, should supply the Ibo with this new insight, coupled with a recognition of the fact that Christ died equally for all men, sex difference being only a kind of "division of labour" by which humanity is enriched, multiplied and nurtured in all the graces of happy living. The *agape* meaning of love as self giving, is other than self satisfying concept of *eros* or even of *philia*, the satisfying joy that comes from the experience of facing life together, bound together by the "love" of fellowship. Love as *agape* used in the context of the surrender of persons in creative, self-fulfilling sexuality, becomes a function of Christian vocation of home making. I shall be arguing later that this meaning does not exclude the possibility of such Christian vocation of home making being carried out in a polygamous setting. After all self-giving love is not a quality that is restricted to two human persons only, and can not be equally exercised in group living, which may happen to be a people's most natural and spontaneous way of organised home making. However, what we are concerned with now, is to indicate that this concept and the "living" of love through sexuality, when properly taken into Christian ethics, as we are now beginning to understand it, can enrich Ibo life immensely. Hitherto sexuality is either a child bearing function or erotic indulgence sometimes bordering on perversion. Both in the presently practised Christian ethics in Ibo-land as well as in traditional Ibo morality there has been some form of sanctimoniousness attached to the meaning and practice of love and sex, which all along, has tended to reduce the self-fulfilling qualities in them. The ideal Christian ethics which we have been reconstructing, should re-educate the Ibo Christian in this as in many other life-situation-norms, and take on non-Christians along, because such norm could be shown for what it really it, universalistic norm, although the Christian with the special grace of the Holy Spirit, would have greater chance of living out such "good" life through the fellowship he shares with God through Christ and also with the Church of Christ.

(3) *The acceptance of unavoidable suffering*

As we have already indicated in a preceding paragraph, Ibo traditional society in its pursuit of "the good" as *ndu* (life) had looked upon suffering as real calamity that can hamper *ndu*. It therefore used all sorts of means to avert suffering. Divination together with the propitiation of one spirit or the other, sacrifice, "medicines" of well being through what European writers have called fetish, "magic" or "charms" were used to ensure that one does not get inflicted with such suffering. The Ibos believe, as we have already indicated in previous chapters, that such suffering or pain or abnormalities in nature like a child born blind, the lame, the dumb and the deaf, chronic diseases, or death by drowning—that all these forms of suffering, proceed from some divinities as punishment for crimes (*aru*) committed either by the person suffering them, or by his parents or by someone in the lineage. The questions that Job's friends put to him about confessing his crimes, for which he was inflicted with the sufferings that had befallen him, (Job chapters 4-27 the three cycles of speeches) would indicate that the Jews of that period in the Old Testament believed the same. Even in the time of our Lord the question of his disciples as to who sinned, the parents of the man born blind or the man himself, to explain why he was born blind, suggests that the belief continued in the New Testament period (St. John's Gospel chapter 9 verses 1-5). Morality for the Ibo, as we had already seen, would be meaningless if harmony between community and nature did not prevent such sufferings, and because the gods and spirits could never be found unreliable, men must be responsible for bringing such sufferings through unconfessed and unatoned evil deeds or through malicious acts of wickedness. The new thing Christ brought into human history about the vicarious nature of unmerited suffering, is one of the norms Christian ethics must instill in the Ibo. Not that always the sufferer or his immediate kin relations has sinned, but that through such suffering the greatness of God's power may be manifested.[42] Furthermore the nature of the world in which we live,

---

[42] We cannot enter into the argument here as to whether or not God's intention for man includes suffering and disease and whether all the evil that befalls man in pain and "unmerited" or unavoidable suffering results entirely from human ignorance, folly and sin. This partially is Ibo traditional belief. I am not quite sure that this is tenable in Christian theology although the origin of suffering is attributed by some theologians to the Fall. Without stopping to argue it in detail I tend to disagree with M. M. Makhaye's assertion: "Disease follows from human ignorance, folly and sin". I believe that part of the mechanism of man's physiology includes within it the possibilities of disease. Some diseases we agree result from ignorance, folly and sin, but not all. See M. M. Makhaye "Sickness and Healing in African Christian Perspective (with application to counselling)" in *Relevant Theology for Africa*, edited by Hans Jurgen Becken, Durban: Lutheran Publishing House, 1973, p. 158. Note also the efforts of the World Council of Churches in organising Christian Medical Commission to educate Christians about the spiritual and psychical dimensions of health and healing. See the Healing

although as God's creation it is good, yet its reality in terms of ambiguities, even if in the elementary forms of darkness following light in the rhythm of succeeding days and nights, or in the existence of polarities like the vice within a virtue (excessive tolerance might degenerate into irresponsibility and so on), should be recognised. The Christian ethic of trust in God through faith, and assurance as to the love and concern of God for his children, should be a corrective to this fear of "unjustifiable" suffering which to the Ibo includes death. Childlessness is another aspect of this problem. It is unacceptable to the Ibo that a man should live and not have children. One of the main causes of Christians taking on additional wives to the one married according to Church rules, is this question of childlessness. There is no doubt that Ibo value places high on its list the continuation of the "life" of the lineage, long after its founder had died through the various generations of his offspring. Here the Christian ideal of faith in the goodness of God and trust in his power to give the best to his children, should be a means of enlarging the Ibo man's views in such a way as to accept the possibility of childlessness. It does mean, of course, that childlessness should not result from reckless living in early youth, nor again should it be the outcome of too much anxiety which could cause great harm, which otherwise could not have occurred (these are elements which Christian faith and life of mature Christian behaviour could help and instruct members in).

The Ibo approach to healing (and this can very well be a means of understanding the high premium he attaches to *ndu* (*life*) and to wholeness) through physical, spiritual and psychological means, should be understood by Christian ethical values. The western approach to healing mainly as a physical problem which the best physicians in the western world are already correcting, is still very much in evidence in Christian values practiced in Iboland. Christian ethical values have a great deal to learn (and by so learning adjust its horizon by widening it) from the more healthy aspects of Ibo attitude towards suffering, wholeness and healing. There is a great deal of truth in the Ibo understanding of unmerited suffering of some individuals resulting partly from broken harmony between man, nature and the spirit realities of existence, for which a kind of "atonement" is necessary. Take the great pain of poverty, unemployment and discrimination. This surely

---

Church", Geneva: W.C.C. 1963 and Contact Monthly Journal of C.M.C., W.C.C. Geneva.

breaks the natural harmony between God's various orders of creation and "atonement" is needed in the form of "sacrificial" redistribution of resources, power structures and the re-education of the people as to the correct attitude of accepting human beings as humans pure and simple, and not as high and low, great and small, learned and ignorant (we have already pointed out how the absence of such correct attitude among the C.M.S. missionaries in Iboland from about 1890 diminished the growth of proper Christian values in the various congregations). A good deal of the teaching on Christian social ethics, and the approach to the demands of redistribution of resources in this age of technology, when the rich are getting richer and the poor poorer in Iboland as elsewhere, requires new insights from this approach to suffering resulting partly from broken harmony. Secondly, in Ibo value of wholeness, a man suffering, whether "meritedly" or "unmeritedly", depended on the fellowship of his relatives, his neighbours and his kinsmen living and dead, for moral and practical support towards his recovery of wholeness again. The Christian norm should endeavour to institutionalise this and employ it in its rebuilding of real community consciousness in which the fellow believers show the sick and the suffering, the kind of emotional, cognitive and actional involvement traditional society would have provided for him as psychotherapeutic group. [43] (Is this not one of the attractive techniques of the Aladura Churches?).

The deeper question confronting the Ibo in this whole problem of suffering and evil in the world, is why is he the one inflicted with such "suffering" like childlessness, having a lame or dumb child or subjected to abject poverty? Despite what has been said above about accepting this in the spirit of the vicarious nature of the suffering of Christ—the righteous who died for the unrighteous "that he might bring us to God" (I Peter 3, verse 18), the Ibo Christian today still wants to combine spiritual, psychological and physical approaches towards getting rid of or even avoiding the chances of such sufferings as he still refuses to accept that his *chi* would condition him to that state. His belief in the existence of many chance-situations in life, trying to vitiate the good and auspicious lot which his *chi* would normally allot to him, makes him (even as a strong Christian believer) seek ways of more "spiritual" channels, for the controlling of life so as to exclude such suffering. The problem is further complicated

---

[43] M. M. Makhaye, Ibid.

by situations like this: A and B suffering the same type of sickness go to the hospital, A is cured and B could not be cured and he remains an invalid. B asks the question "why myself?" In answer to this question he might want to combine the scientific cum physical approach of the doctor he consulted at the hospital with possible additional knowledge (like the one a diviner or a prophet of the Aladura Churches might give him), and the additional energy (like the "spirit-force" believed to reside in "medicine" concocted for him by the native medicine-man (nwadibia) or a prophet). In this way, part of the attempt at solving the problem created for this Christian by the fact of suffering, is to combine scientific approach to healing with psychological symbolism (the charm worn) and spiritual force. Christian faith must include in its ethical values of dealing with health, wholeness and suffering in Iboland methods that combine these three dimensions of Ibo life experience—symbols, spirit reality and material or scientific means. The reconstructed Christian ethics we have been developing should indicate how best to do this. We will come back to this theme in a subsequent chapter (chapter VIII).

(4) *Law and grace*

The origin of the pairing of law and grace in an antithetical setting is Saint Paul, especially his teaching in Romans chapters 4 to 6 in which he contrasts the law of Moses and the faith of Abraham. Through identical faith in Christ a Christian believer receives grace, by which he is enabled to live the righteous life of moral uprightness. Ibo traditional morality does not know grace in the meaning that Christianity associates with the word. True enough the general predisposing "luck" or good fortune which a man's *chi* endows him with, plays identical role to that the Holy Spirit plays in giving grace to the believer. Furthermore we had pointed to what John Macquarrie calls "common grace" with which he supports his argument that to speak of original sin is also to presume "original righteousness". [44] In this the Ibo would share. It is therefore the function of ideal Christian ethic to supply the depth of meaning of the idea and life described by the New Testament in its teaching on grace. It starts with trust or faith in God, then it moves on to confidence in the form of assurance through knowledge of the dependability of God and ends in that attitude to life where love, joy, peace, patience, kindness, goodness,

---

44 John Macquarrie, Three Issues in Ethics, *op. cit.*, p. 122.

faithfulness, gentleness and self-control manifest themselves in an individual's character. This harvest of the Spirit (compare Galatians chapter 5 verse 22) appears in the Christian man possessing it outwardly as an effortless production or put in the language of Saint Paul in the epistle quoted—"against such (noble living) there is no law". No law can be placed beside such noble life to be its yard stick, because such life far outshines any code of behaviour a community can draw up! Put the Ibo traditional morality side by side with this, you see how much Christian ethics must give to the Ibo to enrich his moral life in this respect. His endless struggle for the means of satisfying the moral demands of the community, both living and dead, his struggles to unleash the "life-force" and the "spirit-energy"—the *élan vital,* to use the phrase of Henri Bergson, through sacrifices, "medicines" and divination, will end in the joy of knowing the Redeemer and his "Grace abounding". We had already pointed out that the Church having been institutionalized, must have laws or rules by which to administer its structures of interaction, leadership and role playing. This must not be confused into deriving norms of personal life from the rigid demands of a code rather than by following Christ in a loving manner and respecting him by enjoying his fellowship through having identical devotion to God as the Source of all value and meaning. The rigidity of the moral demands of Ibo traditional code, greatly needs the life giving and the fresh breath of "grace".[45] There is so much search in Iboland especially now (witness the "bonanza" of mushroom salvation-Churches) for meaningful "aid" with which to grapple with innumerable problems of life situations, greatly complicated by social change. This results mainly from dissatisfaction with Ibo rigid moral code as well as the crack in the system of that traditional code itself, as its centre cannot hold all the

---

[45] Elizabeth Isichei commenting on this rigidity of Ibo moral law said that Ibo religion "created whole classes of unfortunates, to whom Christianity was to come as a liberation—the old women forced to drink poison to prove their innocence from witchcraft, the slaves who were purchased for sacrifice, the *osu* who were the untouchables of some (Ibo) towns, the mothers of twins and other categories of infant whose birth was seen as abominable". It is a great pity that in course of time Christianity gave to Iboland another code of laws that the same Isichei remarked "Later both European administrators and the Ibo themselves were to agree that the sanctions introduced by English law—and the Christian religion were infinitely less effective". Hence our need of real Christian ethics in which grace is operative and not law. See Elizabeth Isichei, "Ibo and Christian Beliefs: Some Aspects of a Theological Encounter", *op. cit.*, p. 129.

experiences of modern life, and the failure of Christianity and modernistic technical culture to provide viable alternative. It is part of the thesis of this study that reconstructed and revitalised Christian ethics which relates itself to the realities of Ibo life can destroy the rigidity of law in the old code and yet use that code's understanding of life to breathe into Iboland the fresh breath of divine grace through Christ.

(5) *Sharing of material resources and power*

The extended family concept in Ibo lineages has built into the system the practice of anyone, who is in a position to help others with his resources, let him do so. This has created a very resilient framework for bearing one another's burdens. The experience of recent civil war in Nigeria is a great tribute to the Ibo "family" structure when well over half a million Ibo people displaced from various parts of Nigeria in which most had lived as their homes, were "accommodated" by their kinsmen at home. We had already indicated how, with the advent of modernization and its market economy, those Ibos who "succeeded" were able to educate their relations in universities at home and abroad thereby extending the influence and spread of technical culture in the villages we studied. The main motive for such assistance in Ibo tradition, is to ensure that men were made available to repay the benefactors in their old age, as well as continue the training of others. There is nothing wrong with this institutionalised enlightened self-interest as the means of extending "progress", only that when placed side by side with the Christian ideal of loving and helping one's neighbours like the cousin or nephew in need of education, one should do it as an end in itself. Love in this form of help should have as its only element self-giving service by which worth (if you prefer, divinity) is invested upon the beneficiary without the conscious calculation of reward or of the biting self conceit that would wish the beneficiary to bow down and worship the benefactor, and where that is not done the latter expresses his conceit in such statements as "after all that I had done for that young man, he does not now regard me as somebody". This is not to encourage ingratitude on the part of cousins and nephews who receive such great help, but to emphasize that Christian ethics in its ideal and therefore its real meaning, should teach the Ibo brought up in his traditional practice of sharing, to add more self-effacing quality of agape-love to his giving.

Another problem the Ibo faces in this context when truly challenged by Christian ethics, is that he is so accustomed to the many demands of the extended family, that he does not have the leisure to develop trained habit of giving to the general cause for humanity and the broader needs of universal brotherhood. Even Church contributions have to be enforced in a legalistic manner, and one of the causes of "dryness" in the Church life of Iboland, is that the greater proportion of its members do not have any idea at all about the virtue of Christian giving. There is of course a great deal of evidence of very poor people giving over fifty percent of their annual income to Church work; and this applies too to some less poor people, but these are just the exceptions. Traditional society's value of a "big" man qualifying for that role, through generosity and hospitality and patronage to his followers, so as to enlarge their number as well as retain their allegiance, can benefit from a more spiritualised concept of generosity like: "When you give a dinner or a banquet, do not invite your friends or your brothers or your kinsmen or rich neighbours lest they also invite you in return and you be repaid". (Luke's Gospel chapter 14 verse 12) Christian ethics should be able to dilute Ibo traditional moral habit that has become very calculating and reward conscious. In Ibo life generosity and the sharing of resources, have become a bit mechanical rather than being spontanuously life enriching and proceeding from self giving love, without strings attached.

In the sharing of power Ibo traditional society's emphasis, that "when a child washes his hands clean, he may be permitted to eat from the same bowl with adults", indicates the openness of that society. Although deferance, respect and authority are due to the older from the younger, yet the egalitarian concept engendered by achievement motivation and the belief that "he who owns (power) today may not own it tomorrow", because "no condition is permanent", evens out the exercise of power. Where the need of Christian value is very great in using authority and power responsibly, (knowing that there is no authority except from God, and that each one would give account to God of how he has used the powers with which he had been enabled to serve) is with the new and emerging political men of this generation. The new urban-industrial ethics which we had already identified in this study, is not yet formalised in Iboland, although we have tried in this study to analyse some of its characteristics. It is our belief that in this matter of the exercise of power—be it political, scientific, entrepreneural or industrial and financial, Christian ethics should be properly expressed, to give the breath of life to the Ibo basic way of life.

In that way, the Ibo Christian as well as non-Christians, can see it as their own relevant way of life which will provide the channels for modernistic technical culture in Iboland. We shall discuss further the place of the modern-industrial and urban values in the reconstructed Christian ethics that we are building up for Iboland. Because it is an ethic that takes into serious consideration the self image modern man has of himself such Christian ethics will no longer be seen as irrelevant to the demands of technical culture.

Before we end this section on the comparative study of Ibo traditional morality and Christian ethics in relation to the sharing of resources and power we want to make one more observation. The tradition of sharing resources and power was developed in Iboland many centuries ago when manners were simple and luxuries were few.[46] Everyone had one skill or the other, with which he could make contribution to the common life in this tradition of sharing resources. Even a young boy of seven had his little errands to run by which he learnt the moral truth of being a member of a body like the patrilineage. This ability to give to the community of his own best, how ever little that was, where the uncle for example would give him his first female goat to look after, helped the little boy as a human person to start the individuality so valued in the Ibo traditional culture. Several avenues were open to him to still make contributions, small but expressive of his young and tender abilities, until he grew up to be able to make the bigger and more expensive contributions. The sharing of resources did encourage therefore the Ibo positive value about the human individual per se. It also developed in the society ideas that stressed "one's autonomous capacity to realise whatever his personal potentialities might be".[47] There were no parasites in such a society. Today technology has brought in diversity of manners, complexity of habits and highly skilled specializations. A large number of

---

[46] Cf. The views of Olaudah Equiano or Gustavus Vassa the African: "As our manners are simple, our luxuries are few", contained in his autobiography, first published in 1789. Equiano was an Ibo, born around 1745 and was captured and sold into slavery to Virginia and later secured his freedom and wrote the autobiography and this account of his Ibo life and society is one of the earliest written accounts we now have. See his: The life of Olaudah Equiano or Gustavus Vassa the African, in two vols., London: Dawson of Pall Mall, 1969 edition, Vol. 1, p. 11.

[47] See the views of Richard N. Henderson about the Onitsha Ibo's growth into vigorous individuality despite Ibo's sense of communality in his book: The King in Everyman: Evolutionary Trends in Onitsha Ibo Society and Culture, New Haven and London: Yale University Press, 1972, pp. 521-522.

Ibos do now make traditional demands on their relations who can afford, without themselves explicitly contributing something to the common resources as even a young boy of about seven would do in the "good old days".

The moral insight Christian ethics should bring into this "unnatural" situation is the re-emphasized sense of individuality by which, those overwhelmed by the complexity of the new technological situation, should still do whatever they could to contribute to the resources, so that no one remains a parasite and dehumanized individual waiting for the more successful uncles and cousins and brothers to bear their burden, under the guise that the Ibo traditional morality provided for such concern over one another. The tradition is commendable but its corruption by modern aberrations should be corrected by Christian ethics, through proper emphasis on these two values namely: the worth of the individual person to be nurtured by everyone being trained to be useful and make his proper contribution to the society. Secondly the Weberian emphasis on the doctrine of "the calling", by which every individual looks upon whatever he is called upon to do as the duty by which his being the "elect" child of God, can be made known through the devotion with which he does it. Christians can therefore set the pattern through internalizing the Christian ethics we are recommending and take the non-Christians along as the norm has been there in Ibo traditional morality, only that the forces of social change are trying to destroy it, and Ibo morality by itself, without the revitalization from such values as the reconstructed Christian ethics can give to it, will be unable to bring the norm back again to effective use.

(6) *The Will of God*

We are not concerned here with a theological or philosophical discussion of the general meaning of the will of God either in Christian or Ibo tradition—how it is determined in history, or how it is applied to individual or communal decision making. Rather we are concerned with examining what in the experience of Ibo traditional moral life is regarded as the will of God and show how it compares with the Christian understanding. The aim of such comparative study, as in the preceding paragraphs, is to indicate what the two systems can beneficially take on from each other, towards the proper reconstruction of the Christian ethics we are recommending for Iboland. Such an ethic would be relevant to Iboland, because it utilizes the social and religious factors which for several centuries had informed life and developed experience and culture in Iboland.

We have given a brief account of Ibo cosmology in chapter III. Apart from the supreme Deity (*Chi-ukwu or Chi-neke*) who is vaguely believed to be the over-all-in-charge of the created order, and *Ala* (the earth goddess) charged more directly with upholding the Ibo moral code, there are also the metaphysical forces that appear to have the attributes of man without really being human nor mortal. We have also shown that they are free in the sense of mobility and powerful in the influence they exercise over man. Such influence is exercised through the permanent forms they take, for example at the shrine or localised oracle or in the form of the spirit of ancestors symbolised by and "localised" at the *Ndebunze* Shrine. Only the specialist like *Nwadibia* or members of very secret cults, and in some rare cases *Ọzọ* titled persons, know how to find out the will of these gods through divination, magical rites and "medicine". In times of illness or social upheavals or when an individual needs further re-assurance about his life course, it is these specialised persons who could "see" the gods and spirits and interpret their will to such individuals and communities. But such interpretations are in addition to the already "revealed" body of the will of the gods for the community codified in the Ibo moral norms called *omenani*.

For the individual and for his life as a moral agent, working in society and making success of life, or finding life so much of a problem, the important spirit is his *chi* (personal god or guardian spirit), given to him even before birth. Again we had given a general description of *chi* in Ibo cosmology in Chapter III, but an understanding of what to an Ibo man corresponds to the knowledge of the will of God for him, demands another line of insight into beliefs about *chi*. A man lives in this world, his *chi* lives in the other world and before his birth his *chi* had joined in council with the creator spirit to apportion his fortune to him. From then on, this *chi* goes on "revealing" to him through practical activities in historical situations what the will of God or the gods is for him. Proper names like *Chima* (*chi* knows), *Chibuzo* (*chi* leads the way), *Nkechinyere* (that which ever *chi* gives), suggest this belief that a man's knowledge of the will of God for him is through his *chi*. Proverbs give clearer insight into this belief. "A man does not fall down except where his *chi* consents that he should fall". To accept that it is the will of God to "fall down" (which might mean falling from fortune to poverty, from grace to grass or from rank to file) is to accept that one's *chi* has "spoken" it. To die becomes the will of God because one's *chi* has complied with it. (*Chi onye adigh nizu onwu anegh egbu ya.*) To the Ibo the greatest condemnation is the one uttered by his *chi*. Where such a man is again convinced that men's accusations against him have no substance, he would name his next child *Chiebonam*, believing that his *chi* has not condemned him. Very interesting is the name *Nebechi*: wait upon *chi*, he will yet reveal to you the will of God! Should we then in relating Ibo moral ideas to Christian teaching equate *chi* with God? Up to a point, yes, in so far as *Chi-ukwu*, another variant for God used in Ibo Christian literature, means the *Great Chi* (the Over Soul). God becomes more personal to the Ibo in his individual approach to the divine will for personal moral life in the concept of the personal *chi*. [48] Some general association of the will of the spirits or gods with fate, exists among the Ibo in the *chi* concepts which we have now discussed. The knowledge of the will of God in a positive way for one's moral life, does not seem to appear in Ibo thinking; although the sense of benediction for individual's life appears in proverbs and names, it is God's will in connection with punishment that seems to be more generally known through divination and historical occurrences. The will of God for the Ibo set in his traditional moral frame work, is not easily knowable, [49] as even in Christianity the individual set face to face with conflicting choices, does not find the will of God too easy to determine, so as to make a more accurate moral choice. To both, God is still "a God who hidest thyself" (Isaiah chapter 45 verse 15). Never-

[48] I am acquainted with a young Ibo man whose "conservative" Christian parents gave the name *Chukwudi* (God exists) at his baptism, at 18 he changed it to *Chidi* (Chi exists) and argues that apart from being more modern "*Chidi*" brings his convictions about God home better than *Chukwudi*. Some 50 years ago *chi* was reserved by Christian writers to Ibo "heathen concepts!"

[49] Ibo salutation name for the masquerade as the representative of the spirit world appearing in this world is *amama amacha amacha*: the known and yet the unknown.

The idea of chance element and the "unknowableness" of the affairs of this world, is further illustrated in this Ibo consolation dirge which young ladies easily improvise, with which to sympathise with a bereaved member of their age set called Charity. Note that by that name the song is modern as "Charity" suggests a "Christian" name.

Charity nwamgbeke gharaba	Charity the daughter of Mgbeke leave off (be comforted).
Charity nwangbeke gharaba	Charity the daughter of Mgbeke leave off.
Ije U wa adigh nhanya	The affairs of this world are not equal.
Ije Uwa adigh mpiakota	The affairs of this world do not admit of mathematical rationality.

theless there is a great deal the Christian insight can give towards the reconstruction of the Ibo man's moral perspective in respect of this concept of the will of God in ethical formulations found in this traditional life experiences.

Christian knowledge of the will of God starts with the life, work, resurrection and the glorification of Jesus Christ. The Old Testament preparations for this Christ-event revealed God's will to man through, not only the historical dealings of God with his covenant people Israel, but also through the prophets. Nevertheless it is only in Christ can anyone "see" God, for Christ is the image of the Invisible God. Christ's summary of the will of God for man is surrender to God through faith, and then walking with Him through obedience and participation in God's work of reconciling the world to himself. This further constitutes Christian ethics not into "a system of virtues and vices, of laws and counsels, of rewards and punishments. All this is not lacking, but it appears within a frame work of concrete, personal decisions". [50] Christian ethics, as will of God for man revealed by Jesus Christ, requires life of personal decisions day by day so as to walk closely with God in Christ. In any given life situation, a Christian living this life of I—Thou relationship with God, endeavours to deduce the line of action that constitutes the will of God for him, from the past actions of God through Jesus Christ. Such past actions manifested:

(1) Very close sharing in the person of God through prayer and obedience.
(2) Extending God's love, care and concern to all in need of such love, care and concern.
(3) Being mindful that the judge of Christ's actions was not the fault finding Pharisees or the religious-ceremony-protecting high priests or even the law enforcing Pilates nor the fickleminded crowd, but God himself.

So all deference for the continuing of the work of God as Christ himself has said is "My Father has never yet ceased his work and I am working too... In truth, in truth, I tell you, the son can do nothing by Himself; He does only what He sees the Father doing: What the Father does, the son does" (John 5 verses 17 and 19). [51] Further help

---

[50] Paul Tillich, Biblical Religion and the Search for Ultimate Reality, Chicago: The University of Chicago Press, 1968, p. 45.

[51] See Bruce Reed, Biblical Social Ethics: An Evangelical View, in J. C. Bennett (ed.), Christian Social Ethics in a Changing World, New York: Association Press, London: S.C.M. Press, 1966, pp. 105-118.

in determining whether what one regards as pertaining to the will of God is really so, can be found in checking how far what we decide to do is a furtherance of the fruit or "harvest" of the Spirit in love, joy, peace, patience, kindness, goodness, faithfulness, gentleness and self-control (Galatians chapter 5 verse 22).

It is with this kind of insight that Christian ethics should displace the incipient fatalism and calculation associated with the will of God in Ibo traditional code. Modern, complex and pluralistic society which is developing in Iboland is full of areas calling for decision-making where knowledge of all the factors—technical, financial, political and administrative, tends to dismiss as irrelevant any idea about the will of God in that decision. Part of the thesis of this study is that no situation to a responsible person is void of moral judgment, and no decision is without its historical consequences and it is within such historical situations and consequences that Jesus says "my Father has never yet ceased his work". No responsible Ibo man, believer or non-believer, does not, both instinctively and sometimes explicitly, recognise the reality of the spirit world in which God still works. No real moral decisions in all honesty of intentions, possibly with attention to the technical and other details, will fail to relate to the will of God whether we acknowledged it or not. Hence the importance of the reconstructed Christian ethics which can take in the concept of our common humanity including those aspects of Ibo traditional morality that bear witness to it. We will discuss this further in Chapter VIII to show that our reconstructed Christian ethic by drawing from Ibo traditional life experiences, as well as from scientific and technological life experiences, can provide one common norm for all Ibos in these three historical life experiences. When the proper approach to knowing and doing the will of God is taken from this perspective of personal fellowship with or personal decision for God, sin is seen clearly to be nothing but deciding against God, forsaking his fellowship and therefore acting or doing things that completely deny the demands of love, joy and peace. The end product of this way of life comes to the same thing as that of committing *aru* (abomination) in the Ibo moral code, namely destruction of the harmony and peaceful "equilibrium" between man, nature and the spirit world. But in view of the fact that in the former, sin is seen in its true psychological nature as existing in the human person making the decision, whilst in the latter it is mainly the social code that is infringed, and the human person whom the broken harmony would affect, is left untouched in the "sinning" stage, the Christian meaning of sin is more expressive of the nature of things and should be adopted.

Another insight that Christian ethics can give to Ibo society in this matter of the will of God is this: God is other than man, and He is the Ultimate Reality. We mortals despite our privileges in the Christ-event, cannot comprehend and carry out *all* of God's will on this side of eternity. This is why Christian teaching contains a great deal of eschatology—the belief that the greater demands of love, peace and joy, will find fulfilment at the end of time within more spiritualised existence. The Ibo concept of *Uwa Ozo* (next world) points dimly to this eschatological dimension of man's fulfilment, but confounds its full meaning by picturing it as a replica of this very present world. Here Christian ethics can enlarge Ibo traditional concept thereby giving the Ibo more meaningful living and decision-making that satisfies Ibo man's perennial yearning for justice and *ndu* (life).

This brief attempt at the comparative study of Ibo morality and Christian ethics does not suggest that only these six subjects could be so compared. We used only these six simply to indicate the need for such study even where we might be charged of making arbitrary choice of themes to compare, and the stance from which we are comparing. There is no doubt that comparative study of any kind involves the subjective "value judgment" of the person comparing, because the scientific criteria of choosing and valuing are not clearly objectively determinable. Nevertheless the attempt at building up theological insights from the real life-experience of societies like the Ibo, cannot bear much fruit without such comparative analysis, to point out living issues as well as dead issues in the situation. Dead issues will of course be buried, while living issues will become bases for the necessary reconstruction in theology, thereby ensuring that such theology is living theology, or in the idiom of this study, that we endeavour to produce Christian teaching on ethics from our African non-Christian background which will match, as far as possible the true life experience of African peoples like the Ibo.

Some Comparison of Urban-Industrial Values with Ibo-Traditional and Christian Ethics

In comparing urban-industrial and modernistic ethic, as it appears in Iboland with Ibo traditional morality as well as with Christian ethics, we wish to call attention to three facts. There is as yet no outspoken denial of God or of the "life-force" from the spirit world uttered manifestly by the "devotees" of modernistic ethic operating in Iboland at present. There is the break down of the "traditional" codes: Ibo and Christian, owing to the gathering of peoples from various areas to the new towns, and owing to the failure of the Ibo as well as the Christian systems to answer to the self image modern man has of himself. This has resulted in the lack of clearly defined moral norms by which Ibos value the new life style generated by technical western culture. It is our strong conviction, from the data available to us, that Ibos will want to contain technological advantages without denying the reality of the spirit powers in human affairs. In other words, according to the trends we have observed, the Ibo's reluctance to separate the material realm from the spiritual realm, is likely to make technological progress a non-secularised life-style, whereas it is increasingly becoming secularised in western experience. Secondly there are aspects in the nature of technological civilization itself, which require that the Ibos, if they will benefit fully from its promises, must develop and internalise the qualities of life that uphold those aspects. Integrity, responsibility, wider loyalty and disciplined use of resources are some of the qualities that relate to these aspects. Both Christian ethics and Ibo traditional morality, have the basic ethos on which these qualities can be fully developed and used in the more successful application of technology to the improvement of *ndu* (life) among the Ibo. The third fact we wish to call attention to in this cursory comparison of Ibo morality and Christian ethics with urban-industrial ethics in Iboland, is the place of symbolism in technical culture. Ibo life is, by and large, symbolic life. Technology together with its structures of townlife, industrial organisations, markets, expertise, skills and success-oriented search for profit, prosperity and progress emphasizes positivistic approach to life. Positivism and creative symbolism, as we know, do not often go well together. There is no doubt that in Iboland technological pseudo-symbols appear in the form of the "gadgets" of modernity—radios, television sets, motor-cars, high-rise houses and the like. Many "modern" Ibos in a joking manner will ask you how many "visible symbols" of modernity exist in your village?

Already by applying the adjective "visible" to the word "symbols", the unreality of these objects of conspicuous consumption, as the Americans refer to them, is easily portrayed. But if attention is paid to them intensely, to the neglect of the proper symbols of Ibo life-experience in which the material and the spiritual dovetail to create a metaphysical understanding of life, and thereby deepen the meaning of existence, technological culture becomes a real danger. The moral problems of urban-industrial and technological life in Iboland would then assume such proportions of great magnitude that could completely erode the foundations of Ibo self-hood. The effective answer to such problem is to use revitalised ethical norms of the Christian ethics we are recommending for Iboland to show up these technological conveniences for what they really are—mere tools or "gadgets" for servicing *ndu* (life) and should therefore be made subject to the symbols that have made life meaningful in Iboland for these past centuries. The work of interpreting the new and fitting them into meaningful existence patterns of Ibo life, is the concern of this study. For we believe that Ibo traditional life, Christianity and technological modernization are facts of existential reality in Iboland today, and they must be adjusted to one another on the foundation of life-experience that is strong and deep enough to carry the structure the new facts will erect. With these few observations we end this comparative study of the three ethical manifestations in Iboland in the hope that when we gather up, in a subsequent chapter, all the threads that our data have provided for us, we will be able to show that an effective Christian ethic that takes Ibo life-experiences into itself, through the reconstructed pattern of ethics we have drawn up, will provide adequate guidance for the problems emanating from urban-industrial and technological experiences in Iboland. But before we gather up the threads, a brief look at three non-African thinkers who have written on topics relevant to our study from their non-African background will be helpful. Dialogue with such positions that are not quite the same as ours can provide objective analysis by which our position is clarified and discussion is deepened, to the mutual benefit of the two positions. The three writers we want to hold dialogue with are W. A. Visser 't Hooft, A. Th. Van Leeuwen and Hendrik Kraemer.

CHAPTER SEVEN

THREE EXAMPLES OF THE CHRISTIAN APPROACH TO MEN OF OTHER FAITHS: VISSER 'T HOOFT, VAN LEEUWEN AND HENDRIK KRAEMER

Introductory Matter

The title of this chapter suggests straight-away to the reader that this is a diversion from our track already beaten out by the six preceding chapters. Hitherto the scene had been Iboland and all the actors and interactors whether they came from among Christians of Europe, Sierra Leone or the West-Indies or from the traders, innovator-colonial administrators or technocrats of Europe and America, faced Ibo traditional life and society directly with their message, materials and methods. Why then introduce these three theologians, who incidentally happen to have all been Dutch and had not known much of Iboland, let alone confronting it directly with their own words, wares and workshops? We all know the value in Shakespeare's plays of the "intrusion" of the Jester—the "Pucks", the "Trinculos" and the "Touchstones". Coming almost entirely from outside the play-plot as it were, these characters in those plays inject objective meaning to our view of life, they enable us to see ourselves and the actors more clearly and more objectively and sharpen the "contrasts" of life more acutely for the play to go on with less drabness and "routine". Not that the three erudite scholars whose views on the central thesis of our study are hereby examined, could in any way be regarded as "theological jesters", but that their "intrusion" from the "outside" is bound to add pep and reflection which will save our study from the drabness of the "one-way-traffic" of introspective subjectivism. Hence the need for this short dialogue with them.

The central thesis of our study is this: Effective Christian morality for Iboland (and by extension, other areas in Africa similarly situated) must be based on sound relevant theology, which has been developed in conscious awareness of Ibo life as it is presently experienced through traditional Ibo moral values, Christian teachings and modern technological influences so as to reflect them. This thesis presupposes and affirms four propositions, namely:

(1) Relevant theology anywhere necessitates that the word of God be interpreted to a people in the context of their experiences and way of life (culture) and that for Iboland this interpretation must be related to Ibo world view, their institutions of cultural life as well as their symbolic interpretations of reality.

(2) The significance of the word "relevant" in the thesis is to indicate that the moral norm to be developed though Christian in its inspiration, orientation and content, will be basic enough to take in the universal moral needs of man that both the new technologically influenced Ibos as well as non-Christians will accept such a norm as workable guidance for the demands of private as well as social life.

(3) The word "effective" as used here is to point to our belief, that because of the problems of interaction between religions and cultures leading to the gradual decay of the Ibo moral code, and the absence of another effective and normative guide to life and values, this new Christian morality to be developed must provide such norm. Furthermore this will lead to the emergence of religiously based new culture even as the old Ibo life style was religiously oriented.

(4) By basing the new norm on Christian theology, because Christianity by being interpreted through Ibo religious tradition and culture purifies that tradition, we further imply that the success of upholding and championing the new values, turning them into a social and ideological force, depends to a large extent on Christians. These Christians (and this would mean real effort at enlarging the recruitment and the constituency, more on these later) must show real evidence of the "additional grace" of the new life in Christ, through the Holy Spirit, and constitute themselves into the inner core, the innovators and the cultural elite, not of privilege, but of service in the spirit of their Master who brought into human experience new "civilization" through self sacrifice.

Because the three theologians we have mentioned have, in varying degrees touched on one or more of these four elaborated meanings of our thesis, we now proceed to look at their writings, picking out of course only such of their views that are immediately relevant to our concern, namely, how do we relate Christianity to the Ibos who for many centuries lived and developed a non-Christian way of life.

W. A. Visser 't Hooft

Our study of the relevant views of Dr. William A. Visser 't Hooft is taken mainly from his book, *No Other Name: The Choice between*

Syncretism and Christian Universalism. [1] As the sub-title indicates the main emphasis of the book is on two themes both of which relate to the main thesis of this study, namely the problem of syncretism to the Christian Church and secondly the meaning of Christian universalism.

To clarify the proper meaning of "syncretism" Visser 't Hooft identified three ways some writers had used the word. "Some speak of syncretism when ever a particular religion makes any use of concepts which have their origin in the life of another religion". [2] This is not syncretism, for every religion that steps out of its original environment has to be communicated through the "expressions and concepts" which are familiar to the people to whom the religion is being communicated. To speak of syncretism in this connection makes every religion syncretistic and this will make nonsense of the word, concludes Visser 't Hooft. The proper word for this exercise of passing "on the original message as clearly as possible and without greater modification of its original content than is inevitable, [3] is translation. Another group of writers use the word to indicate that a particular religion has taken into its own life ideas or practices which have their origin in another religious world. This, Visser 't Hooft, again argues is not syncretism but rather absorption, as long as the foreign elements absorbed become part of the original structure and not used to modify it. He goes further to remind us that Dr. Kraemer has pointed out that absorption is not syncretism. [4] Real syncretism should be reserved for the view that says all religions lead to one God, all their teachings should be pulled together to provide a common religion for common humanity. He quotes from Professor Oepke who puts the matter clearly as follows: "Real syncretism is always based on the presupposition that all positive religions are only reflections of a universal original religion (Urreligion) and show therefore only gradual differences". [5] Real syncretism denies any specific revelation but always looks for the common denominator in religions.

In the second chapter Dr. Visser 't Hooft surveys the various historical forms of syncretism and such survey has enabled us to see more clearly what is meant and what is implied in the meaning and

---

[1] Published in London by the SCM Press, 1963.
[2] W. A. Visser 't Hooft, *op. cit.*, p. 10.
[3] Ibid., p. 11.
[4] Ibid. He quotes this from H. Kraemer, Religion and the Christian Faith, London: Lutterworth Press, 1956, p. 397.
[5] A. Oepke, Das neue Gottesvolk, as quoted by W. A. Visser 't Hooft.

the concept of syncretism. The historical analysis of ancient as well as modern forms of syncretism further indicates the inverterate human desire to "create" the way of his own salvation. The Christian religion is precisely the opposite of this human craving. Visser 't Hooft's very judicious comment, at the end of his historical survey of syncretism is this: "A God who speaks in an infinite variety of ways but never decisively really throws man back upon himself, for it is then up to man to determine how and where he can reach ultimate truth".[6] It is this denial of the uniqueness of revelation in history, the kind we have in Christianity, that clearly marks out what syncretism is. From this clear understanding of what is and what is not syncretism, its pretension to supply humanity with a universalism which it badly needs, now that all the world is constituting itself into a "parish" due to technological devices in mass communication and travel facilities, is challenged by Christian universalism which is the second topic from Visser 't Hooft that we want to discuss.

The New Testament struggled from its earliest period to extract the Christian Church from the attempt to submerge it under existing religious systems. The Judaisers attempted in various ways to bring the young Church under the yoke of Jewish laws, religious observances and rigid codes of behaviour including circumcision. The first synod of Jerusalem as reported in the book of the Acts of the Apostles, bore witness to the determination of the Apostles not to yield to this pressure. Antioch, Ephesus, Corinth and Rome were cosmopolitan cities where the apostles spent so much of their time and energy to fight against the existing practices of mixing cults and combining older indigenous forms of worship with any new form that appealed to them. "Jesus" could have been added on easily by Simon Magus of Samaria (Acts 8 verse 10), at Ephesus the magicians and practitioners of the divination art commonly called the *Ephesia grammata,* as well as the devotees of the cult of Artemis, strongly desired to incorporate the name of Jesus into their magical practices (Acts 19 verses 11-20). Saint Paul of course fought hard against this and all other similar attempts we found in the New Testament. Rather he showed how Jesus Christ should be understood as universally satisfactory to man's universal need for the knowledge of and the fellowship with God. The biblical records clearly portrayed Jesus Christ as the unique, one teacher for all mankind who is the one Lord (Eph. 4 verse 5),

---

[6] *Op. cit.,* p. 48.

the one shepherd of the entire human "flock" (John's Gospel 10 verse 16), the one mediator between man and God (1 Tim. 2 verse 5) and the one name through whom all mankind can receive salvation (Acts 4 verse 12). From such biblical sources, Visser 't Hooft concludes that the Church's Universalism is basic to the nature of the Faith itself. Therefore the kind of universalism of religions which syncretism attempts to give, is superfluous to the Christian Church. The Church must therefore be the witness to point to the one Lord Jesus Christ, the Lord of all men. The Church came into being to proclaim this good news and not to add one more form of spiritual experience to the many which existed already. "The Christian Church cannot therefore participate in the search for a synthesis or confluence of the existing religions. Such a combination will not be an enrichment for humanity, for it could only be achieved by treating the religions as human ideologies of which man himself is the centre".[7] Visser 't Hooft however believes that the Christian Church can enter into dialogue with men of other faiths but only in the sense of creating understanding rather than of finding a common denominator between these religions and Christianity. It is a mistake, he further argues for Christians to think of themselves as men practising religion in the sense that Islam or Hinduism or African traditional religion is a religion, where man is searching for God and trying to attain "salvation" by his efforts. "For the whole New Testament speaks of the Saviour whom we have not chosen but who has chosen us. It is possible to reject him, but it is not seriously possible to think of him as one of the many prophets or founders of religion. A Christianity which should think of itself as one of many diverse contributions to the religious life of mankind is a Christianity that has lost its foundation in the New Testament".[8] The Christian Church therefore should endeavour to state its theology clearly, using the thought-form of the environment in which it operates, but not using such thought-forms to introduce into its structure ideas which change the meaning of biblical truth in its substance,[9] one of such truths being the universal nature of the Church. It is to preserve this universal nature of the Church that makes it necessary that the Church, where ever it exists, should naturally be itself "at home" in the environment; the Universal Church by that fact of its universalism, cannot be "foreign" to any

---

[7] Visser 't Hooft, *op. cit.*, p. 116.
[8] *Op. cit.*, p. 117.
[9] Ibid., p. 123.

nation other than the "foreigness" that belongs to its essential nature as the revelation of God to man. Visser 't Hooft concludes this section of his book, which deals with the universalism of the Church, by urging the Christians to have the freedom and courage to interpret the Gospel in such a way as will bring it closer to the cultures in which, up till now, it has been generally proclaimed in a western, and therefore, in a foreign form. "It is clear that real risks are included", he warns, but goes on to add: "But our desire to arrive at a truly adequate communication of the Gospel must be stronger than our fear of syncretism. ... The time has come when the 'multi-coloured' wisdom of God must express itself in new Asian and African expressions of Christian thought and life".[10] It is because we share this conviction of Dr. Visser 't Hooft that we undertake this study which is an attempt to give African expression to some ethical aspects of the Christian faith. We will now turn to another writer whose views bear relationship to our interest—Dr. Arend Th. van Leeuwen.

A. Th. van Leeuwen

The contribution of Dr. van Leeuwen to this study is taken from his book: *Christianity in World History—The Meeting of the Faith of East and West.*[11] The book does not pay particular attention to Africa, it makes few references to general situations that are common to many non-Western, non-Christian areas of the world to which Christianity has been taken by western missionaries. As Dr. Kraemer observes in the Foreword "The main aim of the book is to interpret the peculiarly dynamic character of Western civilization and its world-wide explosive effect, particularly in the present revolutionary stage of technocracy, which is creating an unprecedented crisis for all religions, Christianity included".[12]

Secondly the book, according to Kraemer also, "is really born out of a passionate devotion to the missionary obligation of the Church and a deep concern for helping to trace new ways for its fulfilment".[13] It is mainly from these two considerations, namely the influence of western technological culture on the Ibo, and the finding of the new and the best ways for the Gospel to fulfil its promises for the Ibo,

---

[10] Visser 't Hooft, *op. cit.*, p. 124.

[11] Published in London: Edinburgh House Press, 1966, translated by H. H. Hoskins.

[12] A. Th. Van Leeuwen, *op. cit.*, p. IX.

[13] Ibid.

that we find Van Leeuwen relevant to our study. The main thesis of the book is that Christianity is "submerged" in modern western civilization which includes secularization, and in this secularized western civilization the "ontocratic" non-Western world receives Christianity *incognito*, so to speak.[14] By "ontocratic" Van Leeuwen means having an understanding of reality in terms of a total order of harmony between nature and man, between the spirit world including one's ancestors (to state it in Ibo's cosmic terms) and the natural world of men and their society; or in the words of Richard Shaull "ontocratic" means "an understanding of reality in terms of a total order of harmony between the eternal and the temporal, the divine and the human. The divine order is identified with nature and society, especially with the state conceived as the 'embodiment of cosmic totality'. All structures of society are given a sacral character; they dare not be tampered with or changed".[15] In enlarging upon this thesis, Van Leeuwen surveyed biblical history to show how prophetic faith in the living God was able to overcome the "Ontocratic" pattern of society in Israel, and how Jesus Christ triumphantly carried in himself this prophetic tradition not only to fulfil it but also to make it available to the new Israel which includes "Jews, Greeks and barbarians". It was this great fact that constituted western history into a Christian history, the crux of which is the Incarnation.

> "*Word* and not silence; *made flesh* and not concept; *grace*, instead of merit or spiritual techniques. *Faith* and not direct knowledge of the divine; *History*, instead of Myth. Recognition of the flesh and hence of matter as realities of our present life. *Paradox, Tension, dialectic* ... And love of one's neighbour as oneself, corresponding with the love of God, replacing the sacred, and founding the *person*".[16]

It is the decision of faith in this "Word made flesh" which has led the western man into the Christian way, that has constituted the

---

[14] Van Leeuwen, *op. cit.*, p. 16. Cf. Leslie Newbigin's paraphrase of the thesis in these words: "The thesis of this work ... is that the process of secularization is the present form in which the non-Western world is meeting biblical history". In Honest Religion for Secular Man, London: S.C.M. Paperback 1966, p. 27.

[15] Richard Shaull, "Revolutionary Changes in Theological Perspective" in J. C. Bennett (ed.), Social Ethics in a Changing World: An Ecumenical Theological Enquiry, New York: Association Press, London: S.C.M. Press, 1966, p. 23 fn.

[16] Denis de Rougemont, Man's Western Quest, as quoted by Van Leeuwen, *op. cit.*, p. 43.

Western history, which in its modern expression as technocracy and secularization had spread throughout the world. Attempts have been made within the history of the western Church to create the "onto-cratic" frame work once again, but such frame or pattern was again broken by the living power of the prophetic tradition nourished in the bible. Van Leeuwen goes on further to suggest that now that the western missionary effort in evangelising the non-Western world is being frustrated by forces set in motion by Christianity itself, for example science, technology and secularization, there is an urgent need for developing an ecumenical theology of history. Such theology should develop the logical connection between "westernization" and the new planetary mode of human existence on the one hand, and evangelization on the other.[17] Outlines for such an ecumenical theology of history are drawn in such views as: "We have ventured to suppose that in the spread of modern western civilization throughout the world something of the spirit of *Christianity incognito* is at work",[18] or "Christianity today has entered a phase of its history in which it presents itself no longer in the form of a self-contained *Corpus Christianum,* but in the bifurcated form of a greatly reduced, weakened and divided Church on the one hand and of a victorious 'secularized' civilization on the other".[19]

Many references Van Leeuwen makes to Christian history and western civilization show such close relationship between western civilization and Christianity that makes it appear that the two are identical. Despite the attempt to emphasize that "one must of course distinguish the two" and avoid confusing "the preaching of the Gospel with the spread of Christian civilization", yet he emphasizes how the Gospel historically has given rise to Christianity, and Christ-ianity has given rise to Christian civilization, which to Van Leeuwen, is the same as western civilization. We find this close identification of western civilization with Christianity a bit dangerous even though we accept the historical connection between the two. It is more accurate to accept that many roots of western civilization, including its modern emphasis on technology and secularization are traceable to the Christian faith and its theocratic influences (even this is a debated subject) but that, to say the least, the two have travelled away from each other, to develop their distinctive identities that clearly distinguish them.

---

17 *Op. cit.*, p. 431.
18 P. 18.
19 P. 16.

It is therefore doubtful how much "Christianity" non-Christian peoples will have by adopting secularization. We will be arguing in favour of using Christian theological frame work to develop an ethic that will be appealing and effective among non-Christians of Iboland which include the "lovers" of secularization and modernity, but we do not hope that that has any much chance of bringing Christ personally to the life of such Ibos, the kind of thing Van Leeuwen hopes would happen to non-western "ontocratic" societies when they adopt secularization. The contribution of Van Leeuwen, and others who have written on secular-theological approach to contemporary missionary activity of the Church, is too early to be properly assessed.[20] The insights such theological analyses give to our study are to be taken with the necessary caution involved for example, in this instance of somewhat easy identification of Christianity with western civilization; in Ibo society today Christianity is being rejected precisely by those who see this identification as neo-colonialism and Christianity as "the whiteman's religion".

Another aspect of Van Leeuwen's contribution which we will view with caution is the suggestion that the ontocratic is wholly evil and must be thrown overboard. Part of the concept covered by the word ontocratic is the Ibo world-view in which the spiritual is not divorced from the material. Nature is matter as well as "spirit" to the Ibo. To the western mind such close identity between the two is not so clear, but the new emphasis on the "theology of nature" and the necessity for preserving the environment and avoiding "pollution" and "desecration of nature", seem to be a search for greater understanding of the "sacredness" of nature, or put into Ibo cosmic terms, "reestablishing the close link between nature and spirit".[21] Van Leeuwen like any

---

[20] Friedrich Gogarten as quoted by Van Leeuwen defined secularization as "human existence comes to be determined by the dimension of time and history". Van Leeuwen, *op. cit.*, p. 331, Gogarten made significant contribution to the Secular theology using Barth's and Bonhoeffer's concepts especially the latter's "World come of age" idea. Richard Shaull's revolutionary theology and Harvey Cox's "Secular City", all contribute towards finding the best way of communicating the Gospel. See also Carl F. Hallencreutz, New Approaches to Men of other faiths, W.C.C. Geneva, 1970, pp. 66-67.

[21] A group of African theologians expressed elements in the African religious traditions which the African fails to see in the Church, among such basic elements are: (1) The unity of the spiritual and the material instead of which he finds in the Church that these are divorced. (2) The relation between man and the cosmos. W.C.C. Study Encounter SE/45, Vol. IX no. 3, 1973 "Giving Account of the Hope that is in Us—From an Exploratory Conversation", p. 5. If we accept Van Leeuwen's thesis entirely as he gives it about the "ontocratic",

discoverer of an aspect of truth, namely, the effect of biblical faith's destruction of religious belief that regarded nature as the external manifestation of the Godhead, which to deeply change or tamper with would evoke the wrath of the gods, in his enthusiasm oversimplified the nature of the relationship between man and nature. Recent Christian reexamination of the real meaning of the kind of dominion man is to exercise over nature, is more cautious in trying to discover what "truth" is to be found in treating nature with awe or "sacredness". The very fact that so many phenomena in nature "are meaningless and incomprehensible to man, is extremely meaningful, in so far as it teaches him the limits of his knowledge and task. That is the way in which nature appears in the mighty chapters 38-41 of Job. The abundancy and inexhaustibility, the absurdities and irrationalities of nature (i.e. what man calls so, from his limited viewpoint) reflect in their own way, the majesty and inscrutability of the Creator".[22] The Ibo, in the "sacred" or reverential attitude he holds towards nature while dominating it, reflects more this viewpoint than Van Leeuwen's thesis about the ontocratic societies' acceptance of secularization would permit.

The Faith and Order Commission of the World Council of Churches in their continued search for the Theology of nature remind us that "nature is both man's servant and his sister",[23] and these two aspects have to be kept in balance. Van Leeuwen emphasizes the way "ontocratic" society like the Ibo can accept secularization which treats nature as man's servant and completely neglects the other aspect of nature being man's sister. The Ibo's reverential or "sacred" attitude to nature while accepting the Christian tradition of nature as the "creation of a transcendent God"[24] is their attempt to treat nature as sister and this need not be destroyed. While agreeing with Van Leeuwen that there are elements in the nature of secularization and technological modernity which Ibo society must accept, and thereby in-

---

it means these fine traditions of the African heritage will not find expression in the teaching and life of the Church.

[22] New Directions in Faith and Order, Bristol 1967, Section I: God in Nature and History. Faith and Order Paper no. 30, Geneva, World Council of Churches 1968, p. 18.

[23] Faith and Order Paper, no. 30, *op. cit.*, p. 23, cf. Pope Paul VI's Message to the Hierarchy and to all the peoples of Africa, Vatican Polyglot Press, 1967 no. 8, where he reminds us that in African tradition "all living beings and visible nature are linked with the invisible and the spirit". Man is not limited to earth by life, but has also in him "the presence and power of another spiritual element in virtue of which human life is always related to after life".

[24] Faith and Order Paper, no. 30, *op. cit.*, p. 22.

directly accept Christian values, for example modern man's image of himself in the ethical model of Macquarrie which we have referred to (page 139), we must avoid the one sided desire for handling, changing and transforming nature which puts western technology and secularization in danger of "forgetting what nature has to contribute in her sister-function", for if man "exercises a dominion which more and more makes the display of nature's sister-aspect impossible, man will pay the price for his fault". [25]

One other difficulty associated with Van Leeuwen's desire to demolish "ontocratic" cultures with secularization is the confusion in the meaning of the word "secularization". Despite his attempt to define secularization as he developed it from biblical prophetic faith, to mean "the creative and liberating activity of the word of God" in contradistinction to secularization which means "being conformed to this world", the confusion continues. According to him "it is a curious thing about the history of Christianization that these two contrary processes of secularization are simultaneously at work within it". [26] This rather makes it difficult for non-western people like the Ibo to see how they can accept Christianity through secularization, where the emphasis of empirical Christianity of the West at present tends towards secularization (or what some writers call secularism) which is like "being conformed to this world"—at least that is the aspect of western technocracy that appeals to non-western countries. The considerable differences between the religious institutions of various traditions (even within the Church itself), and the consequences for the relation of sacred and secular, argue for the differentiation of several varieties of secularization; [27] and although Van Leeuwen is aware of these varieties of the meaning of secularization he does not seem to take this into serious consideration in recommending that secularization is the medium through which non-Christian and non-western people could take in Christianity. Some corrective to Van Leeuwen's over simplification about secularization and the "ontocratic"

---

[25] Faith and Order paper, *op. cit.*, p. 2.

[26] Van Leeuwen, *op. cit.*, p. 332. See also E. Jansen Schoonhoven, "A. Th. van Leeuwen en H. Kraemer" in *Nederlands Theologisch Tijdschrift* 23 (1969) pp. 25-36, where he argues that Van Leeuwen does not seem to differentiate between secularization in the Old Testament and modern secularization.

[27] See John B. Snock, "Varieties of Secularization" in the American Academy of Religion, Annual Meeting, Chicago, November 1973, Abstract of lectures edited by Robert Spivey, p. 33.

is already being provided, as we have already indicated by the emergence of the theology of nature or the theology of the ecology. [28]

The final critical point we wish to raise before analysing the helpful points we can make use of in Van Leeuwen's book is a suggestion he made that the Church can only help the non-western world from the present and the future of such non-western peoples; "it is not from the past that she can ever hope to capture the non-western world", he argues (page 420). Such past according to Van Leeuwen is already disintegrating with the impact of the revolutionary history of the West. We agree with Van Leeuwen about the distintegrating influence of the West (Christianity, technology and modernistic secularization all combined) on Ibo traditional society and its life. But if he means "that the past" of the Ibo as nursed up by its traditional religion, social systems and moral code should not be taken into consideration in interpreting Christianity to the Ibo, we disagree with him. The culture of the people as Van Leeuwen himself has analysed in the first chapter of his book, grows out of the total experiences of the people's past, and therefore to interpret to them the Christian faith in the present, we should be guided by their cultural past; even the language of the people grows out of the past and its use in Christian evangelisation of the Ibo is, to speak the least, presenting the Gospel today from the past in the hope of the future. Hence the importance of the thesis of our study which seeks to develop sound relevant theology for the Ibo in conscious awareness of Ibo life which includes Ibo moral values as developed centuries ago, although as they are presently experienced, for the present is always "pregnated by the past with the future". We now proceed to indicate those aspects of Van Leeuwen's book which we find positively helpful in the insight they give to our study.

Van Leeuwen makes a very strong case for the powerful effect of the Christian history. This history which started with prophetic messages in ancient Israel, in which God chose a people to enter into

---

28 Since after the Stockholm Conference on the "Environment" many Christian theologians are now more concerned especially in the United States, with what are the major implications for theology, of the ecological considerations especially with reference to the "harmony of the spheres" emphasized by "ontocratic societies" like the Ibo more than Van Leeuwen's thesis took notice of. See Hugh Kerr, "Ecosystems and Systematics" in *Theology Today*, Vol. XXIX, no. 1, April 1972, pp. 104-119. We are not unaware of the criticisms of Van Leeuwen on this theme coming from India, only that we wish to leave that out. See *Religion and Society*, nos. 12, 13 and 14, 1966-67.

convenant relationship with himself, assumed a significant turn when, through Jesus Christ, God himself intervened in the human religious quest and gave man the revelation of himself. First in the form of Christendom and then western Christian history, it has recently manifested itself in confrontation with non-Christian religions of non-western people both as technocratic secularization as well as the modern missionary movements from the West. Throughout the bible argues Richard Shaull, "there is a strong eschatological emphasis which stresses the dynamic nature of God and the fact that his action in history is moving toward a goal. It is this which has led Professor Van Leeuwen to conclude that the biblical attitude toward that world has made our modern revolution both possible and inevitable".[29] This Christian history has hit Iboland as we have analysed in Chapters IV and V. The cosmic totality of Ibo moral code has been punctured by this impact and the Ibo must, following the thesis of Van Leeuwen become involved in the onward movement of Christian history. This study is an effort to help him understand Christianity better so as to be able to enter more fully into that history.

Another aspect of Van Leeuwen's analysis that is of great help towards a clearer understanding of our study, is his idea about the meaning of "christianization" today. The expectation of earlier missionaries that non-western religions like Hinduism or African traditional religion would be replaced with Christianity was said to be based on false premises. "Certainly one may speak of "missionary failure", if one conceives the ultimate purpose of the mission to be replacing Hinduism with Christianity",[30] argues Van Leeuwen. He then goes on to say that the best Christians can expect to happen in a non-western, non-Christian area like Iboland with which we are concerned, is to confront the people with the inevitable and pervasive technocratic secularization of western history and through such confrontation expose them to the biblical prophetism already contained in the Christian history. Put in another way, as Carl Hallencreutz does, Van Leeuwen's analysis makes the Church's missionary task to include providing liberation from all bondage to "ontocratic" patterns which hinder true personal existence and to "participate in the ongoing

[29] Richard Shaull "Revolutionary Change in Theological Perspective" in B. C. Bennett (ed.), Christian Social Ethics in a Changing world: An Ecumenical Theological Enquiry, New York: Association Press, London: S.C.M. Press, 1966, p. 28.

[30] Van Leeuwen, *op. cit.*, p. 420.

process of secularization in the third world. It should not be concerned with a common religious front against secularism nor with any reconception of traditional religions".[31] We have already indicated above our reservations about the enthusiasm of Van Leeuwen that secularization contains "Christianization ferment". We have also rejected his plea against looking at the past of the people through their non-Christian religion, what Carl Hallencreutz describes here as "reconception of traditional religions". We are however inclined to agree with Van Leeuwen that in the fact of plurality of religious beliefs, ideologies and liberation forces (set in motion by biblical prophetic faith) which make people free to believe, or not to believe, thereby disregarding all forms of "doctrine based on authority", we can no longer hope to build Christendom in the non-Christian world of the Ibo, for example. Therefore the prospects for the result of missionary endeavours will be brighter and, humanly speaking, more realistic if we aim at punctuating life and society of the Ibo with Christian ethos and values, which is part of the thesis of this study.

A third point in Van Leeuwen which we find helpful, is his suggestion about the qualifications Churches in non-western missionary areas should possess so as to be truly indigenous. We are now tired of hearing about the unnecessary odium of foreignness which missionaries from the West have inflicted on Churches, in a place like Iboland, by being all too easily satisfied with exporting duplicate versions of their own particular type of Christianity, instead of finding the proper links within the culture of the people through which the Church can grow in the native soil of the mission area. We ourselves have already contributed to this over emphasized theme in chapter IV of this study. Van Leeuwen's new insight to the subject includes his warning, that making a Church indigenous merely by deepening its roots into the life of the society, so that it can be thoroughly identified with that society (for instance being the "established" Church, enjoying political and national privileges) has its own dangers which we should beware of. Such identification could deprive the Church, as the salt of the earth of its savour or be subjected to the kind of tragedy of the Germanized Christianity under the Nazi regime. This is a very healthy warning and we do well to remember it in the "indigenization pro-

---

31 Carl F. Hallencreutz, New Approaches to Men of Other Faiths, Geneva: World Council of Churches, 1970, p. 69. Cf. the Comment of Paul Löffler, Secular Man and Christian Mission, edited by Paul Löffler, Geneva: W.C.C., 1968, pp. 38 and 39.

cesses" we are developing in this study, for as Van Leeuwen observes, despite the risks and temptations involved in such indigenization, the Church in a place like Iboland "can properly fulfil her calling only when she meets the challenge and the risk in the freedom of faith and not under the shelter of any Western defences",[32] and this freedom is possible only when the Church reinterprets the Christian message in the culture and life experiences of the people as we try to do in this study.

Furthermore in promoting indigenization processes, the kind we are interested in, we should be warned that "there is a real danger that a Church beset with too tender a conscience about her foreign origin and character may waste her energies in adapting herself to aspects of an indigenous culture already consigned to the past and doomed to become out of date".[33] Our attempt to work out a theological position that will recommend that Christians in Iboland take on the full implications of the "extended family duties", the *Ọzọ* title and the sociological demands of polygamy, will benefit immensely from such warning. In the age of rapid social change the Church will have to face series of indigenization exercises, as each decade turns up with new cultural habits which require that the Gospel be re-interpreted to become relevant to such a generation, and this is a type of evangelization that all Churches must gear their missionary orientation towards. For Iboland it will mean that the initial exercise in indigenization processes, must be prepared materially and spiritually not only for re-interpreting the Christian message in the Ibo culture and life, but also in rearing Christians for the ever changing tempo of twentieth century life, which includes secularization and the arrival in greater doses of modern civilization. The missionary activity of the Church in Iboland, and throughout the world for that matter, set in this dimension will be very exacting, tremendous and costly in men, material, spiritual resources and mental energy. It is hoped that this study will make even a modest contribution towards a clearer understanding of part of the strategy of such missionary enterprise in the twentieth century—the century that sees the end of the traditional missionary work, and watches with anxiety for the start of the new and more complicated Christian mission.

The fourth and final point from Van Leeuwen's book (p. 425 f.f.)

---

[32] Van Leeuwen, *op. cit.*, p. 423.
[33] Van Leeuwen, *op. cit.*, p. 424.

which we find helpful in our study is his question whether or not there should be an "Eastern theology" and for our purpose, an African Theology. He observes that in view of the fact that the Asian and African Churches have been educated for long on straightforward transference of Western theological ways of thought, there is an urgent need for creative work on the part of Asian and African theologians—lay as well as clerical.

Despite this need for interpreters of the Christian message to come from Africa and to contain African thought-forms, a Christian theology seriously speaking, has only national or continental or cultural insights but remains pure and simple Christian theology. Missionary theology is a vital part of the Christian Gospel and can not be "Eastern" or "Western", "American" or "African". The vision of the prophetic highway of Isaiah (chapter 35 verses 8-10) along which all walk towards the *shalom* and the *pleroma* of the New Jerusalem, calls for interpreters all along the way, no matter from where they enter and with what historical, cultural and national insight. Their journey is one, its origin is the One Lord and its destination is the same one Lord, hence the theological map is one no matter the contours, shadings and scales. Our study of the patterns of Christian ethics in an African background may contain African colourings from Iboland yet it remains pure and simple Christian theology. We have just used the imagery of the highway from Isaiah chapter 35 along which all those the Lord has ransomed shall return to him, whether they enter the highway from Africa or from Europe. We have also used the imagery of maps and regard our study as an African colouring on the road map that leads all Christians on the highway to the New Jerusalem. These imageries could be very instructive in this question of whether or not there should be African theology, Eastern theology or Western theology. If it is the "colourings" that are labelled as "African", "Eastern" or "Western" theologies, the absurdity will be immediately clear, for no one regards as the map the red colouring that indicates the mountains, or the green colourings that show the forests—these are mere colourings on the map. Another slant to the discussion comes from a statement from an Occasional Bulletin of the Research Department of the Church of England Assembly Overseas' Council which raises the question as to whether European and African Christians are not today called to stand together in the work of bringing under the Lordship of Christ the modern technological civilization which, as Van Leeuwen has clearly shown us, is becoming the common "culture" of mankind, instead of Christians in the two continents struggling to harmonise the differences in their Christianity brought about by their differing cultures.[34]

Our attempt in this study has just been described as that of interpreting Christian message from an African background just as a European interpreter does so from his European background, but our common endeavour is to bring our respective peoples to acknowledge, in the face of technocratic civilization and secularization, that Jesus is the Lord. Towards this common goal all Christian theologies (whether the orientation be African or European, whether moral, systematic or dogmatic) must move, and on that account become inevitably one theology. The theological task of our age therefore must accept that its inspiration may come from the "multi-coloured" Asian, Western, African or Latin-American expressions of our era. As long as all such expressions aim at and fulfil the one purpose of making Christ known, appreciated and accepted, or even rejected (because the Gospel is always a judgment upon men and judgment includes the possibilities of rejection) it is one theology and not "Eastern" theology or "Western" theology or "African" theology. Ecumenicity does not mean only the calling and the attending of world conferences, it includes also thinking together of world problems from world-wide varied experiences of the One Lord Jesus Christ. The missionary challenge of the emerging international culture, made possible by Christian missionary work, technology and secularization, is a challenge for effective and relevant theology by which Jesus Christ is clearly presented as absolutely crucial towards an understanding of the meaning of the emerging world community. From this consideration all theology becomes "missionary theology", meaning the theology that reflects clearly on what Christ means to the situations of secularization, revolutionary changes, liberation movements, search for new identity especially by the oppressed and the disprivileged peoples of the world. In this most exciting but most difficult "missionary" task of the Church, its theology cannot afford to be anything than one dynamic Christian theology of "the Cross and Him crucified" on it whether written by the African, the Asian or the Westerner. We now turn to the discussion of the contributions Hendrik Kraemer makes towards the clarification of our subject matter.

---

[34] Occasional Bulletin, nos. 3 and 4, London: Church Assembly Overseas Council, 1962, pp. 14-17.

Dr. Hendrik Kraemer

Dr. Kraemer was a prolific writer whose thoughts overflowed from one major theological topic to another. It is however as a missionary thinker, strategist and statesman that he is relevant to our study, hence his works that we will call attention to are: *The Christian Message in a Non-Christian World; Religion and the Christian Faith, and From Missionfield to Independent Church: Report on a Decisive Decade in the Growth of Indigenous Churches in Indonesia.*[35] Some of the key topics of Kraemer like syncretism, the unique nature of biblical revelation together with the universalism of that revelation for all mankind, were also handled by Visser 't Hooft and Van Leeuwen and we have discussed them in some brief form while analysing these two writer's relevance to our study. To avoid repeating ourselves, we will briefly show how Kraemer differed from the other two, especially in discussing syncretism, so as to concentrate on other themes that Kraemer has handled in more specific ways, namely the attitude of Christianity to other faiths both as religions as well as moral systems of human salvation.

On syncretism the analysis of Visser 't Hooft which, as we have already indicated, distinguished three kinds of uses which writers make of the word, Kraemer is in general agreement; after all Visser 't Hooft used Kraemer to a large extent. The latter's explicit emphasis on biblical realism sharpened the meaning of syncretism. The concept of syncretism as illigitimate mingling of different religious elements, can only grow out of Christian atmosphere when the pure light of divine self revelation in the biblical tradition shines on man's attempts through the religions to find salvation for himself—what Van Leeuwen described in the biblical phrase as "building a tower of Babel whose top would reach the heavens". Kraemer goes on to say that as a matter of history, syncretism both as concept and a word, resulted from Protestant theological controversies of the seventeenth century. Before then the amalgamation of cults on the basis of naturalistic kinship was a feature of all naturalist religions (which could not have been regarded illegitimate) and it continues to be so even now.[36]

Kraemer therefore argues that the real meaning of syncretism can

---

[35] The Christian Message in a non-Christian World, London: Edinburgh House Press, 1938. Religion and the Christian Faith, London: Lutterworth Press, 1956. From Missionfield to Independent Church, London: S.C.M. Press, 1958.

[36] Hendrik Kraemer, Christian Message in a Non-Christian World, *op. cit.*, p. 203. Van Leeuwen, Christianity and World History, *op. cit.*, p. 417.

only be understood when the religions of mankind are judged by biblical realism.

Translation, adaptation and syncretism proper which we have analysed in Visser 't Hooft are also thoroughly discussed by Kraemer with lengthy clarification of what adaptation is and what it is not. Anti-adaptationists are condemned as unrealistic, whilst over-zealous adaptationists are criticised because "their idea of adaptation, although they intend the opposite, inevitably leads to the weakening of Christianity, for in practice, it is not the endeavour to bring Christian truth to its most vigorous and clear expression by indigenous ways, but to recast Christianity into an indigenous philosophy of life, in which the dominant elements are the pre-Christian apprehension of existence, coloured and sanctioned by supposedly kindred Christian elements". [37] This sounds like syncretism and not adaptation or indigenization, and may not have been described as "the activity of over-zealous adaptationists", but simply the activities of syncretists in view of the fact that the "dominant elements" are pre-Christian "apprehension of existence" and pre-Christian "philosophy of life". One of the problems leading to the debate about "syncretism", "adaptation", "continuity" and "discontinuity" since the publication of Kraemer's *Christian Message in a Non-Christian World* and since after the *International Missionary Conference* at Tambaran near Madras in India in 1938, in our view, could be due to the complicated, or one should say "dialectical" use of these terms by Kraemer, which a lot of people have misunderstood. "Adaptation" is used in one breath as expressing the cardinal facts of the revelation in Christ "by wrestling with them *concretely* (my italics) and so to present the Christian truth and reveal at the same time the intrinsic inadequacy of man's religious efforts", [38] in another breath "adaptation" is "the genuine translation of Christianity into indigenous terms so that its relevancy to their concrete situations becomes evident". [39] One would have preferred that in order to avoid any misunderstanding in the use of the word "adaptation", [40] the function of relevant communication of the faith in clear "indi-

---

[37] Kraemer, The Christian Message, *op. cit.*, p. 317.

[38] Kraemer, *op. cit.*, p. 308.

[39] Kraemer, *op. cit.*, p. 323. Note that Kraemer in Religion and the Christian Faith accepted the need for further clarification of key words and key concepts used in The Christian Message in an Non-Christian World. See Religion and the Christian Faith, *op. cit.*, p. 232.

[40] Some clarification of key concepts have been given in his subsequent book Religion and the Christian Faith.

genous terms" could be expressed by the word "adaptation" as in the last quotation; whilst the analysis of non-Christian religions by subjecting them to the judgment of biblical realism to show their inadequacy could be expressed in another word.

Kraemer emphasizes the use of cultural anthropology as a vehicle for the clearer understanding of the cultural usefulness of non-Christian religions. From such clearer understanding we can then re-interpret Christianity and make it indigenous to a people like the Ibo. We feel certain therefore that Kraemer would support our stand in this study. When he expounds the deep meanings of his major theme, namely, the uniqueness of biblical realism, he does so in such a way that makes it difficult to forget that biblical realism, when translated into concreteness in the application of the Gospel to the Ibo for example, would mean not only using their cultural and historical religious experiences, but also doing so in such a way that keeps the Gospel still unique, even when the culture through which it is interpreted had grown out of the people's non-Christian religion. To do this would mean conversion of the spiritual values in non-Christian religions to which Kraemer would have no objection. From the survey Carl Hallencreutz prepared on the debates about the approach to men of other faiths by Christians since after Tambaran, some people who had felt uneasy about Kraemer's exact meaning of "continuity" and "discontinuity" had attacked his approach.[41] There might be the need as Kraemer himself expressed later for definite clarification of what is meant, for example by the phrase, "conversion of the spiritual values in non-Christian religions" or, "the obligation to strive for the presentation of the Christian truth in terms and modes of expression that makes its challenge intelligible and related to the peculiar quality of reality in which they (Churches of the mission field) live",[42] yet his meaning is clear enough for us to make our deductions. The same goes for his often repeated warning that "paganism and the prophetic revelation of biblical realism are not continuous with each other".[43] The deduction we wish to make from these quotations is that the first

---

[41] C. F. Hallencreutz, *op. cit.*, p. 43. Cf. E. C. Dewick's acceptance of the validity of the appeal to religious experience as the faith of the religious man testifies to divine revelational activity outside the Church. E. C. Dewick, The Christian Attitude to Other Religions, Cambridge: The University Press, 1953, pp. 136 ff. Hallencreutz also calls attention to Kenneth Cragg's uneasiness with Kraemer's view of "discontinuity". Hallencreutz, *op. cit.*, p. 43.

[42] Kraemer, *op. cit.*, p. 302.

[43] Ibid., p. 338.

two statements argue for continuity with non-Christian religions, while the last statement argues for discontinuity. This is one example of Kraemer's dialectical dimension in which two seeming contradictions stand by each other, but which in fact are the two sides of the same coin. This we believe, results from his handling of crucial issues about the real content and meaning of the Gospel, as well as the proper method of transmitting it. We will discuss these two points further, that is, how far we can use non-Christian religions as the "human starting point" towards the people's fuller understanding of Christianity, and where the communication of the Gospel must avoid the use of non-Christian religions with which it can have nothing like continuity what so ever. Meanwhile we take up Kraemer's analysis of religions and their moral systems in the light of Christianity's biblical realism.

Christianity is the revelation of God to man in Jesus Christ prepared for by the prophetic religion of Israel. Its essential nature in comparison with religions of man, is that it is the voluntaristic manifestation of God to man unaided by man's search, whilst religions are man-made attempts at obtaining salvation by human effort. Put simply in this form we see clearly why Kraemer says religions like the Ibo traditional religion could not have prepared the way for Christianity. Biblical revelation is an "objective act of God in which His will and His mind in regard to the condition of man and the world and their need become revealed and claim absolute and *unique* (our italics) validity".[44] This uniqueness of Christianity through this objective act of God's revelation, means in effect God's recognition of the impotence of man to know God in a real divine human personal relationship. Personality on human level can only be penetrated into by another personality through the willing act of self-exposure to the other person. This is more so in divine Personality. Therefore God man can never know unless God reveals himself to man. This is the crux of the difference between Christianity and the religions, and it is this uniqueness of Christianity, or this new fact of God-man relationship, which Kraemer highly emphasizes. It is this act of God in Jesus Christ which assures man of a new beginning in his relationship to God. This constitutes the Gospel, and for it man has no other substitute, no matter the sublime height he may have reached in his man-made religious history. Here we are perfectly in agreement with Kraemer about the given facts of the Gospel message, namely, that God of his

---

[44] Kraemer, Christian Message in a Non-Christian World, *op. cit.*, p. 143.

own free will acted in history, and in Jesus Christ became man who "lived, died and ascended" and on withdrawing of his bodily presence from his disciples, he sent to them the Holy Spirit who taught and inspired them towards personal faith in God to whom they were now reconciled through this Jesus. From such conviction and through the missionary activities of the apostles the Church grew.

The ethic that developed out of this act of God's revelation is not given in the bible as a religious or moral philosophy. [45] Both Jesus as well as St. Paul and other apostles deduced the type of behaviour consonant with this new situation of divine-human relationship instead of writing out a blue print of Christian ethics as a fossilized system of code and philosophy. "It is, however, an adulteration of the concrete and radical religious realism of the Bible and the Christian Faith to take these derivations as the essential and abiding invariables of the Gospel. This intense religious realism of the Bible proclaims and asserts realities. It does not intend to present a "world-view", but it challenges man in his *total* being to confront himself with these realities and accordingly take decisions". [46] All the amount of ethical deductions St. Paul for example, made from the inevitable response of man to this new relationship with God, becomes meaningful only for those who become "new creature" in Christ, observing, as we have indicated in chapter VI, this new relationship as "sons of God" and "heirs of Christ" by not defrauding their fellowmen, not selling their bodies to a prostitute in sexual immorality, and so on. Kraemer therefore concludes that Christian ethic, as it has been developed from the Bible, and throughout Christian history, is entirely "incommensurable with all other ethics in the world" [47] because of its motive force and also because of the ends it serves in being the fruit or the result of the new fellowship with God. It is in the effort to discover how we can concretely reach the totality of the personality, by using the structures and the institutions of Ibo society as the channels through which the Ibos can manifest this fruit of Christian faith in daily living, that the need arises for indigenization of the Church. This means the re-interpretation or "the making concrete the challenges of the faith to real life situation". Every generation and every culture are called upon to do this and as Kraemer has reminded us, this work of "genuine translation presupposes a thorough grasp of what Christian

[45] Kraemer, *op. cit.*, p. 64.
[46] Ibid.
[47] Kraemer, *op. cit.*, p. 85.

truth is and of the material in which it must be expressed"; [48] Hence the effort in this study to reflect theologically, from some aspects of the Christian faith, and anthropologically as well as sociologically, from some understanding of Ibo society.

It is not our concern in this brief examination of the relevance of Kraemer's thoughts to our study to go through all his brilliant analyses of non-Christian religions, and the various changes or restatements of convictions he developed in various writings during the course of his many studies and the long period of his theological reflections. Such survey has been ably done by men like Carl Hallencreutz. [49] We can only call attention to his insistence that non-Christian religions could never be the results of the *logos spermatikos* or the embodiments of *praeparatio evangelica.* [50] Although Kraemer would admit that no one can stop God from revealing himself in any way he (God) would choose, he nevertheless insists that biblical revelation does not receive "light" from the religions of man, or from their concerns about nature which will show any further "truth" about God. "For after that in the wisdom of God the world by wisdom knew not God, it pleased God by the foolishness of preaching to save them that believe" (1 Cor. 1 verse 21).

Kraemer quoted this passage from St. Paul's first epistle to the Corinthians to show once more that the realm analysed in biblical revelation and the realm of the religions of man are two "categories entirely different". He would concede that through a process of subjecting the religions to the scrutiny of biblical thinking, and by applying the methods of theological science of religion, "one may discover in this way, gradually, a number of pointers in the direction of, or definitely away from the Gospel". [51] With this proviso Kraemer still rejects that the religions of man can be seen as *praeparatio evangelica* because the Gospel has its definite *sui generis* character. Hence the religions can never be fulfilled by the revelation of Christ. [52] One can easily agree with Kraemer in this emphasis that the revelation of God, as

[48] Kraemer, *op. cit.*, p. 323.

[49] Carl Hallencreutz, New Approach to Men of other Faiths, Geneva: W.C.C. 1970. See also his: Kraemer towards Tambaram: A study in Hendrik Kraemer's Missionary Approach, Uppsala, 1966.

[50] H. Kraemer, Religion and the Christian Faith, London, Lutterworth Press, 1956, pp. 348-352.

[51] Ibid., p. 350.

[52] Cf. A. Th. Van Leeuwen, Christianity in World History, London, Edinburgh House Press, 1966, p. 416.

contained in biblical realism, is absolutely a new initiative of God to which the religions of man have nothing to contribute; but when it comes to the "conversion" of the spiritual values in non-Christian religions, as we have already indicated, we find that it is necessary and useful to do so by forging some tenuous link between Christianity and a non-Christian religion like that of the Ibo.

We had already indicated that we would discuss further how we can use non-Christian religions as "the human starting point" (Kraemer's phrase) towards the Ibo's fuller understanding of Christianity (which is continuity) and at the same time show where Christianity must avoid the non-Christian religion because between the two there are no links (which is discontinuity). Our thesis has already indicated our belief that Ibo traditional religious experiences, cultural expressions and the unconscious responses of man to the obedience of God through traditional ways of life, can be used as channels of communicating the meaning of the Gospel to the Ibo. The emphasis Kraemer consistently makes is that in doing so we must not adulterate the Gospel itself—hence his great fear of syncretism, a subject to which we will return presently. The Christ-event as God's unique act of his self disclosure through which man is invited by God himself to close and personal relationship with him, is absolutely discontinuous with non-Christian religious attempts of man to achieve salvation. The contents of the Gospel is new, distinct and therefore discontinuous with the Ibo's search for *Chukwu*, but the interpretation and the relating of the Gospel to concrete day to day living in Ibo society can draw from the background of the people. We are repeating this over and over again because it appears that the debates over Kraemer's concepts about "continuity" and "discontinuity", "specific revelation" and "general revelation" are unnecessary when real concrete situations are faced. It could have been very illuminating if Kraemer himself had worked out in practical detail how he could have converted the spiritual values in non-Christian religions of the Amboina people,[53] for example. If he did this, he would have retained some "continuity" with their past including their religious cultural past. He could not have done the "genuine translation" which he advocated strongly

[53] The tiny island of Amboina belongs to the archipelago of the South Moluccas, West of New Guinea (now Irian Jaya) Dr. Kraemer toured this place in 1926, part of his report on the Church there is contained in H. Kraemer, From Mission Field to Independent Church, London: S.C.M. Press, 1958, pp. 13-26. Kraemer himself in Religion and the Christian Faith said that the "whole controversy of "continuity-discontinuity, was "superfluous", *op. cit.*, p. 352.

without thorough knowledge of the people which anthropologists now tell us can only be gained by knowledge of the people's religion.[54] Therefore Kraemer's system of the communication of the Gospel contains both the principle of discontinuity as well as of continuity with the non-Christian religious background of the people to whom the Gospel is taken. Therefore the "continuity" and "discontinuity" debates were in the first instance unnecessary. The same "both/and" idea can be seen in his writings in respect of God's specific revelation in Christ and God's self-disclosure to man in history and creation. In his exegesis of the mythical story of Genesis chapter 3 he says: "the truth about man is that *he, in religious, moral and psychological respects, i.e. in his total being, finds himself through the fall in an inescapable dialectical condition; related to God—separated from Him; sought by God ("Adam where art thou": God's self-disclosure to man) and haunted by Him—rebelling against Him and yet groping towards Him*".[55]

Kraemer here admits God's self-disclosure to man despite man's rebellion and the fact of the Fall. That self-disclosure has continued in all history and ages and cultures[56] despite the special unique and "once-for-all" self-disclosure of God in Jesus Christ. There are therefore even in Kraemer's system features of both general and unique revelations of God, only that in the application of this truth to missionary activities of the Church, we must be careful not to act or speak glibly as if the general revelation in non-Christian religions is an unbroken companion of the Christ-event, and we are prepared to accept this warning of Kraemer, for it checks us against the undiscriminating mixture of religious beliefs that blurs the radical demands of God in Christ. Kraemer having been a missionary once, is much concerned with how best the Gospel is communicated but it does seem that he very often emphasizes the depth of the uniqueness and the vision of "the ideal Christian message" rather than work out the

---

[54] See Robin Horton, "A Definition of Religion and its Uses", Journal of the Royal Anthropological Institute, No. 90, part 2, 1960, pp. 201-226.

[55] H. Kraemer, Religion and the Christian Faith, London: Lutterworth Press, 1956, p. 251.

[56] Cf. Prof. H. H. Farmer's "The Idea of revelation is found... in all religions; we could even say in all cultures", Revelation and Religion, London: Nisbet, 1954, pp. 105 ff. Cf. Tillich's view that in the relation of Christianity to non-Christian religions we could apply "dialectical union of rejection and acceptance". See Paul Tillich, Christianity and the Encounter of the World Religions, New York: Columbia University Press, 1963, pp. 30-33.

details of the empirical implications to show practically how some of his great ideas of mission could have worked out in a place like the Ibo society. Of course to demand this would amount to expecting too much from Kraemer whose main task as he conceived it was "to investigate into the great human fact: Religion: in the light of Biblical Revelation, particularly in the light of Jesus Christ".[57] This great concern about biblical revelation makes Kraemer lament that empirical Christianity has failed to realise the contents and the promise of the revelation in historical actuality. Kraemer however handles the contents of biblical revelation in a prophetic manner showing how biblical realism is different from religion and when Christianity, resulting from biblical revelation becomes concrete as empirical Christianity, it becomes like one of the religions. Hence his emphasis that "Christianity as a phenomenon in history has to be considered as a form of religion just like the others... This thesis must constantly be repeated in order to avoid the frequently occurring identification or partial identification of Christianity, one of the religions, with the Revelation of God in Christ".[58] It is correct therefore to say that Kraemer's vision or gaze was fixed primarily on "the Revelation of God in Christ". It is in that light that he sees the religions of man, and speaks convincingly about biblical realism in terms of "discontinuity" with the religions and regards it as the only revelation or the unique revelation.

Kraemer's prophetic insight into the divergence between biblical realism and its expression in empirical Christianity raises very important question about the relationship between Christianity as the historical institutional Church and Christianity as the unique revelation of God in Jesus Christ. The revelation is greater and other than the empirical manifestation in the institution historically called the Church. What is preached is the revelation and yet it is the Church that communicates this revelation to the non-Christians, and it is from and through the Church that the revelation becomes known. Therefore to the non-Christian people the easy identification of the Church with its message, that is the revelation of God in Christ, is easily understandable. It is only through the processes of teaching and the re-interpretation of the Gospel in the people's thought form that the

[57] H. Kraemer, Religion and the Christian Faith, *op. cit.*, p. 6.

[58] Kraemer, Religion and the Christian Faith, *op. cit.*, p. 82. Cf. Christian Message in a non-Christian World, *op. cit.*, p. 145 "erroneous identification of empirical Christianity with the revelation in Christ".

distinction can once more be brought out in a mission area. Hence the importance of baptizing the people's culture into Christianity.[59] This brings us once more to the last point we want to discuss here in this summary, namely, syncretism.

We have already indicated Visser 't Hooft's analysis of syncretism which is developed from Kraemer and have accepted the three kinds out of which only one is the real meaning of syncretism, namely, the denial of the specific revelation in Christ which leads to the attempt in finding the common denominator in religions, with which the definite contents of God's revelation of himself in Christ are mixed, blurred and adulterated. We therefore follow Kraemer in accepting that syncretism has meaning only in Christianity or in biblical realism's search light being placed on the religions of mankind; after all with the religions of mankind syncretism as the mixing of cults, gods and rituals is as natural as water is to fish. Therefore this "matter of fact" feature of religions does not deserve to be given any special name. We are however aware of the vast amount of literature emanating from the "History of Religions" and other sources on the subject of "syncretism" in this "matter of fact" meaning of the word.[60] Search for common features or the analysis of the same phenomenon occurring in various and different historical and cultural locations are treated under "syncretism"; when religious ideas and varied interpretations can be fitted into a more comprehensive and overarching meaning-scheme, "syncretism" is invoked; when a particular context of meaning gives indication of having been influenced by another context, it is described

[95] Kraemer did this when he condemned the edict banning the burning of candles in the Church and performing of ritual lamentation for the dead by Amboinese Christians. See Kraemer, From the Mission Field to Independent Church, *op. cit.*, pp. 21-22.

There is need for thorough study through the insight of theology and sociology about this discrepancy between the Church as "The Revelation of God in Christ" and as a social institution with all the human weaknesses in jostling for leadership, role playing, channels and chains of command and sanctions of commendation or condemnation. It will be very instructive to see what such joint study can reveal. A combination of the theological analysis of Kraemer with the historical cum sociological analysis of Weber of Troeltsch will definitely prove rewarding in such a study. See Max Weber, Protestant Ethic and the Spirit of Capitalism, New York, Charles Scribner and Sons, 1958. Ernst Troeltsch, The Social Teaching of the Christian Churches, 2 vols. Trans. by Olive Wyon, New York: The Macmillan Company, 1931.

[60] See Walter H. Capps, "Geo Widengren on syncretism: On Parsing Uppsala. Methodological Tendencies" in *Numen: International Review for the History of Religions*, Vol. XX, Fasc. 3, Dec. 1973, pp. 163-185, in which some current literature on the subject is mentioned.

and examined under the umbrella of "syncretism". From our specific meaning and understanding of syncretism these various examples of "syncretism" appear ridiculous. Ideas are bound to interact and religion as a phenomenon of human existence, must have features that appear in several different historical and cultural locations as a matter of course, and need not be examples of "syncretism". We make this short comment on "syncretism" as an academic exercise of analysis and the search for "genus and species", or as descriptions of religious traditions that contain "fusion, union or coalescence",[61] so as to indicate clearly the meaning and context of what we accept as syncretism. From the academic point of view of the historian of religions, this might be regarded as a very narrow view of "syncretism", but from our standpoint it is the only meaningful understanding of the word, that is that syncretism has meaning only in Christianity.

This chapter has provided for us the opportunity to clarify the theory of mission and the methodology of missionary activity which our thesis can support and by which it can be defended. We have here identified three usages of the word "syncretism" for example and by pinpointing what is syncretism proper, we have shown that our study suggests how to avoid syncretism while at the same time we re-interpret Christianity to the Ibo as an exercise in "genuine translation" of the faith for its greater and effective acceptance, appropriation and revitalization. We have gained some insight in the usefulness of secularization as an indirect means of some Ibo accepting Christian norms even when they are not within the membership of the Church. It will help us to organise the practical suggestions we will make to the Churches about how they should handle certain aspects of Ibo cultural institutions like the *Ọzọ* title, polygamy and the extended family and lineage responsibilities so that Christianity can take the ideas and practices associated with them into its own life (what Kraemer calls absorption). We have seen in the concept of the Universal Church, resulting from the unique revelation of God in Jesus Christ, that no people should find the Church a "foreign" body (other than the foreignness that belongs to the nature of the Church itself as a colony of heaven on earth) because the essential meaning of the universality of the Church is that it relates to the total experiences of man every-

---

61 Walter H. Capps, *op. cit.*, p. 183. Kraemer, Christian Message in a non-Christian World ,*op. cit.*, p. 203 (already referred to in note no. 36).

where, be it cultural, psychological and spiritual. The Ibo Christian therefore can be taught to feel at home from the totality of his being, as contained in his past and his present experiences, both as a Christian as well as a member of his society.

In that society reality for example is a system of ideas in bodily form, life is spiritualistic, but only because it is manifested in human and other symbolic forms. *Aru* as ritual avoidance or religious prohibition is a spiritualistic idea containing a powerful force with contamination-potency, and yet its meaning is in the bodily appearance of a cock crowing in the night or a woman giving birth to twin babies. This is why a thorough going separation of spirit and matter is not easily acceptable to the Ibo. Interactionism between the two (spirit and matter) is the method the Ibos employ to avoid thorough going separation between an idea, or spiritually loaded event like the revelation in the Christ-event, and its empirical expression in the historic Church. When Christianity is clearly presented as the unique revelation of God in Christ (which Kraemer rightly emphasizes) with its high level spirituality, and at the same time interpreted in the bodily form of the visible Church through the Ibo life experiences and culture, the Ibo will be more involvingly caught up by the mystery and the reality of the Church, "the Body of Christ". This we hope should minimise the divergence between "the Revelation of God in Christ" and "Christianity as a phenomenon in history" to which Kraemer has consistently called attention.

Having made this excursion into the theoretical approach of Visser 't Hooft, Van Leeuwen and Kraemer to the missionary work of the Church, we can appreciate the more and subscribe to the statement with which a group of African theologians meeting at Ibadan in 1966 summed up their thinking:

> "We recognise the radical quality of God's self-revelation in Jesus Christ; and yet it is because of this revelation we can discern what is truly of God in our pre-Christian heritage: this knowledge of God (in Christ Jesus) is not totally discontinuous with our people's previous traditional knowledge of Him". [62]

[62] Biblical Revelation and African Beliefs edited by Kwesi Dickson and Paul Ellingworth, London: Lutterworth Press, 1970, p. 16. The literature is immense on the argument for and against "continuity" and "discontinuity". We have indicated a few in footnotes. Hallencreutz's New Approaches to Men of Other Faiths, *op. cit.*, is a good guide to the literature on the topic. We want to observe however that Roman Catholic theologians as well as Asian and African writers

Bishop James Johnson, the African Anglican Bishop who succeeded Bishop Crowther on the Niger (in which Iboland is included), reminded the Pan Anglican Congress in 1908: "Christianity is intended to be the religion not of one particular race of people only, but of the whole world. But in different countries it will wear different types, if it is to become indigenous to every soil. It should have in Europe a European type. In Asia an Asiatic type—different types of one and the same religion with different formulae of faith and different ceremonies of worship; for not otherwise can Christianity wear anywhere a national character, not otherwise can its attitude be what it should towards national customs which have much in them to help to promote indigenousness to it". [63]

With these statements as further support to the thesis of this study, and not forgetful of the necessary caution one should take when communicating the Gospel of the unique revelation of God in Jesus Christ to the Ibo, for example, we now proceed in the next chapter to indicate the practical possibilities of developing Christian ethics in an African background.

---

tend to favour "continuity" theories. In Europe, America and Britain there is a division with Barthians and American Fundamentalists tending towards "discontinuity". Our position as already indicated is both "continuity" and "discontinuity".

63 E. A. Ayandale, Holy Johnson: Pioneer of African Nationalism 1836-1917, London: Frank Cass, 1970, p. 302.

CHAPTER EIGHT

CHRISTIANITY AND AFRICAN CULTURE: THE IBO EXAMPLE

Introductory Matter

The main concern of our study is to answer these questions: How does the Ibo Christian assess and respond to the demands of his culture, which are facts which he can no longer ignore? This culture and its demands have grown out of non-Christian, traditional religious influences. Secondly, how can the Ibo at the same time as he responds to the demands of his culture, remain faithful to the Christian Faith? In addition to the demands of his culture, he must also respond to the influences of the recent past, influences that result from the existence of the Church for over one hundred years, from the confrontation Ibo-life has with Western technological civilization and secularization and the influences from the crack in the Ibo traditional moral code which has resulted from that code's interaction with both Christianity and technological secularization. The frame-work for answering the questions posed by our thesis has been developed in the preceding seven chapters. After the introduction in chapter I, Ibo traditional society and religion are discussed in chapters II and III so as to indicate the major aspects of the Ibo culture and its value orientation. Chapters IV and V contain the history of the development of Christianity and the influence of technological culture as well as the various levels of interaction between Christianity, technological culture and Ibo life. From such interaction it has become clear that many Ibos live in three worlds of three competing norms: the old traditional way which is no longer as compact and effective as in the past and yet it is of great consequence to the people; the Christian values which are not yet well understood and internalized but all the same are very challenging by demanding total allegiance; and the utilitarian modernistic demands of technological secularization and its culture. This technological culture is not clearly defined and yet it remains very attractive. Some Ibos regard it as a liberating force from the shackles of the authoritarian traditional moral code and the "perfectionism" of Christian morals, which as we have just indicated, are not properly understood. Christian morals still remain uninterpreted to the Ibos in the people's thought-forms and unconscious imagination as well as in the social outreach of their daily life. Chapter VI shows where these three normative influences differ and where they agree with each other, indicating what can be best learnt from each value system.

Because the Ibos are used to having religious background for their ethical norms, and the traditional religion in its teaching and world view is now inadequate to explain most of the experiences of today, the Christian religion becomes the only satisfactory existing religion (there is little or no Islam) from which an ethos could be developed to take in Ibo present experiences. Hence the need for this Christian ethics in an African background which we are concerned with. We have already in chapter VII indicated that the theoretical approach we are adopting in relating the Christian Faith to Ibo traditional religious life-experiences is a combination of the principles of "continuity" and "discontinuity". In the Christ-event, that is, the self-disclosure of God to man in Christ Jesus who through his life, death, resurrection and glorification shows man how God loves and cares for him, Ibo traditional religion and life can contribute no new insight. It is the direct action of God's intervention, it is God's initiative and direct message to man. This is "discontinuity". In the understanding of how this Christ-event can be an effective feature of daily life within the structures of Ibo social life, practices and relationships, some continuity with Ibo life experiences as influenced by its traditional religion, customs and exchanges (culture) becomes inevitable. This is "continuity".

Furthermore we have shown in chapter I that this study deals also with culture change due to the meeting of those religions and cultures we have been discussing. It is not always realised that one of the latent (meaning not included in the major aims) effects of missionary work is the disruption it introduces into the culture of the missionary areas. Decay in the Ibo moral code started when Christianity preached directly against some Ibo beliefs like the spirit-world of the Ibo and the earth goddess (*ala*) and her sanctity around which a good deal in that moral code was built. That was the start of cultural change in Iboland. Hence our conviction that a new ethical norm, built on the Christian Faith but interpreted through Ibo life experience, will lead to a new cultural vitality which could once more integrate the Ibo society towards a more meaningful experience than what obtains now in the absence of any such effective norm. While comparing Ibo ethical ideas with those of Christianity in chapter VI we pointed out the immense potential for service there is in the Christian concept of duty including what we followed Weber in describing as the "doctrine of the calling". It is through service to the community as well as through clear understanding and the application of freedom to human persons and human societies that Christianity can encourage creativity by which cultural vitality is developed. [1] This is part of the relationship between Christian ethic (properly understood and concretely applied to help provide an alternative norm to a missionary area) and the problem of social change in such missionary area.

From our study of Ibo traditional society and religion it becomes clear that, like other preliterate peoples, the Ibos were religious and organized their cultural life around their religion. It is equally true that they had traces of scepticism. They also had traces of secularism in their traditional religious life especially in their attempt to use religion as the means to attain well-being, success and safety. Hence the Ibos could not have been spoken of as "sacralists", in the sense of being opposed to technical development due to their religion, as Van Leeuwen had suggested. (See our discussion in chapter VII). It is our conviction therefore that the Ibos, judging from their past experience of combining the sacred with the secular, will find attractive an ethical norm that builds on convincing religious beliefs like the Christian Faith (convincing because they are relevant), and supported by empirical factors of Ibo life-experience. With this clarification of a few points that can be summarised from the preceding chapters of our study, we now proceed to develop the pattern of ethic we have been pointing towards throughout his study.

We had attempted in chapter VI a definition of ethics indicating the various meanings of the word, but we did not in such definition, include the various sub-divisions into which the subject matter of ethics can be divided. There are, for example, four such possible subdivisions in the specialised field of ethics, namely, meta-ethics which like metaphysics "goes beyond", in this case "beyond ethics", to analyse and to define the foundations and the language of ethics. The emphasis here is on analytical work of ethical terms or predicates or statements. We are not concerned with this branch of ethics. Then again we have descriptive ethics and applied ethics with which we are not directly

---

[1] Egbert de Vries has reminded us that "creativity flourished through Christianity in the first centuries of the Christian era, in the Renaissance and Reformation". See his "From Tradition to Modernity" in *Man in Community: Christian Concern for the Human in Changing Society*, edited by Egbert de Vries, New York: Association Press, London: S.C.M. Press, 1966, p. 36.

concerned. If we give examples that relate somehow to applied and social ethics, it is only for the illustration of points made. It is with the fourth sub-division of ethics that we are concerned, namely, normative ethics. Professor Richard B. Brandt defined normative ethics as a philosophical "inquiry aiming to state and defend as valid or true a complete and economic set of general ethical principles, and also some less general principles that are important for what we may call 'providing the ethical foundation' of the more important human institutions".[2] We are concerned in providing for the Ibo, in the light of the situations we have described in this study, some ethical norms which relate to their experience, for example in the values like justice, and obligation, co-operation and harmony, reprehensible action (*igba-ajo-ihe*) or *ezigbo madu* (the acceptable person). Because these values relate to the general factors that enable people to live at all together in Ibo community-life, they can be understood by all, irrespective of their religions or lack of religions. From such background of some form of consensus, the people will see the necessity for observing these values in order to co-exist at all, especially in the modern community. The importance of new and far-reaching ethical principles adequate for the modern Ibo, will then become abundantly clear. These ethical norms or principles, as we have already indicated, will be Christian while its application is wider than the Christian Churches in Iboland to include all the Ibo. We aim at providing Christian "civilization" or a way of "cultivating values of social interaction" among the people from the Christian faith, a way that is superior to, and capable of supplanting, the traditional religious norms without destroying traditional social life and its more acceptable customs like *ifenru* (paying customary tribute in recognition of seniority ranks within the patrilineage), for example.

Outline of Suggested Ethical Principles

(1) *The Nature of Man*

Man is created by God, he is given capacity for desiring things which he can pursue and achieve and so he does not remain static,

[2] Richard B. Brandt, Ethical Theory, Englewood Cliffs, New Jersey: Prentice Hall. Inc., 1959, p. 7. See also the division of "ethics" into these four by the Working Party on the Ethics of University Education of the Netherlands University's Council in Higher Education and Research in *The Netherlands Universities Foundation for International Co-operation* (NUFFIC) Bulletin I, Vol. 18, 1974, p. 16 and 17.

this is what our forefathers symbolised in the ram-headed god called *ikenga*. Secondly man is born into this world first of all through his parents into his community of many ancestors, and then into the lineage unit, later he grows up into the village, town, country and world communities. He is not meant to live in lonely isolation. His immediate association and membership is in this world of matter, nature and other human beings who influence him and whom he influences. With these he plays, fights and shares all the co-operation by which life is made creative, its joys and sorrows sustained by the various links of relationships like friendship, marriage, age sets and workmates. Hence the possibility of developing personality. But despite all the facilities of this common life in community and in the world of visible existence, he feels affinity with a kind of unseen "spirit-world" through his consciousness of self transcendence. Thirdly man is endowed with reason and intellect, he discovers the various behaviour patterns of nature, man and other created parts of the world. He knows what preserves his life and regards it as good and knows as well what destroys himself, his friends, his community and regards that as evil. He makes things, creates new effects and organises systems by which new technics are generated and greater facilities provided for the living of his life. Fourthly in the course of doing things he controls nature and in dominating it with his creative skill he still remembers that he shares some kind of affinity with nature. Where he does not any more fear the "spirit-owner" of a forest as his forefathers did, he treats the forest and all other forms of nature with a "sisterly" feeling, knowing at least that the wanton destruction of all forests would leave the lands bare, and there will be no more trees for his grandchildren to use. Fifthly he accepts a kind of responsibility for the way he behaves. He knows that a good manure will result in the good yield of his yam harvest, smallpox can be avoided by vaccination and by the general cleanliness of home, village and town. He no more attributes to God what really he has been responsible for. For example, if he had contracted venereal disease which had destroyed his procreative organs, he does not blame God for failure to have children, for it is part of man's nature to understand the general routine of cause and effect within nature and created beings. [3]

---

[3] This very simple introduction to "who man is" takes in a good deal of Ibo understanding of man. It contains the biblical doctrine of man's creation, it avoids the error of Marxist materialistic determinism as well as Idealist over spiritualistic nature of man bordering on Gnosticism. It provides the basic nature

(2) *The World in which Man lives and Man's Capacity for Living in it*

This world is God's creation in which all men share equally as human beings the privilege of making it a happy place of abode for man's fullest development. It has within it opportunity for man to survive or to destroy himself. Dynamism, as a principle of rapid succession in the stages of man's development of his mind, is part of the noticeable "laws" with which the world operates, releasing for man spiritual values such as creativity, opportunities for service and freedom. God's power, will and demands manifest themselves through man's obedience in co-operating with God as he (man) exercises creativity, service and freedom. This is the concept our forefathers symbolised in the *Chi* idea. Furthermore man's existence in this world is marked by some routine patterns or "natural laws". For example, man's body grows and decays, in its growth man feels hungry and he is therefore desirous to find food, secure shelter and protect his young. These constitute his basic needs as well as the source of his anxieties, strivings and therefore greed. He has the power of procreation and so he has and rears children, sometimes with the excessive desire to perpetuate his individual line of the human species. In the struggle for food, shelter and opportunities for the work of procreating and caring for children, he comes into clashes with other men and realises and knows within himself what is his "duty", "obligation" and "rights" or even the "wrong" ways of satisfying these basic needs. He has the capacity of "soul-life" by which he appreciates kindness, acts of mercy and hospitality and other people's concern for him (which is a form of love). He also feels inclined to do these things for others and has the capacity to feel happy when he can do so well enough to see other people's conditions bettered. Because of the many channels through which he is linked to various persons, groups and avenues of mutual help and co-operation, man discovers that his world is made up of many institutions and orders of social links and controls. Hence the many levels of the lineage or levels of kinship relationships, many associations like the age sets, guilds of dancers, blacksmiths and trade unions. Through these various communities we find in the world, whether they be in the form of cultural ethos or interpersonal relation-

---

of man's need for communalistic existence through responsibility, avoids too wide a gap between the natural and the spiritual and removes the ugly image of God as "striker of terror". This prepares the ground for the Christian image of God whom we can approach as "Abba Father!" It further combines biblical sources with "scientific matter of fact" approach.

ships or institutions, God's creative purposes bear fruit for men; the new emerges out of the old, and culture, as customary ways of living together and appreciating as well as tolerating one another, is developed. Moral codes, as man's attempts in various units and communities to regulate how best to enjoy living together, are also developed. Their principal aims are to help man reach what he knows as his "authentic" self-hood, even when this knowledge is very limited. Hence we see in various cultures of the world that the essence of all moral prescriptions, is the search for that which best protects and enhances the true humanity of the persons concerned, despite the divisions of men into the rulers and the ruled, the poor and the rich, the great and the small. Hence the world is the place where we find materials for decision-making and for the development of virtue or vice. [4]

(3) *The Failure of Man Always to Decide as He Should*

It is a vital experience of all mankind that many many times over, we mean well but decide badly about a given situation. At other times we know the "right" course of action, at least "right" in the sense that there is no deceit, no falsehood, no depriving of the other person, and yet we depart from such right course of action either because of fear or favour of other persons. Why is this so? There is the possibility that the course of action contains so many technical points of which we have no knowledge at the time of decision, so we just decide ignorantly and the decision turns out to be "wrong" in the sense of the harm it inflicts on others or on ourselves. On the other hand the circumstances of daily existence change so quickly, and habits already learnt with which we decide on alternatives, become unable "to lead us accurately" in handling the new situation. This looks like ignorance plea already entered above but differs from it because our "fault" here is our unwillingness to wake up to the new habit or attitude of

---

[4] This short statement about the ethical presuppositions about the world and man's existence in it adopts definite positions like the belief that ethical consciousness is part of the nature of man even when he is incapable, of his own power, to fulfil its demands. Cf. St. Paul's "The good that I would, that I do not, and the evil I would not that I do". Romans 7 verse 21. To have moral consciousness is implicit in man's existence on earth and is within the concept of God's creation of man. What is not implicit is man's ability to realise his ethical potentialities to the full. See also H. D. Lewis, Morals and Revelation, London: George Allen and Unwin, 1951, pp. 11-19. The phrase "Natural law" used here implies simply "the general law found in nature" like the moral consciousness we have spoken about. It does not therefore refer to the traditional "Natural-Law" theories. See Chapter VI, footnote 29 on page 145.

mind with which to cope. Whatever the reason, the situation is still the same, namely, that man does not always decide and act as he should. He has the consciousness of what is the "proper way" or what he "ought to do" or what helps his situation best (and a man's situation is that he is created always to live in community), he nevertheless goes ahead and behaves as if he were meant to live by himself alone. Sometimes he blames himself for doing what he has done, indicating that he has a conscience within him (no matter how that has been developed). Sometimes the society, fearing that if each person continues deciding in this sort of wrong way it could lead to the destruction of the entire community, works out a code and some principles of checking, punishing and eliminating incidences of such wrong decisions and wrong doings. This is how our forefathers developed *omenani* and used *ala* (the earth goddess) to help in checking the evil doings of some members of their society. But despite all such provisions man still discovers that he continues to have inclination to decide wrongly, selfishly and without the strength to stand up against such inclination. Even where one person has done as well and as good as he honestly knows how, and his community knows him to be a "good" man (as good as he can be), he can be drawn into so much calamity like sickness, loss of property, children and position. He suffers and shares in the sin of his community. In all these instances it becomes clear to all, that in reality man has both capacity for good as well as for evil, which is sin, and that the world in which we live, through the actions of men, is a place for the experience of joy as well as of sorrow. Despite the wisdom of our forefathers contained in their proverb "let the kite perch and let the eagle perch also, which ever says the other will not perch, let its wings break off!", there are many who "perch" and refuse others to "perch". This becomes a clear evidence of concrete sin which we call selfishness. Our forefathers resorted to all sorts of activities to rid society of these evils and teach men to desist from them. They used sacrifice of various sorts, they used ritual avoidances, they used *nso-ala* (taboos and ritual cleansing), organised the sacred society of the *Ọzọ* title to consecrate men into "guilds of noble rank" who show the example of virtuous living, and yet sin and evil remained, because they were attempting to remove them from society instead of from inside the wills of men from where decisions are made. The spirit nature in them, when roused by the conscience which is also in them, gets agitated and they ask has *Chineke* (God the Creator) brought us into this world to struggle for the good and never attain it? Even *ndu,* (life) which is their highest desire, is vitiated and threatened by sin and evil like poisoning, greed, war, armed robbery, kidnapping and selling into slavery. God in his wisdom knowing that all the prescriptions our forefathers had, touched only the outside of sin and evil, revealed to all mankind (our forefathers included) the spirit and inward way of conquering sin and evil in human heart. This spirit and inward way is the way of love, and Jesus Christ as God who lived in human flesh and died for the love of all mankind but rose again from the dead and lives in the eternal glory of the Spirit world, gives daily to those who believe in him this Spirit power for conquering sin. The search in Iboland for "spirit power" for overcoming the evil minded persons, for realising the good life (*ndu*) through well being, either in physical health, or in the service of fellowmen or in the success of our work, by which we show that we can sincerely and honestly benefit our fellowmen, through our good agricultural product or carpentery or by teaching—all that search has ended in Jesus Christ. The thing we have been searching for, as a people, in the upper ceiling is just there in the very low ceiling. But someone would want to ask why has evil continued in the world as well as in Iboland and Jesus had been known in Iboland for over one hundred years and in some other places for much longer? The answer to this question is simply this, many in Iboland as elsewhere, who follow Jesus through his Church, have not really bothered to follow his way of love which involves self sacrifice, obedience to God rather than to our selfish inclinations and the knowledge of how God deals with man through man's humility. We shall discuss these points a little further to indicate the difference life in Jesus Christ makes to the ethical situation of a people, the Ibo as well as any other group; for although all of us endeavour to lead the good life, it is, as our fore-fathers used to say, "beating and bending the iron without heating it red-hot in the furnace". Only those who live by the power of Jesus have "heated the iron" of their life in the fire of his Holy Spirit and his love, and can bend it to the unselfish life of love. [5]

---

[5] What we have done in this section is to introduce in non-theological or philosophical terminologies the fact of conscience and sin in the moral life. We have not stopped to examine the modern psychological explanations of conscience. Up to this point we have discussed ethical considerations common to Christian Ibo as well as the non-Christian, for ethical incidence as human experience is common to both, but the power to fulfil the ethical demands as the Christian sees it in Christ, is impossible without the life in Christ. The

(4) *The Moral Power of the Christian Life*

The distinctive element in the Christian ethic is the special context within which the moral life is perceived. It is no longer the effort of ɩn unaided person to attain what he regards as the "*Summum Bonum*" for all such good "ends" of life perceived by man are faulty in the sense of being limited in scope, comprehension and achievement. After ɩll, man himself that conceives it, is finite and limited in his knowledge. The special context of the Christian ethics includes the normative place of Jesus Christ and his teaching, not necessarily as a good "outside" example to be imitated, but mainly as the source and the inspiration of a new style of life. In other words Jesus Christ as God's revelation of what reality means becomes the announcer of what is "the good", namely, love. Secondly by his redemption and reconciliation, he offers man as a believer, forgiveness by which sin is battled against in the believer's life. Thirdly by the power of the Holy Spirit he has given to the reconciled and forgiven believer, he (the believer) receives power, grace and inspiration to live the good life with the service of love to God and to fellowmen. The Christian set in this "moral milieu", daily, through meditation upon the word of God and by sharing in the fellowship of the Church, receives clarification of his thoughts. This he does through the help some interpreters of the Christian moral teachings can give him, so that he can face the practical decisions of concrete issues of daily life, as these are not in any way "given" or commanded. Only, because of the power of the Spirit, and through loyalty to Christ in obedience to God, which enables him to depart from sin (now seen as rebellion to God) day by day, a believer is given light with which to make the decisions. By such decisions, moral vitality is generated and maintained in the community. Every Ibo man can easily understand the necessity for the power of the Spirit of God in the moral life of an individual, because, all the emphasis on

Christian Ibo must therefore bear special responsibility for the development of the Christian norm and endeavour to take the non-Christian along in understanding at least the need for such a norm. This is a new type of evangelism. We also speak of sin in the more generic meaning of the word as breaking religious or moral law, or committing offence or fault, reserving its more theological meaning as rebellion against or alienation from God for later use. The Ibo idea of sin as *aru* (pollution, abomination or ritual danger) has also within its meaning, some sense of alienation in the concept of the break of the harmony between the source of benevolence (which can mean God although this for the Ibo includes nature, the spirit world in which the ancestors share) and man.

individual *chi*'s support for successful living points to the human need for this kind of help. Of course the *chi* concept could not fulfil what it points to because of the lack of true knowledge of, and the proper fellowship with God. Such knowledge and fellowship has come through the life and work of Jesus Christ. For God no man can know unless God reveals himself to man, and this he has done in Jesus Christ. We now rejoice in the fullness of sharing in the power of God through the Holy Spirit whom we receive as believers in Jesus Christ. When we christen a child with the name *Chidi* we affirm our belief in the certainty of the power of the Holy Spirit of God to aid that child, as well as all children of faith in the Saviour, towards the triumphant life of moral integrity manifested in the harvest of the Spirit—full of love, joy, peace, patience, kindness, goodness, faithfulness, gentleness, self-control. (Gal. 5 verse 22). This moral life through faith in Jesus Christ is nourished, as we have said in chapter VI, by real fellowship with God through daily acts of penitence, self-sacrifice and prayer, and by sharing in the apostolic teaching (including bible reading, study and understanding); by sharing in the sacrament of the body and blood of our Lord in remembrance of his death, passion and abiding presence; as well as in the consistent fellowship with the Church of God in the work of spreading the good news about the Saviour. No one certainly can possess the joy of the triumphant life through Christ and remain indifferent to telling the good news abroad. For the essence of good "news" is that it be published. Hence Christian ethics and the mission of the Church dovetail into one another in theory and practice. [6]

For those interested in theoretical models, Christian special approach and emphasis in ethics, as we here present it, can be seen not primarily as agapist, although the significance of the agape of God for man in Christ is the source of our love exercise to God and to fellowmen; it is not necessarily situational ethics, although we apply our love—reinforced moral decisions to concrete situations; it is not necessarily as the ethics of obedience to the gospel, although it could not have been possible without the Christ-event which constitutes the gospel

[6] In the history of the Church periods of intense moral revitalization of the common life in the body of Christ, the Church, had led to new enthusiasm in the evangelistic work of the Church. Cf. for instance in Britain, the period of the Evangelical Revival saw the founding of the Church Missionary Society (1799), the British and Foreign Bible Society, the missionary activities within Britain itself of the Methodist Movement led by John and Charles Wesley.

into good news for man; rather it becomes the ethic of gratitude—thankfulness to God for his mercy in creative and redemptive work. This eucharistic ethic will always be lived, celebrated and acted in rememberance of him who makes such a life of moral triumph possible. The Ibo, as well as almost all African peoples, love celebrations as memorials and symbolic occasions for recharging the affairs of daily life and man himself, set in this material world of such routine and perplexing affairs, with the spirit-source of reality. This eucharistic ethics will of course remind the Church of the importance of enacting the sacramental symbols of the bread and wine to remember him who commanded us to "do this in remembrance of me". And as the Church recaptures once more the meaning of the sacrament of the Eucharist and prays daily at the end of such service "send us out in the power of your Spirit to live and work to your praise and glory", [7] the implication of eucharistic theology for ethics recaptures its central place in the life of the Church in Iboland. [8]

From this kind of understanding as to the real meaning of Christian ethics, its source of power in individual life as well as its being practicalised in such daily living of market or farm, of school or town council offices, the place and meaning of the "virtues" like justice, hospitality, achievement, co-operation, duty and benevolence or the

---

[7] Anglican Service Book "An Order of Holy Communion", Alternative Service Series Three, London: Cambridge University Press, 1973, p. 27. Gratitude to the Ibo when publicly enacted, stresses not only expression of thanks but also a desire to entreat for more favours by offering greater allegiance to the benefactor through pleasing him by actions and words. When all these facts, sentiments and the unconscious associations built around the celebrations of gratitude in Ibo culture are transferred by appropriate teaching to the Eucharistic ethics of the Christian Church as herein analysed, the effect on the total life of the people, through deeper devotion to God and the new life it will uphold, will be really terrific, the Spirit of God being their helper.

[8] The basis of Christian ethics given in this outline (numbered 1-4) is an attempt to interpret the kernel of such an ethic in Ibo thought form while indicating that Christian ethic is the ethos or life style necessarily emerging out of the Christ-event and man's response to it. It does not enter into the debates about the various emphases of Christian ethics but at the same time it takes in the Pauline emphasis of "a man in Christ" being a new creature, the Barthian emphasis of "Christ alone", the Paul Ramsey's agapism and the Catholic emphasis of the sacramental importance of Christian life through the Church. It also takes in the Joseph Fletcher as well as Paul Lehmann's concern for situations of decision and action. The Reformation's emphasis on "by faith alone" is also within its frame work. For books by these writers see footnote no. 16 in chapter VI (p. 138). Add this to the comparison of certain Christian ethical ideals with the Ibo moral concepts in chapter VI pages 150 to 167, the picture of the reconstructed Christian ethic we have been recommending will emerge.

Ibo supreme good of *ndu* acquire their correct stance. They are seen properly as the result of fellowship with God, as channels or tools with which we bear fruit through the Spirit in expression of our gratitude to God.

(5) *The Place of the Church in the Ethical life of the People*

We wish in this section also to suggest the general relationship there is between religion and morals. Our analysis of Ibo traditional religion and society indicates the close relationship between religion and Ibo society. We do not, however, subscribe to the view that morality cannot exist without religion. Morality or ethics as the reflection upon and the attempt of man to pursue what he rationally conceives as the good, is a faculty of man's nature. The fact that sin of pride in rational achievement vitiates human reason and limits its reach in the knowledge of reality (because reality is far greater than man and his conscious experience, hence the fact that man in this realm sees "through a glass darkly") does not destroy this capacity by such limitation. Further the concept of autonomous ethics is beset with the problem of its relativity due to the variety of historical, cultural and the human personal units and blocks that operate within this autonomous ethics. Despite this problem of relativity as well as other problems associated with ethics existing on its own without religion, especially the Christian religion, it is still an empirical fact of human existence that even men without religion do have their type of ethical concerns.

We make this short observation because if the Christian can "sell" his Christian ethics of fulness of manhood (which really is in Christ) to the Ibo now seduced by secularization and modern technological life, he can only do so logically by presuming that he has a "moral sense" so as to be able to appreciate where and why the Christian ethic has something so "attractive" to offer. Both St. Paul and our Lord presumed this in their hearers (Romans 2 verse 14, Matt. 7 verse 11) and it is a good pedagogical methodology to start off someone, from what he knows (and that must be credited to him first) so as to lead him to what he does not know.[9] Nevertheless the very close relationship between religion and morality is a matter of un-

---

[9] We share H. D. Lewis' view: "The refinement of ethical ideas usually comes from religious sources, and we have derived our noblest ethical ideals directly from religion... But the fact remains that it is possible to be moral without being religious". H. D. Lewis, Morals and Revelation, *op. cit.*, p. 16.

doubted reality. It is more so in Christianity. A man cannot be a Christian without believing in and identifying himself with the "Christ-event". Equally so the life of moral triumph of the Christian is achievable only to the "man in Christ". This is not a mere tautology in which the Christian equals "the man in Christ" but a serious statement of first principle, namely, that without Christ the Christian moral life of those who belong to the "registered membership" of the Church is impossible. The transition Church in Iboland (transition from mission and European garbed Church to an indigenous Church, "native" and "traditional" to the Ibos) must take this seriously. To this effect, we offer some suggestions in relation to the organised life of the Church, as we will be discussing suggestions relating to Ibo culture later.

The worship of the Church must reflect love for Christ through appeal to the total personality of the Ibo. Sacramental and symbolic worship does this better, judging from the Ibo life style, culture and speech patterns. (There is much use of proverbs and picture language.) The whole of Ibo life is full of symbolic usages and exchanges. Liturgical worship centred on the Holy Communion should do this better than the sing-sit-down-read, stand up, talk and talk-rhythm of most of non Roman Churches in Iboland. Images and artistic representation of the various historical fact of the life of our Lord, and other good artistic representation of the life of faith, can be used in stimulating meditation as we know that the highest cannot be uttered—it is best symbolised. Teaching the Bible and the life of prayer should be rigorously pursued, making them the prelude to meaningful worship. We do not need to repeat suggestions we have already made elsewhere [10] but we only wish to stress the need for using as much of the cultural experiences of the people as possible. For example spontaneous ejaculatory prayer in the spirit of "Abba, Father" is well known to the Ibo; bring this with clear teaching into their Christian life. Domestic shrines had helped the Ibo in traditional religion to "domesticate" religion; educate the Christians to have the family altar. Priests and *nwadibias* (medicine-men also as diviners) healed, divined and prayed, teach the ordained and lay apostolates of the Church to cultivate and grow in their understanding of the nature of man who needs wholeness through his body, his mind and his spirit. Spiritual

---

[10] Edmund Ilogu, "The Problem of the Indigenization of the Church" in *The International Review of Missions*, Vol. XLIX, No. 194, April 1960, pp. 167-182.

healing should be explored and institutionalised in the more orthodox Churches so that they become not the preserve of the Aladura Churches and questionable "Healing-Home-Churches".[11]

The organization of the Churches' life in Iboland must eschew too much emphasis on money contribution as the hall mark of membership. Rather teaching, praying and sharing in the fellowship of joys and sorrows together, should be emphasised, for these are the more basic foundations of Church membership. Ordained ministers must be told in clear terms that we are the ministers of the Word and Sacrament and not superintendents of "groups" and "districts". To realise this is to make us ever humble searchers for the hours, the places and the resources from where we can find "sustenance" so as to be able to sustain our people in the prayers, the preaching of the Word and in the breaking of bread. The use of ex-communication from Holy Communion as sanction against breach of the laws of the Church, must be reviewed so as to leave the Sacrament to continue being a means of grace rather than a punishment weapon.

This interjection of a few practical points in the middle of some systematic discussions of ethical principles might appear as bad organization of thought. The answer to such criticism is that the Church, in addition to being the household of God in which every member is joined together "upon the foundation of the apostles and prophets, Christ Jesus himself being the corner-stone" so that it can grow "into a holy temple in the Lord" (cf. Ephesians 2 verses 20 and 21), is also a historical institution having structures of ordinary routine and administration. These structures can tarnish the spiritual origin, the frame-work and life of this "body of Christ" and make it no longer capable of inspiring men with the ethical life of triumph we are very much concerned with. To avoid being carried away by the ideal picture of the Church with its great possibilities for the ethical life of the Christians, these practical matters of the social realities of

---

[11] The World Council of Churches should make available the results of studies, researches and consultations which its Christian Medical Commission (CMC) provides. The local Churches especially in the Third World need such information and guidance very urgently. To restrict such studies to the few "ecumeniacs" will still leave the "grass-root" Churches incapable of providing more authentic services to Christians in places like Iboland than what the less orthodox Churches like the Aladuras of Nigeria are providing. Universities' Departments of Religion are in duty bound to explore intensively the relationship for human personality of Religion, Psychiatry and Sociology.

life in the Church do help us to realise, how great our need is even for sanctification with wisdom in routine things.

Part of the spiritual qualities which we receive from the Holy Spirit by being faithful to the Lord includes hope. Just as we have touched on the importance of faith and love in the moral life of believers, we should remind ourselves that hope is the quality that enables us not to give up even in the face of the irritating common chore, or the irritating practical routine things that could drain off the spiritual energy with which we could have maintained the daily demands of love, justice, hospitality and duty, for example. Hope continues to urge us on towards the next stage until the end. But the end of the Christian life of love is the meeting with Christ, the object of our love—for all love's journey ends in meeting. Our final meeting with Christ surely is not on this level or spate of history, it is beyond history at the dawn of life in "the world-to-come". As we have indicated in chapter VI the uncompleted ethical demands of love or of duty, of joy or of justice, even our Christian ethical ideals of being "perfect as your heavenly father is perfect", or to attain "mature manhood, to the measure of the stature of the fullness of Christ" (see Matt. 5 verse 48, Eph. 4 verse 13) cannot be fully realised on this earthly existence. There is no place for complacency, no sense of pride of achievement, but in hope, the work of Christian moral growth is continued until it ends in our meeting with our God and Saviour. The importance of eschatology in the Christian ethic is its continual reminder to us, that God himself is the end of all such endeavour, just as he is the source of our knowledge of what is good, and also the giver of the power to Christians to carry out the ethical demands always in faith, hope and love. But once more we remind ourselves that it is through the practical things of daily life, the routine as well as the special, the cultural as well as the social—it is through these temporal things that we prepare and pass into the eternal of eschatology. We will turn now to the discussion of some of the cultural practical things in the life of the Ibo Christians.

Christianity and Ibo Culture

A great deal has been written about the relationship of religion and culture in general and the relationship of Christianity and non-Christian culture in particular.[12] We will therefore leave off repeating

12 The Bibliography contains a good selection of them. The books mentioned

what others have already discussed and go straight away to the examination of the way the three Ibo institutions we have earmarked for consideration can be related to Christianity. These three are: "extended-family" and lineage duties, polygamy and the *Ọzọ* title. The need for this kind of examination is that if the Christian ethical norms and value we have been recommending very strongly will become effective in people's life, they will do so in proportion to how much their effectiveness is related to the working out of some, if not all, of the institutional ways in which the Ibo express their acceptances and rejections. The importance of normative ethics in a situation of social change like that of Iboland, lies in its ability to show: what values the people regard vital; what decisions of everyday life are influenced by such vital values; and how the greater majority of the people internalize such values and in what activities. The Ibo traditional society values norms associated with *ndu* (life) justice, hospitality, co-operation and achievement to mention just this few. An Ibo who becomes Christian, a real man in Christ, bearing the fruit of the spirit in love, joy, peace, patience, kindness, goodness, faithfulness, gentleness and self-control finds he has grace enough to live "naturally" in a harmonised and expanded meaning of his traditional values with bearing the fruit of Christian moral virtues just mentioned. The persistence with which many Christians in Iboland desire to express their preferences of values in institutions like *Ọzọ*, polygamy and extended-family or lineage duties, suggests that these are some of the institutions in which people are prepared to invest their "meanings" of "virtue", Christian and traditional. We had shown in chapter IV how early missionaries in Iboland had hoped that these institutions origin-

---

here are those that: (1) indicate the influence of religion in the development of culture through the value orientation it gives to the choices, decisions and actions of the people; (2) those that indicate particularly how Christianity in a new environment like the Ibo "Christianises" aspects of the life style of the people leading to the emergence of new orientations that eventually mean the growth of a new style of life:

(1) J. Milton Yinger, The Scientific Study of Relegion, New York: Macmillan, 1970, especially chapters 3, 7, 8, 9, 10 and 11.
Glenn M. Vernon, Sociology of Religion, New York: McGraw Hill, 1962.
Anthony F. C. Wallace, Religion: An Anthropological View, New York: Random House, 1966.
Robert M. Bellah, Tokugawa Religion, Boston: Beacon Press, 1970, as an illustration of a particular religion on a particular culture.

(2) Max Weber, The Protestant Ethic and the Spirit of Capitalism, translated by Talcott Parsons, London: George Allen & Unwin, 1930.
H. Richard Niebuhr, Christ and Culture, New York: Harper & Row, 1951.

ating from the people's traditional religious life and culture would soon die away. After over one hundred years of the existence of Christianity in Iboland they are still living issues, about which many genuine Christians are agitated. They ask: Can Christian virtue which they have harmonised with their Ibo traditional values, having subjected the latter under the purifying grace of Christ, find expression through *all* of the living institutions of their community life including, for example these three we have mentioned? Because *Ọzọ*, polygamy and lineage duties are for them living issues among living dynamic and active society like the Ibo, we can no longer within the Christian Church treat them as if they were dead ruins. There is the need therefore to place these institutions under the searchlight of the Christian way of life which we have been developing for Iboland, so as to give some guidance to the Christian Church there.

Extended-Family and Lineage Duties

The conference held at Onitsha May 12-14 and June 3rd and 4th in 1914 between the missionaries and the native Christian leaders on how to Christianise some Ibo "native customs", as well as to decide which ones should be so christianised, failed to achieve any tangible result. Almost all the various examples of "native customs" that came before the conference were regarded as "heathen practices" about which a Christian man should not concern himself. Extended-family and lineage duties were among the topics so discussed. The things involved in extended-family and lineage duties which are still outstanding today include *ife-nru* (customary giving of seniority tributes), widow inheritance, libation and ancestor reverence. In 1914 the list was formidable but a good number of the items which the Church authorities rejected then as unworthy of a Christian man's attention, have, without real noticeable authorization, become part of Christian practices. Examples include second burial and memorial for dead father, uncle or brother, *ine omugwo* (celebrations connected with child-birth), initiation into the lineage's masquerade society or the lineage's dance group. Any Christian who cares can join or do any of these today in Iboland. Some clergy frown at some of them but do not seem to have sufficient reason or authority to stop such Christians. We too have neither theological nor historical reasons to suggest that a Christian should not do or take part in any of them. Even the masquerade which used to be the messenger of the earth goddess, and the ancestors is more or less an entertainment these days. Those of us who belong to it guard its "secrets" mainly as "loyalty-drill" rather than belief in any real secret to keep! Even widow inheritance is now a matter of acceptance between the wife to be "inherited" and the brother in law or father's son, that would inherit, except that in the Anglican Church the prayer book list of prohibited kindred and affinity in marriages still contains that a man may not marry father's wife. People can get over this by having the marriage blessed rather than take a full ordinance wedding service of the Church.

We are now left with two items *ife-nru* and ancestor reverence through libation and other associated ideas about ancestors. Two activities are involved in *Ife-nru*: when an animal is killed certain parts of it must be given to the senior brother and uncle, where the young man killing the animal has lost his father. If his father is alive it will be for the father and the uncle and also for the senior brother. The second activity is the carrying of tribute gifts in the form of fire wood, eight pieces of yam, palm wine and sometimes a few other items on the great feast day of the lineage or clan by the younger to the elder. Items taken vary in different places. Some Christians already do this. We recommend that it should be universally done as the Ibos did it in the past by all, Christian as well as non-Christian. It is a means of recognising the lineage tree when the line of seniority is clarified once a year by the exchange of these tribute gifts on the appointed day. Furthermore Christians should see in it an occasion for re-establishing their membership in the community of blood relationships, just as through the Church they share in the Community of Spirit relationships. In these days of the growth of cities where children are born, who do not easily recognise their membership in the community, this yearly exchange of tribute no matter where people actually live will strengthen their sense of belonging to counteract the evil effects of the anomie of city life.

Belief in the continuity of the lineage through a link that connects the dead, the living and the children of the future, is a very strong and healthy cultural feature of Iboland. Christianity has removed the irrational fear of ancestral spirits as the source of evils like sickness, barrenness and some epidemics, especially where the ancestors have been neglected and the duties of allegiance due to them fall by default. Yet Christianity has not been able to destroy the belief in the existence of some unexplainable link between us and our forefathers. But the question is, should Christianity destroy such a belief? Is there nothing in the Christian faith that echoes this belief? Our recommendation therefore is that all Ibos, Christian as well as non-Christian acknowledge this link with our patrilineal ancestors in the pouring of libation and in the giving of pieces of kola nut. If the non-Christian in Ibo towns and villages will agree to fix their big celebration in honour of the ancestors on All-Saints-Day, then all should have a big celebration indeed; the Christians more so for we are once more reminded in All-Saints-Day Holy Communion about the great cloud of witnesses observing how we run our Christian race of faith and they can now include even our ancestors in the flesh whose one great delight in their life time was to see the prosperity of the descendants they had sired. And who is best qualified to lead the life of integrity, service and honour by which the village can be preserved in peace and prosperity other than the Christian! While All-Saints-Day should remind Christians primarily of the labours of love in faith of those through whom the Gospel reached us—St. Peter, St. Paul, Crowther and Nweje, it should in addition remind us of those who founded our clans and villages and lineages, without which, humanly speaking, we could not have had a Church or the Gospel. Furthermore when we pour libation or give out pieces of kola nuts we do so as symbolic expression of our honour to our ancestors instead of the "heathen thought" of worshipping them, for we have and worship one Lord God Almighty. We also, in real depth of affection, lift up our souls to Him Who descended to the dead to do his utmost for their soul's true weal. We cannot fully believe in the communion of saints and in the resurrection of the body without seriously thinking of our common humanity with those who had begotten us and yet knew not the Lord Jesus. We can not determine what their place is in God's economy of redemption, for God alone knows, but our faith and our belief is definitely too small if we do not spare a thought or a word of prayer about them to Him who alone can present us all faultless before His presence with exceeding joy. The Ibo belief in continuity with the ancestors, together with the symbolic honour to them through libation, can provide for Christians, together with All-Saints-Day, moments for such thought and prayer both for our ancestors in the faith as well as our ancestors in flesh and blood. [13]

This is a crucial point not only for theology, but also for sociology. The Ibos as a people have got built-in systems for the rootage of

---

13 Cf. The views of A. Shorter, W.F. in African Culture and the Christian Faith: An Introduction to Social and Pastoral Anthropology, London and Dublin: Geoffrey Chapman, 1973, pp. 59-61.

human relationship. In these days of irresponsible freedoms as are exhibited in many towns and cities, where many do no longer have any roots in the community, the Christian Church in Iboland must not help to destroy existing roots of the people's belonging. If the Church in Iboland cuts off its members from the community by not sharing in the symbols of the community's solidarity, it reduces immensely the chances of influencing the people. The Christians are to come apart from among the peoples—the non-Christians of Iboland—by the quality of the life that is hid with Christ in holiness and purity of living, not by resisting the community of flesh and blood. Secondly by christianising the cultural fact of community solidarity, like belief in the links with ancestors, the Christians are gradually working for the day when the already crumbling traditional religious teachings will have nothing more with which to conjure, and the people, always in need of religious explanations for human existence, will find Christ their all sufficiency. And although we may not easily hope for a Christendom in Iboland, we can by this measure, hope that it will expose the untenableness of traditional religious beliefs.

Polygamy

A great deal has been written about polygamy as a traditional marriage system in all Africa of which Iboland is a part. [14]

In discussing polygamy and the Christian Church in Iboland we will distinguish between two kinds: people who are converted into Christianity while they still have many wives, and secondly, those who after marrying one wife as Christians slide back into polygamy and still retain their membership in the Church. At the present state of biblical studies and research into New Testament teaching, we are unable to substantiate theologically the contention of some debaters in Iboland that the New Testament did not explicitly lay it down as the Christian "law", ideal and intention for every Christian to be the husband of one wife only. We have already mentioned in chapter IV the attitude of the African Church Incorporated and the United African Church that only the clergy were required by biblical injunction to marry only

[14] Arthur Phillips (Ed.), Survey of African Marriage and Family Life London: Oxford University Press, 1953; A. R. Radcliffe-Brown and Daryll Forde, African System of Kinship and Marriage, London: Oxford University Press, 1960; Thomas Price, African Marriage, I.M.C. Research Pamphlet no. 1, London: 1954; Report of All-Africa-Seminar on the Christian Home and Family Life, Geneva: W.C.C., 1963, E. G. Parrinder, The Bible and Polygamy, London S.P.C.K., 1950.

one wife whilst the ordinary members of the Church could have more than one. This kind of argument, built up mainly from 1 Timothy chapter 3 verses 1-7 and Titus chapter 1 verses 5-9, is best described as argument from silence; because the passages do not mention "members of the congregation" therefore being "faithful to his *one* wife" means that only the leader or elder or bishop is commanded to marry one wife. It is definitely a weak argument to support polygamy for any group in the Church. The passages mentioned above deal with instructions to Timothy and Titus about the qualifications of persons to be appointed elders or bishops in Churches. To deduce facts about marriage rules from such passages, is to go beyond what the evidence provides.

Again those who argue from the phrase "and the two shall become one flesh" (see Matt. 19:5; Mark 10:8) in support of monogamy, in our view, argue from a wrong premise. What our Lord is teaching about in these two passages is his condemnation of easy divorce which the Jews had developed. In its place our Lord indicated the importance of real union between husband and wife. I submit that the emphasis on "the two being one flesh" is a metaphor describing intimacy especially the intimacy engendered by sex relationship between any man and any woman and such intimacy is not impossible between a man and his two or three wives. St. Paul even argued that between a man and a prostitute the two could become "one flesh", only that the prostitute was the wrong person to whom a Christian could make his body to be under bondage to. (Do you not know that anyone who joins himself to a prostitute becomes one body with her? For as it is written "The two shall become one" 1 Cor. 6 verse 16) Therefore we should look for support for monogamy elsewhere. We are not absolutely certain either that polygamy did not exist in the missionary areas where St. Paul worked. The passage in 1 Corinthians chapter 5 verse 1 where St. Paul says "I actually hear reports of sexual immorality among you, immorality such as even pagans do not tolerate: the union of a man with his father's wife", suggests a polygamous home because this young man in question could not have been going in with the father's wife that was his mother, unless the mother had died and the father had remarried, but this sounds unlikely from the words of the text. Probably there was polygamy in those missionary areas and we are the poorer for not having any definite statements in the bible about how such polygamous families were handled in the New Testament Churches. Furthermore most of the biblical passages that relate to marriage, have good advice about happy homes which result from the devotion of wives and husbands to each other, and the proper performance of duties that pertain to each. Such homes, from my experiences in Iboland and a few other parts I have visited in Africa, have been maintained by some families that are polygamous (see Rom. 7 verses 1-4; 1 Cor. 6 verses 16-18 and chapter 7; Eph. 5 verses 22-33; Col. 3 verses 18 and 19; 1 Tim. 5 verses 9-16; Heb. 13 verse 4; 1 Peter 3 verses 1-8). The argument from such movements as Women's liberation and their emphasis on the equality between men and women, thereby concluding that one husband equals one wife, is so circumscribed culturally and historically that it cannot be a good argument in support of the Christian practice of monogamy.[15] Nor even the horror with which European and American women view the idea of another "legally approved" woman sharing their "man", "legally approved" because in Africa polygamy is lawful, just as monogamy is lawful in many western countries. The laws of nations here cannot be good argument in support of the Christian practice of monogamy. Real support for Christian monogamy has to be looked for from sources other than the foregoing arguments and biblical passages I have pointed out. In Matthew chapter 19 verses 3-12 and Mark 10 verses 2-12 our Lord said "The Creator made them from the beginning male and female", meaning that the biblical account of Creation indicated that Adam was given one helpmate Eve, and that was the intention of the Creator. We are aware of some biblical scholars who argue that the Genesis account of the creation is not history and should not be quoted as such.[16] Without entering into the controversy about the problems of the Pentateuch, nor about the myths of origin in non biblical accounts of the Near East, we do accept that the belief of men within the biblical tradition, which was supported by our Lord, was that God meant a man to have one female helpmate

---

[15] Some educated Nigerian women including Ibos answer leaders of such liberation movements that they already have equality within their Nigerian culture with their men folk even in polygamy which they support whole heartedly. See Daily Times, Lagos, Nigeria, Friday August 3, 1973, p. 16, interviews with Mrs. F. Nwakuche and with two wives of Chief W. D. Odibo.

[16] See L. E. P. Erith, "Genesis" in A New Commentary on Holy Scripture including the Apocrypha edited by Charles Gore et. al., London: S.P.C.K., 1929, pp. 36-63, where he says "We must admit therefore that the records of Genesis are to a large extent legendry in character", p. 38, cf. A. S. Peak "books of the Pentateuch contain many inconsistencies which prove that they cannot be a record of literal history". See A Commentary of the Bible edited by A. S. Peake, London and Edinburgh: T. C. and E. C. Jack Ltd., 1926, p. 133.

and that the practice of having more than one "helpmate" developed as a result of man's departure from the divine intentions to which the Christ-event has recalled man through repentance, faith and forgiveness. This is the biblical line of approach which we believe will be more convincing to the Ibo, because to accept the fulness of God's revelation in Christ, is to accept recalling the world as well as the individuals and their character from the paths of their wanderings away from God (that is, in sin, which is alienation from and rebellion against God). One of such paths is polygamy and to retain polygamy is like wanting to eat one's cake and at the same time wanting to keep it. If we have turned to the path of the divine intentions by following Christ, one "Adam" one "Eve" is one example of such original divine intentions. Christians in Iboland who after many years of Christian marriage go back to polygamy should understand it as deviating again into "paths of wanderings" away from God's intention and that they make the revelation of God in Christ ineffective for their life and for their society. To say this is to indicate unmistakably the great pastoral care all the Church owes to them.

This leaves us then with those who become converted whilst having more than one wife. A great deal has been written about this group even from the days of Bishop Crowther in Iboland.[17] After going through many views on this topic, (a few are given in footnote 17) we would also recommend that polygamous converts be admitted, with their wives, both to baptism as well as to the Holy Communion. The charge that this will create two different categories of communicants, and imply double standards of morality in the one local Church which is bound to scandalise some, should be countered with our Lord's teaching with the parable of the corn and the tares (Matt. 13 verses 24-30) "Let both grow together until the harvest" because our Lord himself said "lest in gathering the weeds you root up the wheat along with them". How can anyone be absolutely certain before the

---

[17] Adrian Hastings, Church and Mission in Modern Africa, London: Burns and Oates, 1967, pp. 162-184 where he pleads for a change in the official Christian attitude to converts who are polygamists so as to accommodate them within the Covenant of Grace. Max Warren in his C.M.S. Newsletter no. 196 July 1957 asks whether deprivation of the sacraments is the best approach to people within the Church who are polygamous. The All-Africa Seminar on the Christian Home and Family Life at Mindolo recommended that this group of polygamists be admitted not only into baptism, but also into the Holy Communion with all their wives, but be not allowed to hold post of responsibility in the Church, *op. cit.*, p. 20.

harvest, which is that of the Lord himself, that within the "tares" of the polygamous converts there are not genuine great souls set on fire with the redemptive love of Christ in their hearts?

To end this short look at polygamy and the Church in Iboland a few observations are necessary: Polygamy has been the sociological setting for many homes in Iboland for a long time.[18] The ideal Christian home life is in a monogamous family and this is new. The Church in Iboland if it is not a fellowship strong enough, bound together by the liberating and the strengthening power of the Holy Spirit, cannot hope to use the laws of excommunication from Holy Communion to combat and eventually liquidate polygamy in its life. Monogamy not being a sociological way of Ibo life, can only be seen as part of the new life in Christ. It is only in proportion to the reality of this new life in Christ that all the "appurtenances" of that life can become attractively desirable, valued and possessed; monogamy is one of such "appurtenances". It is only the Church with manifest life in the Spirit which can hope to have monogamy as its accepted practice. To say this is to place the responsibility where it squarely belongs, the whole body of Christ's Church in Iboland, and not necessarily the excommunicated polygamists. These are looked upon sometimes by the ostensibly monogamous with the "holier than thou" attitude, which is again un-Christ like, indicating the vicious circle of our need—the need in the total Church of repentance and revival.

The Ọzọ Title.

We have already introduced what the *Ọzọ* title taking is and the way it faced the challenge from Christianity (chapters II and IV). What we wish to attempt now is to see where it fits in the life of an Ibo Christian today. As we indicated in chapter IV, several meetings have been held since 1914 to 1973 to find how Christianity should re-act to *Ọzọ*. Negative response had been decided upon as early as 1914 but up till the present pressures from Christians wanting to take the title continue to mount and the Roman Catholic hierarchy at Onitsha as noted already in chapter IV had given what one might call provisional approval to their members to take a Christian kind of the *Ọzọ* title. Our general line of approach is that Christians should take the *Ọzọ* title. Secondly, that all Christians irrespective of deno-

[18] See Max Gluckman, Custom and Conflict in Africa, Oxford: Basil Blackwell, 1956.

mination, should have a common front and accept a common type of the title. Thirdly that both Christians and non-Christians share in the lineage's or clan's *Ọzọ* wealth and accept reciprocally each other's title, only that details of the ceremony in Christian title taking should differ from the details of the ceremony in the non-Christian. We will now proceed to substantiate these three propositions.

The first proposition that Christians should take the *Ọzọ* title is one of the logical upshots of the thesis of this study. If the Ibo after one hundred years of Christianity and all the influence of secularization still find the *Ọzọ* a very useful and functional institution of their society, then it is a very important "value-carrying" institution of community life. Now that we are arguing for the infiltration of Christian normative principles into the cultural life of the Ibo (and we have discovered that *Ọzọ* is one of their central cultural institutions), it must be "captured" into the Christian value orientation as part of the strategy for the Christianization of Ibo life. Part of the influence of western type of education and of secularization is the undermining of the religious beliefs of Ibo traditional religion. The *Ọzọ* title's traditional religious background cannot last for any much length of time, reckoning from present evidence. The Christian Church must step in, now that the tide is favourable, and provide the inevitable religious undergirding to *Ọzọ*. [19]

Our second proposition is that all Christians in Iboland should work

---

[19] The literature on *Ọzọ* and Christianity is immense in the form of committee minutes, protest letters to Bishops, appeals from Christians in favour and a few against Christian participation in it. Part of the evidence about its popularity was the demonstration in 1970 by 5,000 Anglican Church members who had taken the title against the order of the Bishop on the Niger that they should renounce it or face ex-communication from the Church. They followed up their demonstration with a three paged printed petition to the Bishop and the Archbishop of the Anglican Province of West Africa in which they claimed among other things: "We as Christians have since disassociated ourselves from idol worship and anything idolatrous previously connected with *Ọzọ* title and refined it to suit our Christian religion and belief". The contention of the Bishop was that this refining "to suit our Christian religion and belief" was done without his knowledge and approval and he suspects that the refining might not be good enough. The people ask why has the Bishop since 1914 failed to provide for Christians the proper Christian version of *Ọzọ*? It is in the face of questions like this that our study ceases being a purely academic exercise and becomes a matter for the real life and witness of the Church in Iboland. We studied six different Committee reports on *Ọzọ* made to the various synods of the Anglican Diocese on the Niger, four positive, one blantantly negative and one reserved in their recommendations. All point to a strong conviction that Christianization of *Ọzọ* is long overdue. See also Chapter II footnote 16.

out a common *Ọzọ* for Christians in Iboland. What is implied in this proposition is that a denominational approach to the title will rob it of the virtue of its Christian witness. Some denominations would want to set up a Christian system of *Ọzọ* that is more attractive, by its lack of deep Christian theological insight, so as to use it as a weapon for attracting the money elite of Iboland into its own fold against any denomination that prefers a more theologically worked out system even though it might lose members by so doing. This will very easily set up again the old ugly competition of Christian groups scrambling for members instead of presenting Christ to the peoples which is the key-note of all evangelization. Such rivalry will automatically fail to really Christianise the *Ọzọ* title as one of the initial movements towards the gradual building up of Christian normative influence in Iboland and the indigenization of the Church therein. The sincerity of the Church leaders, especially the Roman Catholic and the Anglican in whose area of influence the *Ọzọ* title is most widely spread, about ecumenism and *aggiornamento*, will be tested partly from the ease with which they work out one Christian system of *Ọzọ* for Iboland. Such a common system will need mainly a theological preamble specifying the relationship between God's revelation of himself in Christ and the existence of the Church in Iboland as a result of this revelation, and the religious beliefs the Ibo had invested on the *Ọzọ* title. This is to ensure its religious presuppositions but in the light of the fullness of God's self disclosure in Christ. Secondly the preamble will contain a statement about the function of the Church both as the mysterious "body of Christ" carrying on the redemptive work of Christ in the world through the Holy Spirit and also as an institution organised and run administratively by men through which the best in man's creative genius that makes up his culture can be given expression. The *Ọzọ* is one of such cultural creative avenues in music, work of art, servicing of human social institutions which Christian Ibos can now, from their ancient traditions, offer to God to bless, towards the enrichment of their social and cultural life. Agreement will be reached between Christian leaders and non-Christians about the two groups expressing the religious presuppositions of the title in accordance with the beliefs of their respective faiths. This brings us to the third proposition.

Three items are included in the third proposition, namely, that the Christian as well as the non-Christian title taking will involve all concerned in a given village, lineage or clan through all the title holders in that community being present to partake of the social merriments of *Ọzọ*, and divide according to tradition the *Ọzọ* wealth and maintain a common seniority list in the community. The reason for this provision is obvious. In the effort to let Christian value permeate Ibo life, we cannot afford to have a social wall of division between Christians and non-Christians. All must see themselves socially as Ibos. The psychology of Christian's effort to be the salt of the earth where ever he finds himself, works best through identification with the people, while of course, ensuring that the "salt quality" of life in the Spirit through personal fellowship with Christ is evident in love, joy, peace and all of the fruit of the Spirit (Gal. 5 verse 22). The second part of the third proposition is the reciprocal recognition of the title in any given village as one, both for the Christian as well as for the non-Christian. This ensures that *Ọzọ* title taking remains, in any given village, irrespective of Christians participating in it, a culturally unifying factor. If this is not done and Christian *Ọzọ* title taking compartmentalizes itself away from that of non-Christian, the village community becomes divided at an important item of its culture and the hoped for Christianization of this important cultural item will never materialise. The final part of this third proposition is the acceptance by all-Christians and non-Christians that the religious ceremonies associated with the *Ọzọ* will differ as between the Christian and the non-Christian. Already this has been accepted in many parts of Iboland. Non-Christians appreciate the fact that Christians will no longer keep their own *Ọzọ* vigil at the ancestral shrine in the "bush". They will rather keep such vigil in the Church. All *Ọzọ* title holders should endeavour to watch the respective religious ceremonies, Christian as well as non-Christian. If Christians can ever hope to explain satisfactorily to their non-Christian kinsman the superiority of Christian beliefs over their non-Christian ones they must understand the rationale of Ibo religious practices including those related to *Ọzọ* title taking. With the common Christian preamble to *Ọzọ* as already suggested for all Christians in Iboland, the liturgical interpretation of the Christian religious symbolization of *Ọzọ* title taking will necessarily differ as between denominations. A non-liturgical Church cannot overnight become liturgical for the sake of *Ọzọ* title taking service. Therefore such a denomination should work out an acceptable service pattern of its own, whereas denominations like the Roman Catholic and the Anglican will have no difficulty in making the Mass or the Eucharist the central service.

Whatever form of the religious service of *Ọzọ* title taking each denomination works out for itself, the crucial traditional religious elements in *Ọzọ* must be brought out, namely, dedication for community service, sanctification of life and the making of covenant with "the ancestral saints of the community" to maintain purity of life, by which the social life of the community is enriched through the leadership of the new *Ọzọ* man and finally the handing over to the *Ọzọ* man the insignia of his office which have been blessed. In Onitsha for example an *Ọzọ* "holy box" containing some ancestral holy emblems is given to the person. We look forward to a Christian man's *Ọzọ* holy box as it stands in the Church in front of the altar table, ready for dedication and containing the holy bible, a cross or crucifix, a rosary (for the Romans for example) a small white cloth like the altar cloth with the inscription "In This Sign You Will Conquer" written over a cross emblem already drawn on the cloth. This the *Ọzọ* man carries over his left shoulder on ceremonial occasion. Specially designed crucifix, which only the *Ọzọ* title holder may wear on his neck, replaces the cotton ankle ring which non-Christian *Ọzọ* holders do wear. The grand *Ọzọ* stool will, of course, be the place he sits in front of the choir to receive the benediction. These of course are mere suggestions about details which Church leaders will work out, only that the theological dimension of the *Ọzọ* title's religious service must be clearly understood so as to guide actual format and details of the service. Such theological dimension, we repeat, includes dedication, sanctification of life, covenant with the living and the dead in the presence of God to contribute to the spiritual enrichment of life and the receiving of blessed emblems of the *Ọzọ* office.

A good number of the more minor institutions can also be Christianised. Elizabeth Isichei [20] has described the festival of *oma* (the celebration of the female ancestry) at Asaba, which is the same as *Ime Chi l'Agu* at Ihiala. We should incorporate this with all its traditional gift exchanges into the service of the Annunciation of the Blessed Virgin Mary, which in the Anglican Prayer Book falls on the 25th day of March every year. *Ime Obi Umuaka* (the celebration for "the spirit or hearts" of children) should be part of the Holy Innocents Day (December 28). [21] All these suggestions, as we have already

---

[20] Elizabeth Isichei, "Ibo and Christian Beliefs: Some Aspects of a Theological Encounter" in *African Affairs*, Vol. 68, no. 271, April 1969, p. 128.

[21] This seems hard for Churches in Iboland that do not have liturgical patterns in which these Holy Days appear. I fear that Ibos are very ceremonial people

indicated, are the logical upshot of the thesis of this study which seeks to define Christian normative values by which Ibos can live within their traditional culture and gradually, transform, at least some of the main institutions of that culture, into avenues for the normal expression of Christian virtues. In this way the Church in Iboland can hope to become an indigenous Church.

Conclusion

(1) *The Argument*

Ibo society and culture emphasizes considerable individualism as well as communal solidarity. It is through the membership of the community that the individual is assisted, by the built-in values like *ndu*, bravery, justice and co-operation, to aspire towards achievement in status, prestige and the mastery of skills and techniques like those possessed by the *dibias* (diviner-medicine men) oracle managers and their agents. Wealth, demonstrated through such prestige winning and religiously sanctifying institutions like the *Ọzọ* title, allows competition for achieved status rather than inherited positions. Such an open society contains all the possibilities for roles and statuses to go round rather than remain the restricted privileges of particular lineages, clans or other social units. Through group leadership, people at different age levels can be socialised into the norms and values of Ibo society, with sanctions that have been religiously enforced in the form of a moral code. With the arrival and spread of Christianity, technology and secularization, Ibo values and the moral code supporting them started cracking up, because the new experiences have become too extensive for the code and its supporting religious beliefs. The growth of new towns with its concentration of people from various clans and distinctive sub-cultural districts, coupled with the new demands of the economic, political and educational activities, further complicates the situation. This complication has reached such an extent that it now becomes difficult to discern easily what values influence people's decisions; or what rules provide guidance for the socialization of the young or lay the "rules" for what people should expect from each other; or provide patterns of the attitudes people should develop to enable them play roles like those of the teacher, the politician, the public or commercial administrator and the executive. The Christian

---

and that an indigenized Ibo Church will take in more colour and symbolic rituals in its worship to be faithful to Ibo way of life. But this is not our concern now.

Church in this kind of a situation of social change, does not feel capable to deal with the situation adequately because it finds itself divorced from the culture of the people. It is divided in its organizational framework and paralysed due to its lack of any measurable evidence of spiritual vitality which is necessary for it to function as a community force. This kind of situation must inevitably lead to the search for a new value system and a new organizational frame work and motivation. This we have located in a properly indigenized Christian Church in Iboland.

This Christian Church as we have discussed in chapter IV came into Iboland during the period of great disruption in the land. The oracle systems and the wide spread of European trade in slaves, left families broken up, many who went to consult these oracles failed to return, they were said to be "eaten up" by the gods of these oracles. Many people on their lawful pursuits were waylaid by slave raiders and kidnapped and sold to slavers. Mercenaries of the Aro-Chukwu oracle like the Abam people terrorized many parts of Iboland so that people feared to travel away from their own areas. Young children were frequently kidnapped and sometimes sacrificed to the gods of local shrines or sold to slavers. The arrival of both Christianity and the British Colonial authority coincided to provide the needed release from this fairly terrifying situation. These two in turn, together with the western technical culture they engendered, started new social and religious forces which again, in the last one hundred years, have resulted in the social change we have already mentioned. The Christian Church at its initial beginnings in Iboland did not do what St. Augustine of Canterbury[22] did among the Angles, namely, baptising the people's culture into the Christian Church. Therefore the Church in Iboland grew up, as it were, divided away from the cultural roots of Iboland to wear an additional toga of foreignness other than the foreignness that belongs intrinsically to the Gospel itself as a "colony of heaven" on earth. The work of the interpretation of the Gospel through Ibo cultural life experiences so as to provide, from the biblical revelation, new value systems for the people, and therefore for the Church's visible manifestation among the people, becomes the inevitable challenge to theologians of our day.

---

[22] See J. McLeod Campbell, Christian History in the Making, London: Church Assembly Press & Publications Board, 1946, p. 267, where he analysed how Augustine carried out Pope Gregory's advice "to avoid any grave dislocation" of the Angles' customs.

Why should the Christian Church provide for the people this new value orientation? Two main reasons can be given in anwer to this question. One is that the Christian Gospel contains within itself the message of the new possibilities for man due to the reconciliation Christ has made between God and man. Man as a believer in Christ can now understand himself, his neighbours, his communities and the good life they really need for harmonious, happy co-existence. Secondly Christianity like any other religion is, to a substantial degree, the repository of a culture's orientation to the values that will enable the society function as a social interacting unit. The Ibo's emphasis on *ndu,* justice, co-operation, when enhanced by the believer's fruit of the Spirit in love, joy and peace for example, creates new cultural dimensions out of these values, as would make possible new social and integrative force, around which the Ibo can regroup for a new lease of community as well as individual life. There are therefore theological as well as sociological resources within Christianity which make it possible for the Christian Church to be able to be the generator of the new integrative norms of Iboland. The Ibo traditional religion, because of its inability to continue to give satisfactory explanations to present day experiences, can no more uphold such values.

The Church can do this on two levels—individual and community. On the individual side, both the New Testament and the sociological principles of norm development [23] give clear guide how this can be done: belief systems built around the reliable source, the Christ (in New Testament terminology); realization of the need for the norms (the new life of gratitude to the Christ) plus the need for adequate way of life for our time; the obedient application of the norm to interpersonal relationship throughout all the institutions of daily life (the family, industry or business, political activities, cultural activities as well as social links within the community). These help the individual, not only to internalize but also to act upon the norms. On the community side, the sum total of the life of faith through the fruitful exercise of the norms, will create in the society, clear ethos which will guide daily behaviour, generate principles of social expectation and define the attitudes relevant to the proper performance of roles and statuses, especially the new ones present Ibo society call upon the people to bear. In this way individual character could be better devel-

23 John Finley Scott, Internalization of Norms: A Sociological Theory of Moral Commitment, Englewood Cliffs, New Jersey: Prentice Hall, Inc., 1971, pp. 154-169.

oped and the cultural integration of the community becomes possible.

The Church that can do this is one that is indigenised. It provides the moral guidance of the total community—Christian as well as non-Christian. By taking into its symbolic and cultural life the living institutions of the people's way of life like the *Ọzọ* title taking, it eliminates the offensive practice of Christians being divorced from their own culture. The Church instead becomes the spiritual force through which those cultural institutions take on new creativity, because the Christians themselves can now see their accustomed ways of life as new avenues for the glorification of God in Jesus Christ. The objection can be raised that non-Christians who become secularized tend to despise religion as well as Christianity, because its tenets are unacceptable to their more positivistic way of thinking. In the light of this they will debunk such ethical guidance as the Christian religion would provide, which in turn will falsify our argument. To this end our study had already shown how the Christian moral teaching should build its first lessons of moral training on the basic moral impulses of man. Furthermore the African cultural habit of not distinguishing the spiritual too sharply from the material, will continue to make religiously oriented moral values respected. Moreover because some elements of technological secularization contain values derived originally from Christianity (although technological civilization now lives its own independent self expression) religiously oriented moral values can never be totally alien to technology and secularization.[24] The strength of the new moral life in permeating the totality of Ibo life depends, to a great extent, on the Christians who understand the meaning of being "new creature" because each of them is a "man in Christ".

(2) *Wider Implications of the Study*

This will be discussed briefly under two headings: theological and sociological. On the theological level this study follows the line of the

[24] The development of the Theology of Liberation especially in its Latin American version, derives from this belief that secularization contains elements of moral vitality. The emphasis of the Bangkok Conference on "The Meaning of Salvation Today", Dec. 1972 to Jan. 1973, by the slant that conference placed on technology's assistance towards the struggle for social justice as part of the experience of the meaning of salvation, points to the same direction. Ditto the writings of the secular theologians to which we have already referred. See Gustavo Gutierrez, A Theology of Liberation: History, Politics and Salvation, New York: Mary Knoll, Orbis Books, 1973, and International Review of Missions. Vol. LXII, no. 246, April 1973, on the various reports from the Bangkok Conference.

many searches of a good number or writers for what is generally called African theology but which we prefer to speak of as African background to Christian theology.[25] Our methodology in the attempt to interpret the given facts of the biblical revelation of Jesus Christ, follows the well known dictum "facts are sacred but comments are free". The Christian Church can only stand on the fact of the Christ-event. That is sacred and no cultural "pressures" should change it anywhere. It is the foundation on which the Church can either stand or fail to stand. The life that is attendant to the Christ-event is also given as a fact—it must be life in the Spirit and the fruit of the Spirit is well known in love, joy, peace and the rest of it. The organization of the social setting in which such life in the Spirit is lived, is like comment, and therefore free. Hence every African community is at liberty to christianise its traditional cultural institution like Bishop Lucas helped in christianizing the *Jando* initiation practice among the Masasi of Tanzania as long ago as 1913.[26] In the same spirit, Harry Sawyerr has recommended a fresh approach to the liturgy of the Holy Communion Service.[27] As long as the "free" interpretation does not damage nor obscure, nor add nor substract from the Christ-event within the biblical faith, it is a legitimate theological construction to use African thought forms, cultural artefacts and symbols to interpret, communicate and teach the Christian Faith, to the enrichment of the Christian life of our African peoples; for as part of the Report of the Bangkok Conference on Salvation Today puts it: "Culture shapes the human voice that answers the voice of Christ".[28]

---

[25] Many books are now being written to interpret the Christian message from African life experiences for examples see C. G. Baeta (ed.), Christianity in Tropical Africa—Studies presented and discussed at the 7th International African Seminar, University of Ghana, April 1965, London: Oxford University Press, 1968; John S. Mbiti, New Testament Eschatology in an African Background: A Study of the Encounter between New Testament Theology and African Traditional Concpets, London: Oxford University Press 1971, H. Sawyerr, Creative Evangelism: Towards a new Christian Encounter with Africa, London: Lutterworth Press 1968; Charles Nyamiti, The Scope of African Theology, Uganda: Gaba Publications, 1973.

[26] Bishop Lucas was UMCA (Universities Mission to Central Africa) missionary among the Masasi in present day Tanzania. The mission started in Masasi in 1876. See W. V. Lucas, "The Christian Approach to non-Christian Customs" in Christianity and Native Rites, London, 1950, as quoted by T. O. Ranger and I. Kimambo (ed.), The Historical Study of African Religion, University of California Press, Berkeley and Los Angeles, 1972, pp. 221-251.

[27] Harry Sawyerr, *op. cit.*, pp. 118-155.

[28] Bangkok Assembly Report, Section I, "Culture and Identity", Geneva: CWME, 1973, p. 73.

The work of reacting in a defensive manner, against European theological writers who comment on theological issues that have particular bearing on Africa, should be considered as closed. It is unproductive, time consuming, negative and reactionary. More positive approach by African theologians, who use African philosophical and sociological experiences, or religious histories to illustrate constructively themes within the biblical revelation or the Church's systematic theologies, is likely to help build up the body of literature out of which sound theology with African background will emerge. The whole field of symbolism in African religious experiences remains still untapped as well as the significance of such symbolisms for liturgical purposes so as to reach the African's unconscious with "the feel" of the Gospel. Towards such theological goals our study contains a good deal of suggestions that could be taken up and be properly developed theologically. Furthermore our study has suggested that part of the methodological approach to this work of theologizing, is faith, that is that only "the new man in Christ" can theologize. We cannot easily improve upon St. Anselm's definition of theology as *Fides quaerens intellectum.* Without such faith, there is the danger that our theologizing becomes mere projection of purely personal human wishes. This becomes mere intellectualism, and we know that the distance between prophecy and false prophecy is only one single step. Those who abide in the person and in the deeds of the Christ, whose event within the biblical tradition we interpret, can avoid that one single wrong step that might lead to false theological prophecies.

A good deal of theories and insights from the sociology of religion have been touched upon in this study. The theory of Emile Durkheim, [29] that religious representations are constitutive of society and that religious action is very important in stimulating individuals to participate positively in social life, is taken into this analysis of Ibo or any other non-complex society. This integrative force of the traditional religions begins to weaken when such traditional religions are impacted upon by another religion or another value orientation. Furthermore the sociological effects of African traditional religious ceremonies, institutions and symbols, for example oracles, ritual avoidances, sacred animals or sacred bushes are touched upon. This study

---

[29] See his: The Elementary Forms of the Religious Life, Trans. by Joseph W. Swain, New York: The Free Press, 1947; cf. Robert Bellah, Beyond Belief: Essays on Religion in a Post-Traditional World, New York: Harper & Row, 1970, p. 8.

will therefore need a good deal of follow-up to see how much these ceremonies, institutions and symbols served as means of social control and social integration and thereby faciliated interactions between persons, groups and communities. The time is long past when derogatory terms like "fetish", "primitive", "magic" are applied to these facts and facets of African traditional religions and thereby dismiss them as useless, irrelevant and archaic.

Historical materials are supplied in this study about the disruption Christianity brought on Ibo traditional, social and cultural values. Theories of the influence of religion on social change can be further tested from these empirical data. J. Milton Yinger has indicated five logical possibilities in the relationship of religion and social change.[30] This study uses that possibility which sees religion as part of a complex interacting system. Within a given point in time Christianity came face to face with existing traditional religion already facing disruptive effects from some of its own system, for example the disruption the oracles brought to families. From such meeting, influences are set in motion leading to new disruption of values and moral codes and the emergence of new experiences. With greater internalization of Christian norms the traditional values will once more mix with new religious factors towards the development of new forces, which we hope, will create new value orientations adequate for the experiences of life with Christianity, technology, residual traditionalism, the growth of cities and so on. Religious factors will predominate at one stage and in turn receive influences from factors religion has itself released in the society. This mutual interactive influence between religion and social forces towards social change, is one of the sociological considerations that leads us to accept the need for Christianity taking into its system traditional cultural institutions like the *Ọzọ* title, as part of its way of influencing the culture, and the culture in turn will enrich Christianity's life and expression in the given area.

Another sociological implication of our study is the place of religious institutions in individual role playing and the filling of statuses through which social stratification and individual achievements, skills and growth in personality can be stimulated. The place of the diviner-medicine-men in the traditional society and the pastors, missionaries and teachers in the Christian set up, is indicated in the study. Christ-

---

[30] J. Milton Yinger, Sociology Looks at Religion, New York: MacMillan Comp., 1966, p. 40.

ians were the first to build the four corner type of house, plant flowers in their yards, train their families in modern hygiene and with education in mission schools became the elite.[31] The influence of the Church in being the spearhead of a new social influence in the society, which this study recommends very strongly, is deduced from this consideration. Any religious organisation which has clear revelation contents like Christianity has, is bound to influence social functioning of individuals, and thereby exert strong influence upon the society. The effectiveness of this hypothesis will have to be tested in future studies of Ibo society for example, to see to what extent statuses and roles have been better fulfilled because of the influence of Christianity upon their occupants. This brings us straight away to the Weberian thesis which is very much presumed in this study.

One of Weber's emphasis is on the correlation of belief and practical life which leads to his famous "doctrine of the calling".[32] The hope of an African Christian "civilization" emerging anywhere in that continent, as we have indicated in this study, builds on this sociological theory. Already there exists within the traditional value systems concepts of honesty, diligence in one's work especially as a craftsman serving the community with one's skill. What was lacking was the proper motivations as to the goal these values were meant to serve. Christianity with its revelation contents and strong motive force, resulting from faith in the Saviour, when it takes hold of people, supplies not only reasons for and goals towards which such values are to be employed, but also a continually renewed basis for those values. Faith results into action and when such actions are performed with honesty, integrity, dedication and selflessness, a new force for social action and social relationship is bound to be generated. Where Christian men in industry, business, education, government and all other forms of employment see their jobs as a calling by God, through which they can give of their best in this world to the service of their fellow men, but more so to the glory of God, a new civilization is bound to arise. Weber's analysis indicates that it was such application of faith to life which enabled Calvinist puritans to develop the spirit

---

[31] Cf. The Ajayi Thesis that the mission among other things, was the cause of the new elite of Nigeria. See J. F. Ade Ajayi, Christian Missions in Nigeria 1841-1891, The Making of a New Elite, London: Longmans, 1964.

[32] Max Weber, The Protestant Ethic and the Spirit of Capitalism, trans. by Talcott Parsons, New York: Scribners, 1958. See also Max Weber, The Sociology of Religion, trans. Ephraim Fischoff, London: Methuen & Co. Ltd., first published Germany 1922, English Social Science Paperback, reprint 1971.

of capitalism by which western Europe started a new civilization—the industrial civilization. There are, of course, many other aspects of this theory and many variables are involved, for example, the situations, such as historical and political, in which the faith convictions are employed. Furthermore we are not unaware of the amount of debate [33] going on for and against Weber's conclusions in this respect. We however feel convinced that there is a strong correlation between religious faith and practical action. Because of this, we do see in the African's desire for modernity, a possibility that religious and cultural forces can be effective factors towards the desired change to modernity in which the best in African traditional culture is also retained. Only to this extent are we interested in Weber's "doctrine of the calling". We therefore hope, in using the insight of this theory, that the situations and circumstances will be conducive and that the application of the Christian "ethic of thanksgiving" to God by those who really believe in the Christ, will usher in a new social norm by which the whole community is given a new ideology and a new sense of purpose, all leading to a new cultural vitality.

A good deal of the sociological "conclusions" reached in this study will no doubt serve as hypotheses for further testing through empirical studies. For example it will be investigated whether the Christian adoption of traditional institutions like the *Ọzọ* title and all others, will in some ten years' time make the Church more indigenized so that Aladuraism and other forms of healing and problem solving "Churches" will no longer proliferate. Such proliferation will then be deemed unnecessary, because the "Orthodox" Churches have all become relevant to the cultural milieu in which they exist, and have themselves become problem solving to the worshipping individuals. It will be further studied whether such indigenization has led to a renaissance of cultural creativity, especially in such fields as were originally dubbed heathenish and therefore were inhibited by Christianity: traditional wood carving, sculpture, ballad singing, to mention just a few.

---

33 See Benjamin Nelson, "Weber's Protestant Ethic: Its Origins, Wanderings and Foreseeable Futures" in *Beyond the Classics! Essays in the Scientific Study of Religion* edited by Charles J. Glock and Phillip E. Hammond. New York: Harper & Row, Torchbooks, 1973, pp. 71-131. Most important is the 18 paged bibliography of the literature on this subject, mostly on the debate. Here Dr. Nelson upholds the main outlines of the Weber's thesis and further underscores the importance of Weber's efforts to show "at what points certain correlations between forms of religious belief and practical ethics can be worked out". *Op. cit.*, p. 75.

The sociological usefulness of our study will therefore depend on the use it is made of in substantiating or rejecting or modifying theories which we have employed in reaching conclusions which are in fact in the nature of hypotheses.

The use we made of theological and sociological insights in arguing the thesis of this study, is demanded by the nature of the study itself —the moral influences that can be generated by a Church in the situation of rapid social change. The Church itself exists in these two dimensions, namely, as the creation of God in Jesus Christ through the Holy Spirit and as the company of believers bound together in a visible organisation. Theological insight helps us to understand its divine nature whilst sociological empiricism helps us to survey more objectively its institutional ramifications.

APPENDIX I

A GLOSSARY OF SOME IBO WORDS

Agbala an Oracle situated at Awka; one of the four great oracles of Iboland.

Aho name of a shrine prominent in Ihiala Division.

Akoro creeping plant used in religious activities like cleansing from ritual pollution or washing the hands after handling a corpse. It is also used as symbolic representation of various spirits and the means of demarcating the holy from the profane.

Ala Earth, hence name of the earth goddess.

Amadioha God of thunder called *Kamalu* in some Ibo areas.

Aru (*Nso Ala*) ritual pollution, hence contravention of *Omenani* (q v) or doing of things that are tabooed, prohibited or abominable.

Chi Individual's spirit counterpart, sometimes used in place of God the Creator as He relates to an individual person.

Dibia A herbal medicineman who also may act as a diviner, priest or visioner.

Eke, Orie, Afo, Nkwo Names of days which repeat with the suffix *Ukwu* or *Nta,* making up Ibo native week of eight days.

Iba, Obi, Obu the outer house of an elderly person, especially the holder of the *Ọzọ* title, where he receives guests and where the patrilineage assembles for deliberations etc.

Ichi Facial incision which can be an *Ọzọ* title in some places.

Igwe Ka Ala An Oracle dedicated to the sky god and the earth goddess at Umunneoha in Owerri area; One of the four great Oracles of Iboland.

Igwọ Ọfọ ceremonial and ritual cleansing of *Ọfọ* the religious emblem of authority and Justice.

Ifejioku the god of yam and of farmland.

Ihu-Ndoro-Ohia the shrine of *Ndoro Ohia,* a clan god.

Iro-Muo The "delighting" of the gods; *Irọ Urọ* implies intimate and personal playing together as between wife and husband. This is the only traditional Ibo religious worship that contains the idea of man approaching the gods in a relaxed attitude of mutual appreciation suggesting friendship between the gods and men. No wonder it takes place at the time of harvest.

Mbari (*House*) highly decorated house containing the shrine of the earth goddess in Owerri area. Famous for the artistic mural paintings (see illustration on page 37).

Ndebunze, Ndichie the shrine of the ancestors.

Ogirisi, Oha, Ujiji tropical plants used as cultus symbols of certain gods and spirits. The leaves of the last two are edible.

Ogwugwu name of a clan and lineage god.

Okpara the head of *Umunna,* lineage (also of the extended family).

Omenani the approved "doings", "customs" or "ways" of the land; what the ancestors and the earth goddess have sanctioned either to be observed or to be avoided.

Omu Nkwu the tendril of the palm tree, used as symbolic representation of spirits; emblem of what is sacred and therefore separated from common usage or from unauthorised handling.

Osu a slave dedicated to a god or goddess as his or her attendant or priest.

Ọzọ (title) a rank title acquired through expensive social and religious ceremonies. There are various classes and kinds, (see pages 30-31).

Ubiniukpabi (*Ibinukpabi*) the Oracle of *Chukwu* (the Great God) at Aro *Chukwu,* the principal Oracle of Iboland commonly spoken of as the "Long Juju".

Uhie (Drum) "talking" and musical drum hollowed out of a big chunk of wood; in some places it serves as the royal drum and used only on special occasions.

Ulasi Ogboro name of a river god as well as a lineage god, prominent in Ihiala Division.

Umunna The children of ancestor "father", hence the patrilineage.

APPENDIX II

SOME IBO NAMES ILLUSTRATING IBO WORLD VIEW

1. Names that Affirm the reality of God through his beneficent actions to man

Chukwueloka (*Osaeloka*) God's thoughts are very deep.

Chukwujioke (*Chijioke, Chinwe*) God is the divider, he has the portions and he of his own will gives to each person as he thinks fit.

Chukwuemeka (*Nnaemeka*) God (or father in Heaven) has done great things (in giving the family the son so named).

Ikechukwu God's might is manifested (in the gift of the child so named).

Ogo Chukwu God's mercy or benevolence is made concrete (through the child that bears the name).

Okwuolisa (*Okwosa, Olisa*) The word of God is Unalterable.

2. Names that Confess that Reality is mysterious

Amakezeonwu Reality includes the certainty of death, no matter how ever we try to escape it.

Echidime Tomorrow is "pregnant"; it is all uncertain.

Onyemaobi Chukwu? Who can fathom the mind of God?

Onyemaechi Who knows what tomorrow will bring?

Onyeama (*nke diniuru*) No one knows what reality will unfold.

Uwadiegwu The world in which we live is mysterious.

3. Names that express faith and trust in the power of Chukwu (the great Creator God)

Chukwudi (*Chidi*) Certainly there is God (in the sense of trust him).

Chibuzo, Chukwubuzo, Chibueze, Chizoba God leads the way; the king that saves; (and therefore is worthy of trust).

Chukwuka (*dibia*) God is more powerful than *dibia* (or anything).

Kanayo Chukwu (We trust God) so we keep on asking from him.

Mgbeodinma It will surely be fine one day (because God exists).

Ngozichukwuka God's blessings surpass everything.

Nkechinyere What ever *Chi* or God gives, is good.

Nkiruka With faith in God, what lies ahead is yet greater than what has passed.

4. Names that express the blessedness of having children who are the means of continuing the lineage and hence, the human race

Adaiba The daughter that establishes the *Iba* (q v).

Obiajulu My soul is at rest for there is a son to continue the lineage.

Obiewulu The compound ("family") is now established.

Mbanefo (*Udekananwa*) The regions will now know the family (through the son bearing the name).

Nwabundo, Nwabufo, Nwabugwu The child is the shelter, the fame of the lineage, or the family.

Nwachukwu, Nwagbara The child of *Chukwu*, God or the smaller divinities (so the family is established as the gods are established).

Nwakaku, Nwaku, Nwakaego The child is greater than riches.

5. Names that express the enigma about man and his nature

Azikaniwe The children of men are full of wrath, (so fear them and do not put ultimate confidence in them).

Munonyedi Who is on my side, to be sure? (meaning no one).

Madubugwu Man is his fellow man's pride (despite the evil in man).

Onyeduibeya, Onyedumezie? Which man is the sure guide to another man? (meaning no one, so trust *Chukwu* and not man).

6. Names that express the importance of life which death tries to vitiate

Ifeakandu Possessions are not superior to life.

Ndudi (*emeife*) If there is life, there is hope of achievements.

Onwubuya Death is the only "scatterer" (of man's efforts).

Onwuka (*emem*) Death is the one thing that greatly frustrates all my efforts.

7. Names that express the importance of justice in God's world and in men's social relationships

Aso Chukwu Keep the laws of God.

Emefiena Do not purposely injure another person.

Nzomiwu Before making any steps, be mindful of the laws of the gods and of men.

Sọọluibe Give deference to others.

APPENDIX III

SOME PROVERBS THAT EXPRESS SOME ASPECTS OF THE IBO WORLD VIEW AND PHILOSOPHY

1. About the spirits and the spirit world

Nwata bili uno, oketa muo	When a young man starts his new home, he receives his own share of the spirits.
Nnamfa nagbaram Ọgu be ndi muo, ka m'nagbara ha be ndi madu	Let my ancestors defend my cause in the spirit world, while I keep on fighting their cause in the land of the living (Hence the sacrifice of kola nuts, libation, etc.)
Ijérè be nde muo nacho ndikenye, nnamfa nwuru anwu jeziri ebé?	How can you go to the land of the spirits and say there is a shortage of elders, where have our dead fathers gone to?
Efi nenwero ọdu, Chiya anachuru ya ijiji	The cow that has a short tail its *chi* drives away flies from its body.
Oke amana uma taka akpa dibia, ma dibia amana uma bu oke onu	The house mouse should not deliberately bite holes into the diviner's bag and let not the diviner without provocation curse the house mouse; (mutuality between the high and the low, those who see the spirit and the ordinary persons.)

2. On Scepticism

Uche bu afa	It is only with common sense that the diviner "sees" the gods.
Chia n'aka gua n'obi ka ejiagbara ofeke afa, makana odirọ onye furu muo anya, dirisi ndu.	It is by juggling and beating on the chest that divination is made for the uninitiated, for no one (including the diviner) has seen the spirits and still stay alive.

Nwa Aro adasi nwa Aro ibeya na Ubiniukpabi ajuona oha ya	One Aro man does not say to another Aro man that *Ubiniukpabi* has inquired about him. (Because they both know that no such god exists and yet they induced non Aro people to believe that such *Chukwu* existed.)

3. On social responsibility or community life

Ofu mkpisi aka ruta mmanu ozue nde ọzọọnu	When one finger is soaked with palm oil, it quickly spreads to other fingers.
Nwanne onye nagba ajo egwu ọkọ iku anakọ ya	When a man's brother (classificatory) is dancing out of tune, the man (that is the brother watching) quickly develops an itching eyebrow. (He bends his face in shame and pretends to be scratching the eye brow).
Kayiri, kayiri, onwere onye sọsọ ya yiri agu gebu?	This talk about "going together going together", does the tiger swallow any one who goes his way (of life) alone? Meaning that it is good to co-operate with others but if others don't want it, then to heck with it!
Iwe nwanne newe nuru, odieru nọkpukpu	The anger against a brother (classificatory) stops at the fleshy part of the body, it does not penetrate down to the bone. (One can not be very angry against a relative).
Anagwọ ọgwu anya odudo adiținye ya ose	The medicine that is being prepared for the clearing of the eyes, does not require hot pepper.

BIBLIOGRAPHY

Many of the books cited in the footnotes are not relisted in this bibliography

I. ANTHROPOLOGICAL AND CULTURAL STUDIES ON THE IBO

a. *Archival Sources*: National Archives (hereafter N.A.) at Enugu and Ibadan, Nigeria

Anon.

1916—1917 Methods of Breaking and Removing any Juju (extensive confidential reports from Divisional Officers) CSE/1/26/115, NA, Enugu.

1929—1933 Intelligence Reports on Various Divisions in Iboland. EP 1160-1180, Na, Enugu.

Dobinson, Rev. H. H.

n.d. Notes on Conversations and Pieces of Miscellaneous Information Gathered at Onitsha C.M.S. N/5/1: 1890-1891, N.A., Ibadan.

Meek, C. K.

1930—1931 Various Ethnographical Reports on Various Divisions (Iboland) NA, Enugu.

Strong, A. C.

n.d. Onitsha Station Log Book, 1884-1893, C.M.S. N5/1: 1, NA., Ibadan.

Talbot, P. A.

1922 A Report on the Pagan Creed CSE 1/2/18, NA, Enugu.

1922 A Report on Various Superstitions CSE 1/2/20 NA, Enugu.

1922 A Report on Local Jujus CSE 5/2/19, NA, Enugu.

b. *Unpublished Dissertations and Mss.*

Henderson, H. K.

n.d. Ritual Roles of Women in Onitsha Ibo Society, Ph.D. Dissertation, University of California at Berkeley, 1969.

Jeffreys, M. D. W.

n.d. The Divine Umundri Kings of Iboland, Ph.D. Dissertation, University of London at the Library of the School of Oriental and African Studies, London.

Mokwue, J. C.

n.d. Principal Cult Objects Used in Igbo Traditional Religion, long essay, B.A. degree in Religion, 1972, University of Nigeria, Nsukka, Nigeria.

There are about two dozen other titles in this long essay series at the library of the Department of Religion, Nsukka, all on Ibo Traditional Religion.

Smith, S. R.

n.d. The Ibo People: A Study of Religion and Customs of a Tribe in the Southern Provinces of Nigeria. Mss with the authors widow.

c. *Published Articles*

Anon.

1951 Nri Traditions, *Nigeria Magazine* No. 54, p. 252.

Azikiwe, B. N.
1930 Fragments of Onitsha History, *Journal of Negro History XV*, p. 474-97.

Ekejiuba, Felicia
1971—1972 Igba Ndu: An Igbo Mechanism of Social Control and Adjustment, *African Notes: Bulletin of the Institute of African Studies, University of Ibadan*, VII; 1 pp. 9-24.

Forde, C. D.
1938 Fission and Accretion in the Patrilineal Clans of A Semi Bantu Community in Southern Nigeria, *Journal of Royal Anthropological Institute*, 68, pp. 311-338.

Harris, J. S.
1942 Some Aspects of Slavery in Southeastern Nigeria, *Journal of Negro History*, 27, pp. 37-54.

Horton, Robin
1954 The Ohu System of Slavery in a Northern Ibo Village-group, *Africa*, 24, pp. 311-336.
1956 God, Man, and the Land in a Northern Ibo Village-group, *Africa*, 26, pp. 17-28.

Ilogu, Edmund
1964 *Ọfọ, Nigeria Magazine* 82, pp. 234/5.
1973 Worship in Ibo Traditional Religion, *Numen, International Review for the History of Religion* XX, 3, pp. 229-238.

Isichei, Patrick, A. C.
1973 Sex in Traditional Asaba, *Cahiers d'Etudes Africaines* 13; 4, pp. 682-699.

Jeffreys, M. D. W.
1954 *Ikenga*: The Ibo Ram-headed God, *African Studies*, 13, pp. 25-40.
1956 The Umundri Tradition of Origin, *African Studies*, 15; 3, pp. 119-131.

Jones, G. I.
1939 Who are the Aro?, *Nigerian Field*, 8, pp. 100-103.
1962 Ibo Age Organization, with Reference to the Cross River and North Eastern Ibo, *Journal of the Royal Anthropological Institute*, 92, pp. 191-212.

Kalu, Eke
1938 An Ibo Autobiography, *Nigerian Field*, 7, pp. 158-170.

Leith-Ross, S.
1937 Notes on the Osu System among the Ibo of Owerri Province, Nigeria, *Africa*, 10, pp. 206-220.

Ottenberg, S.
1958 Ibo Oracles and Intergroup Relations, *Southwestern Journal of Anthropology*, 14, pp. 295-317.
1961 The Present-State of Ibo Studies, *Journal of the Historical Society of Nigeria*, 2; 2, pp. 211-230.

Uchendu, Victor
1964 The Status Implication of Igbo Religious Beliefs, *Nigerian Field*, 29; 1, pp. 27-37.
1965 Concubinage Among Ngwa Igbo of Southern Nigeria, *Africa*, 35; 2, pp. 187-197.

d. *Books*

Arinze, F. A.
1970 *Sacrifice in Ibo Religion,* Ibadan: Ibadan University Press.

Basden, G. T.
1938 *Niger Ibos,* London: Seeley Service & Co. Ltd. Reprint, London: Frank Cass, 1966.

Echeruo, M. J. C. and Obiechina, E. N., (eds.)
1971 *Igbo Traditional Life, Culture and Literature,* New York: Conch Magazine Ltd.

Equiano, Olauda
1789 *The Life of Olauda Equiano or Gustavus Vasa The African,* 2 vols., Reprint London: Dawson of Pall Mall, 1969.
This autobiography of an Ibo, possibly from Iseke in Ihiala Division, is one of the earliest written accounts about Ibo way of life by an Iboman.

Forde, Daryl and Jones, G. I.
1950 *The Ibo and Ibibio-speaking Peoples of South Eastern Nigeria,* London: Oxford University Press for International African Institute.

Great Britain
1900 *Niger Coast Protectorate,* Report for 1898-9, Colonial Reports-Annual, No. 289, London: H.M.S.O.
1902 *Southern Nigeria,* Report for 1902, Colonial Reports-Annual, No. 405, London: H.M.S.O.

Henderson, R. N.
1972 *The King in Everyman: Evolutionary Trends in Onitsha Ibo Society and Culture,* New Haven: Yale University Press.

Leith-Ross, S.
1934 *African Women*: A Study of the Ibo of Nigeria, London: Faber.

Leonard, A. G.
1906 *The Lower Niger and Its Tribes,* London: Macmillan, Reprint, London: Frank Cass, 1968.

Nzimiro, Ikenna
1971 *Studies In Ibo Political Systems: Chieftaincy and Politics in Four Niger States,* London: Frank Cass; Berkeley and Los Angeles: University of California Press (1972).

Ogbalu, F. C.
1969 *Omenala Igbo* (*The Book of Igbo Custom*), Onitsha: University Publishing Company.

Talbot, P. Amaury
1927 *Some Nigerian Fertility Cult,* London: Oxford Univresity Press Reprint London: Frank Cass, 1967.
1932 *Tribes of the Niger Delta, London*: Oxford University Press, Reprint,, London: Frank Cass, 1967.

Uchendu, Victor
1965 *The Igbo of Southeast Nigeria,* New York: Holt, Rinehart and Winston.

2. HISTORY OF CHRISTIANITY IN IBOLAND

a. *Archival Sources*

C.M.S. Archives, London CA 3/o; G 3/A3/o, CA 3/L and G3/A3/L.
M.M.S. Archives, London PMMS.
University of Nigeria, Nsukka, Nigeria, Department of Religion "Archives":
The Epelle Collections of Mss on Local Church History and Research Materials from *West-African Religion*.

b. *Published Articles*

Bennett, P. A.
1894 A Visit to Opoto, *Niger ad Yoruba Notes*, 1; 2, p. 24.

Dennis, D.
1904 The Rising of the Ekwumekwu, *Niger and Yoruba Notes*, 10; 119 pp. 83-87.

Dobinson H. H.
1895 In the Niger Delta with Bishop Tugwell, *Niger and Yoruba Notes* 1; 8, pp. 13-14.

Johnson, Rt. Rev. Bishop James
1904 The Niger Delta Pastorate, *Niger and Yoruba Notes* 10; 115, pp. 52-54.

Smith, S. R.
1894 Christmas Week Itineration in the Ibo Speaking Country, *Niger and Yoruba Notes*, 4; 46, pp. 82-83.
1905 Oka, *Western Equatorial Africa Diocesan Magazine* 11; 129, pp. 161-165.

Trowell, Bishop
1903 A Visit to Oka, *Niger and Yoruba Notes*, 9; 108, pp. 90-91.

Church Missionary Record 1863-1875.
The Church Missionary Intelligencer 1849-1906, *Niger and Yoruba Notes* 1893-1900 and the *Western Equatorial Africa Diocesan Magazine* 1893-1917 at the C.M.S. Archives in London (157 Waterloo Road) contain many more articles dealing with the planting and the spread of Christianity in Iboland.

c. *Books*

Bane, Martin J.
1956 *Catholic Pioneers in West Africa.* Dublin: Clonmore & Reynolds.

Crowther, S. A. and Taylor, —J. C.
1859 *The Gospel on the Banks of the Niger*, London: Seeley Service 2 vols. Reprint, London: Frank Cass.

Dike, K. O.
1957 *Origins of the Niger Mission 1841-1891*, Ibadan: Ibadan University Press.

Ekechi, F. K.
1971 *Missionary Enterprise and Rivalry in Igboland* 1857-1914, London: Frank Cass.

Epelle, E. M. T.
1955 *The Church in the Niger Delta*, Port-Harcourt: C.M.S. Niger Press.
1964 *Bishops in the Niger Delta*, Aba.

Grimley, John B. and Robinson, G. E.
1966 *Church Growth in Central and Southern Nigeria*, Grand Rapids, Michigan: William B. Eerdmans C.

Hewitt, Gordon
1971 *The Problems of Success: A History of the Church Missionary Society* 1910-1942, London: S.C.M. Press.

Iweka-nuno
1924 *History of Obosi and Iboland in General*, Onitsha: the Author.

Jordan, Rev. Father, J.
1948 *Bishop Shanahan of Southern Nigeria*, Dublin: Clonmore & Reynolds Ltd.

Livingstone, W. P.
n.d. *Mary Slessor of Calabar*, London: Hodder and Stoughton.

Page, Jesse
1910 *The Black Bishop* (Life of Bishop S. A. Crowther) London: Simpkin.

Stock, Eugene
1899—1914 *The History of the Church Missionary Society* in 4 vols. (See expecially volumes II and III) London: C.M.S.

Todd, John, Murray
1962 *African Mission: A History of the Society of African Missions*, London: Burns and Oates.

Walker, F. D.
1930 *The Romance of the Black River: The Story of the C.M.S. Nigeria Mission, London*: C.M.S. The Highway Press.

The various Synod Reports of the Diocese on the Niger, at Onitsha Diocesan Office, 1922 to the present; Owerri Diocese at Egbu; Enugu Diocese at Enugu and Aba Diocese at Aba, contain some historical material.

3. INTERACTION OF CHRISTIANITY AND IBO CULTURE

a. *Unpublished Dissertations and Mss.*

Aruzu, R.
n.d. The Pagans. "An Interview with a Traditional Igbo Philosopher (Ezenwadeyi of Ihembosi)" in Father Aruzu's private possession.

Iwuagwu, A. O.
n.d. The Spiritual Churches in the Eastern States of Nigeria, Ph.D. Thesis, Ibadan University, Ibadan 1971.

Moller, Caroline V.M. (Mrs. S. Ifeka)
n.d. An Aladura Church in Eastern Nigeria, London University Ph.D. (Social Anthropology) 1968.

Obiefuna, A.
n.d. The Christian Education of Igbo Moral Conscience, Alfonsia Doctoral Thesis: Rome, 1966.

b. *Published Articles*

Egbo, E. O.
1972 A Reassessment of the Concept of Ibo Traditional Religion *Numen: International Review for the History of Religions* XIX Fasc. 1 pp. 68-79.

Ezeanya, S. N.
1967 The Osu (Cult.-slave) System in Igbo-land *Journal of Religion in Africa*, I; 1, pp. 36-45. The article ends with the Christian attitude to the system.

Isichei, Mrs. Elizabeth
1969 Ibo and Christian Beliefs: Some Aspects of Theological Encounter *African Affairs: Journal of the Royal African Society* 68; 271, pp. 121-134.
1970 Seven Varieties of Ambiguity: Some Patterns of Igbo Response to Christian Missions, *Journal of Religion in Africa* III; 3, pp. 209-227.

Uchendu, Victor
1964 Missionary Problems in Nigerian Society (mainly on the Ibo) *Practical Anthropology* 11; 3, pp. 105-117.

Umunna, V. Nworah
1939 Nigerian Paganism as a Preparation for the Gospel, *East and West Review* 5, pp. 139-145.

c. *Books*

Nwosu, V. (ed.)
1971 *Prayer Houses and Faith Healing*, Onitsha: Tabansi Press.

4. GENERAL: HISTORICAL, CULTURAL AND THEOLOGICAL MATERIALS ON CHRISTINITY AND THE AFRICAN PEOPLES

Anon.
1951 *The Church in the Town: Addresses Given at a Conference in Accra Gold Coast*, (Ghana) May 15th-18th, 1951, Accra: The Christian Council.
1970 *Les Religions Africaines comme source de valeurs de civilisation: Colloque de Cotonou 16-22 Aout* 1970, Paris: Présence Africaine.

Achebe, Chinua
1958 *Things Fall Apart*, London: Heinemann.
1964 *The Arrow of God*, London: Heinemann.

Aluko, T. M.
1966 *Kinsman and Foreman*, London: Heinemann.

Andersson, Efraim
1968 *Churches at the Grass-Roots: A Study in Congo Brazzaville*, London: Lutterworth Press.

Ayandele, E. A.
1970 *Holy Johnson: Pioneer of African Nationalism 1836-1917*, London: Frank Cass.

Azikiwe, Nnamdi
1937 Renascent Africa, reprint London: Frank Cass 1968.
1970 My Odyssey: An Autobiography, London: C. Hurst + Co., especially chapters 1-3.

Baeta, C. G. (ed.)
1968 *Christianity in Tropical Africa*, London: Oxford University Press for International African Institute.

Bascom, W. R.
1953 African Culture and the Missionary, *Civilisation* 3; 4, p. 499 ff.

Becken, Hans-Jürgen (ed.)
1973 *Relevant Theology for Africa,* Durban: Lutheran Publishing House.

Beetham, T. A.
1967 *Christianity and the New Africa,* London: Pall Mall Press Ltd.

Bosch, David, J. (ed.)
1971 *Church and Culture Change in Africa* (*LUX Mundi 3*) Pretoria: N.G. Kerk-Boekhandel.

Debrunner, H.
1965 *A Church Between Colonial Powers: A Study of the Church in Togo* London: Lutterworth Press.

Desai, Ram (ed.)
1962 *Christianity as seen by Africans, Denver*: Alan Swallow.

Fortes, Meyer
1959 *Oedipus and Job in West African Religion,* London: Oxford University Press.

Hastings, Adrian
1973 *Christian Marriage in Africa,* London: S.P.C.K.

Hetherwick, Alexander
1932 *The Gospel and the African,* Edinburgh: T. and T. Clark.

Idowu, E. Bolaji
1965 *Towards an Indigenous Church,* Ibadan: Oxford University Press.

Jahn, I.
1961 *Muntu: An Outline of neo African Culture,* London: Faber.

Kiplagat, Bethuel A.
1972 Christianity and African Novelists *International Review of Missions* LXI; 241, pp. 130-143.

Mbiti, John
1969 *African Religions and Philosophy,* London: Heinemann.

Mitchell, R. C. and Turner, H. W.
1967 *A Comprehensive Bibliography of Modern African Religious Movements,* Evanston Illinois.

Miller, Walter R.
1947 *Have we Failed in Nigeria*? London: Lutterworth Press.

Mobley, Harns W.
1970 *The Ghanaian's Image of the Missionary,* Leiden: E. J. Brill.

Munonye, John
1966 *The Only Son,* London: Heinemann.

Murphree, M. W.
1969 *Christianity and the Shona,* London: The Athlone Press, New York: Humanities Press, Inc.

Ngugi, James
1968 *The River Between,* African Writers Series, London: Heinemann.

Ojike, Mbonu
1946 *My Africa,* New York: The John Day Co.

Oliver, Roland
1952 *The Missionary Factor in East Africa,* London: Longmans.

Okafor-Omali, Dilim
1965 *A Nigerian Villager in Two Worlds,* London: Faber and Faber.

Oosthuizen, G. C.
1967 *The Theology of a South African Messiah: An Analysis of the Hymnal of The Church of the Nazarites,* Leiden/Köln: E. J. Brill.

Parsons, R. T.
1963 *Churches and Ghana Society,* 1918-1955, Leiden: E. J. Brill.
1964 *Religion in an African Society,* Leiden: E. J. Brill

Parrinder, E. G.
1953 *Religion in an African City* (Ibadan), London: Oxford University Press.

Peel, J. D. Y.
1968 *Aladura: A Religious Movement Among the Yoruba,* London: Oxford University Press.

P'Bitek, Okot
1971 *African Religions in Western Scholarship, Nairobi,* East African Literature Bureau.

Ranger T. O. and Kimambo, I. (eds.)
1972 *The Historical Study of African Religions,* Berkley + Los Angeles: University of California Press.

Rotberg, R. I.
1965 *Christian Missions and the Creation of Northern Nigeria,* London: Oxford University Press.

Sawyerr, Harry
1968 *Creative Evangelism: Towards a New Christian Encounter with Africa,* London: Lutterworth Press.

Shepperson, G. and Price, T.
1958 *Independent African: John Chilembwe and the Origins, Setting and Significance of the Nyasaland Rising of 1915,* Edinburgh University Press.

Shorter, Aylward
1973 *African Culture and the Christian Church: An Introduction to Social and Pastoral Anthropology, London*: Geoffrey Chapman.

Sundkler, B. G. M.
1961 *Bantu Prophets in South Africa,* London: Oxford University Press.
1962 *The Christian Ministry in Africa,* London: S.C.M. Press.

Tanner, R. E. S.
1967 *Transition in African Beliefs—Traditional Religion and Christian Change* (Sukumaland, Tanzania), New York: Maryknoll Publications.

Taylor, J. V.
1958 *The Growth of the Church in Buganda,* London: S.C.M. Press.
1961 with Lehmann, D. *Christians of the Copperbelt,* London: S.C.M. Press.
1963 *The Primal Vision: Christian Presence Amid African Religion,* London: S.C.M. Press.

Turner, H. W.
1967 *African Independent Church,* Oxford :Clarendon Press (2 vols).

Turner, V. W. (ed.)
1971 *Profiles of Change: African Society and Colonial Rule*, London: Cambridge University Press.
(See especially F. B. Welbourn's article Missionary Stimulus and African Responses).

Williamson, S. G.
1965 *Akan Religion and the Christian Faith*, edited by K. A. Dickson Accra: Ghana Universities Press.

Wilson, Monica
1971 *Religion and the Transformation of Society: a study in social change in Africa.* Cambridge: Cambridge University Press.

5. CULTURE, RELIGION AND SOCIETY—GENERAL

Abbott, Walter (ed.)
1966 *Documents of Vatican*, II, New York: Herder and Herder.

Allport, Gordon W.
1950 *The Individual and His Religion*, New York: The Macmillan Company.

Bellah, Robert N. (ed.)
1965 *Religion and Progress in Modern Asia*, New York: The Free Press.

Bennett, John C.
1946 *Christian Ethics and Social Policy,* New York: Scribners and Sons.
1966 (ed.) *Christian Social Ethics in a Changing World,* New York: Association Press, London: S.C.M. Press.

Bergson, Henri
1935 *The Two sources of Morality and Religion* (English Translation) New York: Holt, Rinehart + Winston Inc.

Bonhoeffer, Dietrich
1967 *Letters and Papers form Prison, London*: S.C.M. Press.
1967 *The Way to Freedom,* New York: Harper and Row.

Brothers, Joan (ed.)
1967 *Readings in the Sociology of Religion*, London: Pergamon Press.

Brunner, Heinrich E.
1948—1949 *Christianity and Civilization* (2 vols.) New York: Charles Scribners and Sons.

Calvin, John
1921 *Institutes of the Christian Religion* (2 vols.) Philadelphia, Pa: Presbyterian Board of Publication.

Cogley, John
1968 *Religion in a Secular Age: The Search for Final Meaning*, New York: Frederick A. Praeger Inc.

Coulton, G. G.
1923—1936 *Five Centuries of Religion* (4 vols.), Cambridge: at the University Press.

Demerath, N. J. and Hammond, Phillip
1969 *Religion in Social Context*, New York: Random House.

Eisenstadt, S. N. (ed.)
1968 *The Protestant Ethic and Modernization; A Comparative View,* New York: Basic Books Inc.

Gluckman, Max
1956 *Custom and Conflict in Africa,* New York: The Free Press.

Hagen, Everett E.
1962 *On the Theory of Social Change,* Homewood Illinois: The Dorsey Press.

Lenski, Gerhard
1961 The Religious Factor: A Sociological Study of Religious Impact on Politics, Economics and Family Life, Garden City, New York: Doubleday and Company Inc.

Martin, David
1967 *A Sociology of English Churches,* London: S.C.M. Press.

Niebuhr, H. Richard
1951 *Christ and Culture,* New York: Harper and Row.
1954 (Reprint). *The Social Sources of Denominationalism,* New York Holt, Rinehart + Winston Inc.

Niebuhr, Reinhold
1946 *The Nature and Destiny of Man,* New York: Scribner's Sons.
1965 *Man's Nature and his Communities,* New York: Scribner's Sons.

Parsons, Talcott
1960 *Structure and Process in Modern Societies,* New York: The Free Press.

Scott, John Finley
1971 *Internalization of Norms: A Sociological Theory of Moral Commitment,* Englewood, N. J.: Prentice-Hall, Inc.

Teilhard de Chardin, Pierre
1965 *The Phenomenon of Man, London*: William Collins.

Tillich, Paul
1963 *Systematic Theology* (3 vols.), Chicago: The University of Chicago Press.

Van den Berghe, Pierre
1965 *Africa: Social Problems of Change and Conflict,* San Francisco: Chandler Publishing Co.

Warren, Max
1967 *Social History and Christian Mission,* London: S.C.M. Press.
1971 (ed.) *To Apply the Gospel: Selections from the Writings of Henry Venn* Grand Rapids, Michigan: Wm. B. Eerdmans Company.

Wach, Joachim
1944 *Sociology of Religion, Chicago*: The University of Chicago Press.
1951 *Types of Religious Experience, Christian and Non-Christian,* Chicago: The University of Chicago Press.

Weber, Max
1946 *From Max Weber: Essays in Sociology,* translated and edited by H. H. Gerth and C. Wright Mills, New York: Oxford University Press.
1963 *The Sociology of Religion,* translated by Ephraim Fischoff with Introduction by Talcott Parsons, Boston: Beacon Press.

Wilson, Bryan R.
1966 *Religion in a Secular Society,* London: C. A. Watts and Co.

Wood, William W.
1965 *Culture and Personality Aspects of the Pentecostal Holiness Religion,* The Hague: Mouton and Co.

Yinger, J. Milton
1965 *Toward a Field Theory of Behavior,* New York: McGraw-Hill Book Company.
1970 *The Scientific Study of Religion,* New York: The MacMillan Company; London Collier-MacMillan Limited.

INDEX

ERRATUM

page 120, line 35: for Enlightment, read: Enlightenment